Abraham Joshua Heschel Today

Abraham Joshua Heschel Today

Voices from Warsaw and Jerusalem

HAROLD KASIMOW
EDITOR

WIPF & STOCK · Eugene, Oregon

ABRAHAM JOSHUA HESCHEL TODAY
Voices from Warsaw and Jerusalem

Copyright © 2020 Harold Kasimow. All rights reserved. Except for brief quotations in critical publications or reviews, no part of this book may be reproduced in any manner without prior written permission from the publisher. Write: Permissions, Wipf and Stock Publishers, 199 W. 8th Ave., Suite 3, Eugene, OR 97401.

Wipf & Stock
An Imprint of Wipf and Stock Publishers
199 W. 8th Ave., Suite 3
Eugene, OR 97401

www.wipfandstock.com

PAPERBACK ISBN: 978-1-7252-7351-1
HARDCOVER ISBN: 978-1-7252-7352-8
EBOOK ISBN: 978-1-7252-7353-5

Manufactured in the U.S.A.   08/20/20

In honor and memory of my great teacher
Rabbi Abraham Joshua Heschel
and to his brilliant student and disciple
Rabbi Byron Sherwin
both of whom immensely enriched my life.

Contents

Contributors		ix
Preface and Acknowledgments		xi
1	Editor's Introduction *Shofar: An Interdisciplinary Journal of Jewish Studies 6, 1 (2007)* HAROLD KASIMOW	1
2	In Search of Heschel MICHAEL MARMUR	6
3	God's Omnipotence and Presence in Abraham Joshua Heschel's Philosophy ALEXANDER EVEN-CHEN	32
4	No Religion Is an Island *Following the Trail Blazer* ALON GOSHEN-GOTTSTEIN	60
5	I Am What I Do *Abraham Joshua Heschel Seen from Two Perspectives,* *Secular Jewish and Christian* SHOSHANA RONEN AND STANISLAW OBIREK	98
6	Abraham Joshua Heschel and the Declaration *Dabru Emet* STANISLAW KRAJEWSKI	122
7	Heschel Book Reviews	138
Bibliography		195

Contributors

Rabbi Alexander Even-Chen received his PhD from Hebrew University and is currently senior lecturer in Jewish thought at the Schechter Institute of Jewish Studies in Jerusalem. He is the author of *A Voice from the Darkness, Abraham Joshua Heschel: Phenomenology and Mysticism* (in Hebrew) and has written numerous articles on Heschel in English and Hebrew. His most recent book is *Between Heschel and Buber: A Comparative Study* (Emunot: Jewish Philosophy and Kabbalah), co-authored with Ephraim Meir.

Alon Goshen-Gottstein is the founder and director of the Elijah interfaith Institute. He is acknowledged as one of the world's leading figures in interreligious dialogue, specializing in bridging the theological and academic dimension with a variety of practical initiatives, especially involving world religious leadership. He is the author of numerous books and articles including *The Jewish Encounter with Hinduism: Wisdom, Spirituality, Identity* and *Same God, Other God: Judaism, Hinduism, and the Problem of Idolatry*, both published by Palgrave Macmillan.

Harold Kasimow is the George Drake Professor Emeritus of Religious Studies at Grinnell College in Iowa. He studied with Abraham Joshua Heschel at the Jewish Theological Seminary and wrote his PhD thesis on Heschel's thought at Temple University. He is the author of *The Search Will Make You Free: A Jewish Dialogue with World Religions* and *Interfaith Activism: Abraham Joshua Heschel and Religious Diversity*.

Stanislaw Krajewski is professor of philosophy at the University of Warsaw. He is a leader of the Jewish community in Poland. Krajewski is the author of numerous books and articles including *Poland and the Jews: Reflections of a Polish Polish Jew* and co-editor of *Abraham Joshua Heschel: Philosophy, Theology, and Interreligious Dialogue.*

Michael Marmur is the dean of the Hebrew Union College-Jewish Institute of Religion in Jerusalem. He holds a PhD from the Hebrew University in Jerusalem in the Department of Jewish Thought. He specializes in the thought of Abraham Joshua Heschel, particularly the ways in which Heschel weaves traditional Jewish sources into his contemporary theological enterprise. His most recent book is *Abraham Joshua Heschel and the Sources of Wonder* (The Kenneth Michael Tanenbaum Series in Jewish Studies).

Stanislaw Obirek is one of the most important Polish intellectuals. He deals with religion and contemporary culture, interreligious dialogue, and ways to overcome conflict between religions and cultures. Obirek is a former Jesuit priest and is now Professor of Theology and Religious Studies at the University of Warsaw. He is the author of numerous books including *Of God and Man* and *On the World and Ourselves*, co-authored with Zygmund Bauman.

Shoshana Ronen is a Professor and Head of the Hebrew Studies Department at the University of Warsaw, Poland. Her publications include *In Pursuit of the Void: Journeys to Poland in Contemporary Israeli Literature; Nietzsche and Wittgenstein: In Search of Secular Salvation; Polin, A Land of Forests and Rivers: Images of Poland and Poles in Contemporary Hebrew Literature in Israel;* and *A Prophet of Consolation on the Threshold of Destruction: Yehoshua Oziasz Thon, an Intellectual Portrait.* Her research focuses on modern Hebrew literature, Jewish thought, and modern philosophy.

Preface and Acknowledgments

Heschel once said that "it is gratefulness that makes the soul great." In *Who Is Man?* he writes that "there is a built-in sense of indebtedness in the consciousness of man, and awareness of owning gratitude . . ." In this spirit, I would like to express my own deepest thanks to the many who helped bring about the completion of this book. First and foremost, I am most indebted to my great teacher, Professor Abraham Joshua Heschel, who helped me to see the spiritual nature of the Jewish tradition and respect for the faith of other human beings.

I wish to thank Professors Zev Garber and Nancy Lein who first asked me to edit the special edition of *Shofar* dedicated to Heschel's centennial anniversary in 2007. Their invitation was the spark for this book.

I also owe a special depth of gratitude to Professor Jacob Agus, an exceptional teacher with whom I first discussed the idea of writing my PhD thesis on Heschel. When Professor Agus left Temple University, it was my good fortune that Professor Maurice Friedman, the brilliant Buber scholar and Heschel's friend, agreed to become my major advisor. Professor Friedman discussed my thesis proposal with Rabbi Heschel and later wrote a foreword to my thesis when it was published. I want to express my deepest thanks for Professor Friedman's encouragement and love for the last forty years of his life. I also want to thank my dear friend and fellow student Ken Kramer, Friedman's most devoted disciple, for our fifty years of conversation. I miss him.

I am especially grateful to the scholars from Warsaw and Jerusalem who wrote the essays for the original 2007 volume, as well as to the writers from many parts of the world who wrote new reviews of nearly all of Heschel's books. A number of the reviews were written by Heschel's former students. I am also honored that Jo-Ann Mort, Reverend Benjamin Webb, Professor Peter Huff, and Rabbi Daveen Litwin found the time to write blurbs for this work.

Thank you to my former students at Grinnell College who gave me great joy and challenged me to seek new and deeper understanding of the sacred texts that we have studied together.

Thank you to my friends and colleagues in the Religious Studies department at Grinnell College, especially to my former student, an outstanding biblical scholar Henry Rietz, and to Tyler Roberts, a new, important voice in the philosophy of religion in America. I am also grateful to George A. Drake, former president of Grinnell College, for his interest in my work and for his continuing encouragement.

I am deeply indebted to my dear friend and assistant, Angela Winburn, for her dedication to keeping me on track and her patience throughout—Lord, help her. Angela has been my faithful typist and gentle critic for nearly twenty years. I am also profoundly grateful to Russell Tabbert for his talented editorial skills, and to Angie Vander Leest for moving mountains during the pandemic to help me with this book.

I would like to thank my friend Leonya Ivanov. Our ongoing dialogue and his creative feedback have been indispensable to me.

My profound gratitude also goes to my precious friends John Merkle, Edward Kaplan, and Jacob Teshima, for their extraordinary contributions to the study of Heschel's life and thought. Thank you to Dr. Teshima for providing the photograph for the cover of the book.

Many thanks as always to the editorial staff at Wipf & Stock Publishers, especially to Matt Wimer, who has taken great care to see this book to fruition. Thank you to Purdue University for permission to reprint work previously published in Shofar in 2007.

My deepest gratitude to my wife Lolya, who has devoted her life to "praying with her feet," and to my children and grandchildren. As I have begun to talk about my memories as a Holocaust survivor, I am grateful to them for their understanding and love.

1

Editor's Introduction

Shofar: An Interdisciplinary Journal of Jewish Studies 6, 1 (2007)

HAROLD KASIMOW

GRINNELL COLLEGE (GRINNELL, IOWA)

> A religious man is a person who holds God and man in one thought at one time, at all times, who suffers in himself harm done to others, whose greatest passion is compassion, whose greatest strength is love and defiance of despair.[1]

Rabbi Abraham Joshua Heschel was just such a religious person. With his brilliant mind and compassionate heart, he became one of the most influential religious teachers of America in the twentieth century. Among those who both admire Heschel and have woven his teachings into their work are not only Jews, but also Christians, Buddhists, Hindus, and Muslims

---

1. See Heschel, *Moral Grandeur*, 289. This book is a collection of forty essays written over a period of four decades selected by his daughter Susannah Heschel, herself a distinguished Jewish scholar. Her very moving introduction provides a deeply personal insight into the life and work of her father. In this volume she has made a superb choice of some of Heschel's most significant and enduring essays.

in many different parts of the world, all attracted by his powerful words of wisdom, by the generosity of his spirit, and by his personal integrity. Heschel's impact on Jews and others was due in large part to the fact that many who met him in person or who meet him in his works feel that he is writing out of his own experience. He had the rare ability to speak, and be heard, beyond the boundaries of his own religious tradition.

For Byron Sherwin, Heschel's disciple, secretary, and research assistant, who has written a book and many articles on Heschel, "Abraham Joshua Heschel was a jewel from God's treasure chest."[2] Fritz A. Rothschild, a student and colleague of Heschel, speculates that Heschel's great impact, especially on Jews and Christians, is due to the fact that "Heschel helps us to perceive life as the biblical prophets and psalmists perceived it; he thereby helps us discern in the biblical message the presence of God."[3] Samuel Dresner, Heschel's student and disciple from the time that Heschel arrived in the United States until his death, spoke of Heschel as "*nasi*, a prince of his people. He was *shalem*, marvelously whole. He was *zaddik hador*, a master for our age."[4]

Heschel also had a great impact on a number of the most influential Christians of his day, especially Catholics. He was greatly admired by Thomas Merton, Daniel Berrigan, Cardinal Johannes Willebrands, Cardinal Augustine Bea, who was responsible for the drafting of the Church's revolutionary document *Nostra Aetate*, and even Pope Paul VI. Heschel convinced the Pope to remove a paragraph in *Nostra Aetate* that called for Jews to convert to Christianity.

In his essay "Heschel's Impact on Catholic-Jewish Relations," Eugene Fisher tells us that "when Heschel died, the American Catholic community mourned the loss of one who was, for us, a spiritual mentor and guide, a man whose faith helped form and mold our own faith at its deepest point. When Heschel died, the Jesuit journal *America*, reflecting the mood of the American Catholics throughout the country, took the unprecedented step of devoting an entire issue to a discussion of his work by the leading Catholic thinkers of the day."[5] The well-known American writer James Carroll stated, " To read Heschel was to step aboard the endangered but still seaworthy idea that the most transforming adventure of all can be intellectual. Heschel changed my notions not only of Judaism but of religion itself, and of God."[6]

---

2. Sherwin, *Heschel*, 1.
3. Rothschild, "Varieties," 91.
4. Dresner, "Heschel: The Man," 30.
5. Fisher, "Heschel's Impact," 112.
6. Carroll, *Constantine's Sword*, 47.

Many prominent Protestants also became close friends and admirers of Heschel, including Jaroslav Pelikan and William Sloan Coffin, and no one more so than the great Christian theologian Reinhold Niebuhr. Niebuhr considered Heschel to be "the most authentic prophet of religious life in our culture" and the "commanding and authoritative voice not only in the Jewish community but in the religious life of America."[7] Martin Luther King, Jr., often expressed his deep appreciation of Heschel. He spoke of Heschel as "one of the persons who is relevant at all times, always standing with prophetic insight to guide us through these difficult days."[8] King saw Heschel as a "truly great man," and "a truly great prophet." He viewed him as a messenger of God because his words, "to think of man in terms of white, black, or yellow is more than an error. It is *an eye disease, a cancer of the soul*," expressed King's own dream for the world.[9] Heschel's writings have also made an impact on evangelical scholars. Marvin R. Wilson, one of the best-known evangelical scholars in America, who teaches courses on Heschel, stated to me in a letter, "The writings of Abraham Joshua Heschel have had a greater impact on my life than any other single source except the Bible."[10]

We must not overlook the power of Heschel's literary style as an important reason for people's attraction to his works. This is explored most deeply by Edward Kaplan, who writes: "Heschel's writings convincingly evoke the luminous presence of God For me particularly, he was a great artist. His poetic style enticed my yearning for faith."[11]

In contrast to his widespread influence in America, Heschel has not received the attention he deserves in some other parts of the world, including Poland, where he was born, and Israel, where the prophets gave the world the dream of everlasting peace. This situation is now beginning to change as a number of Heschel's books have been translated into Polish and Hebrew in recent years.

I am therefore very pleased to include in this special issue of *Shofar* some eminent thinkers from Israel and Poland who are deeply immersed in the works of Heschel. I am deeply grateful to all the contributors for their important and moving articles. I am especially happy to see the importance that some of them gave to Heschel's contribution to interfaith dialogue. This is so important today when religious conflict has greatly contributed to the problems of the world. I also want to express my deep gratitude to the

---

7. Niebuhr, "Masterly Analysis."
8. King "Conversation," 2.
9. Heschel, "Religion and Race," 87.
10. In a letter from Marvin R. Wilson to Harold Kasimow (January 29, 1986).
11. Kaplan, *Holiness*, 1.

contributors from many parts of the world who reviewed Heschel's books. Some are leading students and disciples of Heschel, while a few are encountering Heschel for the first time. I hope that these articles and reviews will contribute to the ongoing fascination with Heschel.

This year on the hundredth anniversary of Heschel's birth we need him more than ever to remind us that we are not alone, that we are all created in God's image, and that God loves us and needs us to help perfect the world. Today, when religion is so often used as a force of hate and violence, we need Heschel as a model to help us to see that "in this aeon diversity of religion is the will of God"[12] and that "God is greater than religion."[13] What is most significant for Heschel is not the religion of an individual but how pious, how human the individual is. What is most significant is how you live your life. Heschel can serve as a model of how it is possible for human beings from different traditions to respect and love each other. The Hebrew Bible contains only one verse commanding love of neighbor, but in thirty-six places it commands us to love the stranger. It may be more difficult to love the stranger, but Heschel shows us it is both possible—and necessary.

ACKNOWLEDGMENTS

I wish to express my gratitude to Daniel Morris and Zev Garber, who honored me by inviting me to edit this special volume of *Shofar* for Heschel's centennial birthday anniversary. I have known Zev since I arrived in the United States in August of 1949. We were classmates at Yeshiva Salanter in the Bronx. It is always a great joy to work with Nancy Lein, the splendid managing editor of *Shofar*. I am very grateful for her patience and editorial skills. The friendship and tremendous support of John Keenan, John Merkle, Stanislaw Obirek, and Byron Sherwin has been very important to me. During the years I spent working with Byron on a book on Heschel and other projects, I came to see him as one of the outstanding disciples of Heschel. I wish to thank him from the bottom of my heart for helping me to understand Heschel more fully.

I first met Abraham Joshua Heschel at the Jewish Theological Seminary in New York City when I was nineteen years old. He was my teacher for a course on Genesis, with an emphasis on Rashi's interpretation, and a course on Jewish theology, where we read Heschel's classic work *God in Search of Man*. We were both Holocaust survivors and would sometimes converse in Yiddish, our common birth language.

12. Heschel, "No Religion," 126.
13. Heschel, *Insecurity*, 181.

I was drawn to Heschel's stress on the ethical dimension of Judaism, which aims at ethical perfection, the total transformation of the human being, with a stress on *Aggadah* (spirituality), not just on *halakhah* (law). In *aggadah* the stress is on what is in the heart of the believer while he or she fulfills the demands of God, not just the doing of the deed itself. Heschel believed that the aim of Judaism is to create a harmony between *halakhah* and *aggadah*. For Heschel the ethical aspect of Judaism is as important as the ritualistic.

What really stood out about Heschel was that he was a real *mentsh*. *Mentsh* is the Yiddish word for human being, someone who is truly human, a compassionate being of dignity and great integrity. A *mentsh* is a person who combines compassion with a passion for truth.

Heschel believed that a pious person must be equally mindful of his human relations as he or she is of relations with God. For Heschel we must be "alert to the dignity of every human being." Heschel writes that the pious person is "keenly sensitive to pain and suffering in our own life and in that of others." In his book on the Jews of Eastern Europe, *The Earth Is the Lord's*, Heschel gives the following definition of a saint: "A saint was he who did not know how it is possible not to love, not to help, not to be sensitive to the anxiety of others."[14] Like a few other of his students in the 1950s and '60s, I believed—as I still do—that Heschel was a saint. That is why I have offered a seminar in recent years titled "Abraham Joshua Heschel: A Jewish Saint of the Twentieth Century."

In 1967, Heschel wrote a letter of reference for me so that I could begin my graduate studies in comparative religion. In 1971, in preparation for my dissertation on Heschel, I traveled from Philadelphia to New York City once a week to attend a seminar that Heschel was teaching to his rabbinical students on his book *Heavenly Torah as Refracted through the Generations*. During the summer of 1972, I finished my proposal for my Ph.D. thesis on Heschel and proudly showed it to him. I was thrilled with the comments he wrote for my advisors to read. Heschel, who devoted his life to love and peace, was for me not just a superlative teacher but my hero. He remains the most important spiritual teacher of my life. May his memory be a blessing.

---

14. Heschel, *Earth*, 20–21.

2

In Search of Heschel

Michael Marmur

**HEBREW UNION COLLEGE/JEWISH
INSTITUTE OF RELIGION (JERUSALEM)**

This overview of commentary and scholarship on the life and thought of Abraham Joshua Heschel presents different aspects of Heschel reflected in the rapidly burgeoning literature on his work and personality. Eight dimensions of Heschel, prisms through which he may be perceived, are presented: Heschel as philosopher, as theologian of the deed, as mystic and Hasid, as scholar, as prophet of pathos, as poet and stylist, as twentieth-century symbol, and finally in terms of the influence exerted upon and by him. The question of Heschel's attitude towards symbolism is cited as an example of how he may be perceived through a variety of prisms. It may be that rather than seeking the unifying principle by which the enigma of Heschel may be solved, an appreciation of the multi-faceted nature of his thought and action may provide the most helpful way of conducting this search.

Much has been written about the life and thought of Abraham Joshua Heschel, and the critical and popular literature is still growing. Because of

Heschel's wide-ranging interests, and because his work was written in four languages spanning six decades in a variety of publications, most of what has been written about him is partial in nature. One or another aspect of Heschel's work is considered, and other related dimensions of his thought are downplayed or neglected.[1]

In surveying the burgeoning literature on Heschel, it is possible to present a number of different "Heschels," or different prisms through which Heschel has been discussed and his thought analyzed. The sensitive reader is not asked to choose one at the expense of the others, although in some cases the claim is made to have found the "key" which renders all aspects of his work understandable, or helps discern the kernel from the shell. It is by no means clear that such a master key is in truth to be found. Perhaps the key is this panoramic approach, an attempt to look at the life and thought of Abraham Joshua Heschel from as many different perspectives as possible.

Here, then, are eight different perspectives from which Heschel is often viewed, and a review of some of the most significant examples of each of the approaches in both popular and scholarly literature.

HESCHEL THE PHILOSOPHER

In a review of *God In Search of Man*, Marvin Fox described A. J. Heschel as "one of the few genuine philosophers in this country."[2] The intention behind

---

1. To cite a recent example of this phenomenon, an important work on the image of the Divine relates to Heschel at various points, yet it ignores Heschel's writings explicitly devoted to this theme. See Lorberbaum, *Tzelem Elohim*. References to Heschel can be found throughout the first part of the book, and the bibliography includes both "The Mystical Element in Judaism" and *Torah min Hashamayim*. Indeed, Lorberbaum regards Heschel in a highly positive light, noting that he was one of the few to avoid falling under Maimonides' thrall on the question of the Divine Image. However, the author makes no reference to those of Heschel's writings which deal explicitly with this question. See, for example, Heschel, *Man's Quest*, 124–27; and "Religion and Race," 95.

An important article relating to Heschel as the "prophet of prophecy" makes several acute observations about the Heschelian philosophy of religion, while ignoring some of Heschel's own key works on the theme of prophecy itself. See Schweid, *Prophets*, 234–54. Schweid ignores references to prophecy in *Torah min Hashamayim*, and more glaringly, omits any reference to Heschel's two Hebrew articles on prophecy in the Middle Ages. These articles, particularly the examination of Maimonides' self-understanding as a philosopher or a prophet, are most germane to Schweid's discussion.

2. Maurice Friedman has written in similar terms, asserting that Heschel "does have an original philosophy which, however unsystematic, includes all the aspects of a comprehensive philosophy: an ontology, a theory of knowledge, a theory of values, an ethics, a metaphysics, a philosophy of religion, and applications in many concrete fields" in Friedman, "Contemporary Philosophers," 303. Fox, "God," 77.

this comment was to emphasize Heschel's seriousness of purpose, his willingness to be held up to ridicule, and his refusal to settle for trivial discussions. Despite this judgment, Sol Tanenzapf has observed that "Heschel is not taken seriously as a philosopher, either by his critics or by his adherents, even though he thought of himself as primarily a philosopher."[3]

Opinions differ sharply as to the level of Heschel's philosophical knowledge and intent. Emil Fackenheim suggested that it is an error to read his works in search of philosophical consistency. Rather, the depth and significance of Heschel's work is "profound religious thinking,"[4] and not reasoning in the Western philosophical tradition. In the words of one assessment, Heschel "did not confront philosophy so much as he undercut it."[5] One critic more inclined to take Heschel seriously as a philosopher states that he was "familiar with the whole of Western philosophy."[6] Eliezer Schweid has been almost alone amongst readers of Heschel in emphasizing the link with Hermann Cohen, and points out that Heschel often cites his traditional Jewish sources, but fails to mention the philosophers with whom he is in conversation.[7]

Fritz Rothschild has encouraged future scholars to research "connections and parallels" with process philosophers, whom he lists as Whitehead, Bergson, and Hartshorne, and with existentialists—here he refers to Heidegger, Jaspers, and Marcel.[8] There are indeed veiled (if negative) references to Heidegger in Heschel's work.[9] Elsewhere, Neil Gillman has pointed to similarities with Gabriel Marcel.[10]

3. Tanenzapf, "Heschel," 276.
4. Fackenheim, "God," 53.
5. Davies, "Conscience," 214.
6. Stern, "Irenic Polemicist," 170.
7. Especially note mention of philosophers such as Aristotle, Plato, Kant, and Schopenhauer can be found throughout Heschel's work, although often the references are oblique. For a discussion of Heschel's approach to one of these thinkers, see Perlman, "Heschel's Critique of Kant," 213–26. Schweid, *Prophets*, 236.
8. W. Z. Harvey has referred to Heschel in passing as "among the most exciting of the Hasidic storytelling Jewish existentialist philosophers" (Harvey, "Maimonideanism," 250). See also Friedman, *Witnesses*, 74–88, in which Heschel's relationship to existentialist thought is discussed. A convincing rebuttal of the suggested link between Heschel and existentialism can be found in Chester, *Divine Pathos*, 47–55. Rothschild, "Varieties," 89.
9. See, for example, Heschel, *Alone*, 137; Stern, "Irenic Polemicist," 172: "The work of Martin Heidegger looms behind much of what Heschel has to say about being"; Friedman, "Contemporary Philosophers," 296, who points both to similarities and differences between the two thinkers. Quotations from Heidegger in *Who Is Man?* are mentioned in Goldstein, "Buber's Misunderstanding," 166.
10. Buber is more frequently seen as a religious existentialist, and many comparisons

More attention has been paid to the relationship with process thought. Peri notes a "striking similarity with the thought of Charles Hartshorne," while Tanenzapf and Kaufman have both discussed what they see as the compatibility of Heschel's thought with process philosophy.[11] In their view, the work of Hartshorne is congenial to an understanding of some key Heschelian tenets.[12] Friedman records that he once brought Heschel and Hartshorne together, and recalls that they "had much in common both philosophically and spiritually."[13]

Not all agree that there is much to be learned from this putative link between Heschel and the process philosophers. Both Katz and Schulweis doubt the significance of any such connection, or indeed its very existence.[14] Merkle has argued that there are significant theological differences between aprachHeschel and Hartshorne.[15] Even if it is true that certain theological problems inherent in Heschel's notion of divine pathos could be clarified with recourse to process thinking, this may be evidence of coincidence rather than influence.[16]

Of all the philosophical schools which might have attracted Heschel in the course of his intellectual development, it was the phenomenological method which had the most significant impact. Unlike existentialism and process philosophy, Heschel openly credited the influence exerted upon him by phenomenology. The following paragraph from a 1941 Hebrew essay on prayer makes clear the debt owed to the phenomenological method:

> In all phenomena of spiritual life, we encounter two types of qualities: the quality of actual being, and that of significance or meaning. When, for example, a man stands in a garden and points his finger at a certain flower, two things are revealed to us: the movement of the finger (an occurrence within space and time) and its significance (the intention of the mover, which is

---

have been made between Heschel and Buber, as discussed below. Gillman, "Epistemological Tensions," 81–82.

11. Peri, *Education*, 68. See also Sherman, *Promise*, 36.

12. Tanenzapf, "Heschel and His Critics" and Tanenzapf, "Process Theory," 35–58, especially 40–45. Kaufman, "Heschel, Hasidic Prayer," 163–68; and Kaufman, "Judaism and Process Theology, 59–74, especially 61–63. I have seen the abstract of Nanstad, *Heschel and Whitehead*, but not the entire dissertation.

13. Friedman, *Witnesses*, 13. It is interesting to speculate who influenced whom.

14. Schulweis, "Hartshorne," 58–62; Katz, "Eliezer Berkovits," 138.

15. Merkle, "Heschel's Monotheistic Perspective."

16. Hartshorne's *Omnipotence and Other Theological Mistakes* shows numerous points of agreement with Heschel's views, yet the spirit of the work seems quite different. Perhaps a key difference is the meaning they attribute to the concept of freedom.

evident from the movement). In these two ways the phenomenon (movement of the finger) is interpreted, and any correct evaluation must pay heed to both.[17]

Two salient observations can be made about this paragraph: firstly, that it closely parallels the noetic-noematic distinction at the heart of Husserlian phenomenology. Indeed, the *locus classicus* for the early Husserl discussion of this distinction also takes place in a garden, where an apple tree serves to establish his categorical distinctions.[18] Secondly, this distinction recurs in Heschel's writings. To cite but one example, Heschel explains his concept of depth-theology in the first chapter of *God in Search of Man* thus, "The theme of theology is the content of believing. The theme of the present study is the act of believing."[19] One of the most important and challenging contributions to the critical literature about Abraham Joshua Heschel takes the phenomenological method as the very essence of the Heschelian approach, the key to understanding his entire oeuvre. Perlman's book on Heschel's concept of Revelation seems to rest not only on the assumption that the phenomenology of Husserl unties the Gordian knot of Heschelian thought, but also that apparent inconsistencies and weaknesses in Heschel's argumentation can be explained in terms of this phenomenological insight.[20]

Perlman's claims for the essential integrity and congruity of Heschel's theological approach, and his sense that the apparently disparate components all cohere if they are understood appropriately, are echoed in other descriptions of Heschel's work.[21] "When read carefully and repeatedly," writes Hillel Goldberg, "Heschel's major writings revealed not only beauty and emotion but rigor."[22] Perlman's claim of Heschel's uniqueness among modern Jewish thinkers shows none of the usual signs of academic reserve: "Heschel's theology is radical. It is a total departure from the way Jewish theologians have approached religious problems over the past twenty centuries. Heschel's theology does not possess the slightest parallel of style or method to anything written by any Jewish theologian at any time."[23]

This certainty of Heschel's uniqueness and inner coherence is most reminiscent of the work of Fritz A. Rothschild, although Perlman finds his predecessor too uncritical of Heschel, and insufficiently explicit about the

17. Heschel, "Essence," 347.
18. Husserl, *Ideas*, 214–15.
19. Heschel, *Search*, 7.
20. Perlman, *Idea of Revelation*.
21. See Perlman, "Report," 31.
22. Goldberg, "Heschel," 38.
23. Perlman, *Idea of Revelation*, 3.

phenomenological dimension of his work.²⁴ Perhaps the most profound reading of Heschel from this perspective, although much less broad ranging than either Rothschild or Perlman, is to be found in an excellent essay by Nathan Rotenstreich.

Rotenstreich is less concerned than these others to claim total originality for the subject of his essay, and less insistent that he has discovered the code by which all things Heschelian might be understood. Instead, he presents a balanced view of the intellectual background to *Die Prophetie*, emphasizing the importance of the thought of Max Scheler. He also indicates toward the end of the essay the limitations of the phenomenological method for understanding the Heschelian approach, pointing out that "[p]recisely because of Heschel's adherence to the biblical text, or, let us say, broadly to the Judaic tradition, he is bound to go beyond the phenomenological data."²⁵

This point is made by Heschel himself in his introduction to *The Prophets*: While I still maintain the soundness of the method described above [that adopted in Die Prophetie], which in important aspects reflects the method of phenomenology, I have long since become wary of impartiality, which is itself a way of being partial.²⁶

Rotenstreich's approach, then, points the way to a sensitive reading of Heschel's work, paying appropriate attention to the influence of the phenomenological method he learned in Berlin and retained thereafter.²⁷ It would be unwarranted to claim that the Husserlian approach was always dominant: the influence of Scheler, in such matters as sympathy and wonder, was palpable.²⁸ Others who can be classified in the phenomenological school, such as Rudolph Otto, also influenced Heschel. They may have been more congenial to his overtly spiritual agenda, although Uffenheimer

---

24. Introduction in Rothschild, *Between*, 7–32; Rothschild, "Religious Thought," 12–24; Rothschild, "Varieties," 87–102.

25. Rotenstreich, "Consciousness," 195.

26. Heschel, *Prophets*, xii.

27. Friedman records a conversation in which Heschel confirmed the central importance of the phenomenological approach. See Friedman, *Witnesses*, 55. See also Neusner, "Heschel: The Man," 10, where he indicates that in conversation with Heschel, the latter indicated to him that there was an added element to his thinking which Neusner had not identified. Although in the article Neusner suggests that now we shall never know what the extra dimension was, in conversation with me he has suggested that Heschel intimated that rather than a question of epistemology, ontological and phenomenological issues were still occupying him in the 1950s and beyond.

28. See Staude, *Scheler*, 21–23. See also Brill, "Aggadic Man," 3, where the influence of Geradeus Van de Leeuw is noted.

has argued convincingly that Heschel may have been engaged in a polemic against Otto.[29]

In his important 1943 essay "The Holy Dimension," we find evidence of Heschel's critique of what Husserl called the "presuppositionless" phenomenological method.[30] Without abandoning the method, he brings presuppositions and prior commitments to bear:

> Only those will apprehend religion who can probe its depth with unhalting precision, who can combine the intuition of love with rigor of method, who are able to translate the ineffable into thought and forge the imponderable into words. It is not enough to describe the content of religious consciousness. We must press the man of piety with questions, compelling him to understand and unravel the meaning of what is taking place in his life as it stands at the divine horizon. While penetrating the consciousness of the pious man, we may conceive the reality behind it.[31]

There is no need to posit total reliance on the phenomenological method. Heschel arrived in Berlin with a set of beliefs and experiences which pre-dated his exposure to a particular methodology. Phenomenology was for him a method, rather than a philosophy of life.[32] It was precisely its lack of content which made the approach unsatisfactory.

Before leaving the question of phenomenology, mention can be made of studies dealing with related fields. Kaplan has made use of Depraz's term "phenomenological writing" to demonstrate ways in which the influence of

---

29. Uffenheimer's discussion of Heschel on the prophetic consciousness is important. See Uffenheimer, *Ancient Prophecy*. He discusses the influence of Husserl, Dilthey, Scheler, and Buber on Heschel's conception and suggests that Heschel was engaged in a polemic with Hoelscher's understanding of prophetic ecstasy. Otto is quoted in Heschel, *Die Prophetie*, 140. Note Husserl's comment to Otto in a 1919 letter: "[I]t seems to me that the metaphysician (theologian) in Herr Otto has carried away on his wings Otto the phenomenologist . . . " quoted in Ballard, "Heidegger," 63. See also Kaplan, "Readiness," 27. Gordon Tucker has suggested that the title of an essay by Heschel, "The Quest for Certainty in Saadia's Philosophy," is a veiled reference to Husserl, but Gerson Cohen is surely right when he suggests that the obvious allusion is to John Dewey's 1929 work *The Quest for Certainty*. See Tucker, "Heschel's *Torah min ha-shamayim*" 49–50; Cohen, "Interpreter," 107. James Hyman's dissertation on Heschel includes a discussion of Heschel and Otto, as well as a more general discussion on Heschel and phenomenology. See Hyman, *Alienation*, 103–29, 149–68.

30. See Ströker, "Reflections on Husserl," 249–63.

31. Heschel, "Holy Dimension," 319.

32. Breslauer notes a shift "from an original orientation towards a more pragmatic, utilitarian one" in Heschel's notion of depth-theology (Breslauer, "Theology," 82). See also Ratzabi, "Depth Theology," 22–25.

this method was felt in his rhetoric as well as his reasoning.[33] In *Die Prophetie* a number of references are made to the distance between Heschel's chosen method and that of Freudians, Jungians, and other advocates of a psychological approach. This distance from psychology (as a therapeutic device rather than a concern with consciousness) characterizes every phase of Heschel's work, and even his more positive remarks on the theme demonstrate a lack of sympathy with psychologism, and even with psychology itself.[34] Heschel's views on this question have been examined in essays by Goldman and Barnard.[35]

Some critics doubt that Heschel deserves to be considered a philosopher. In Arthur Cohen's reading, for example, Heschel is "bored with argument" and uses rhetorical devices to compensate for his unwillingness to consider the implications of his own position.[36] Olan and Ben-Horin have also dismissed Heschel on the grounds that he in turn dismisses reason.[37] Some have been more sympathetic, suggesting either that his views hint at "a supra-rational certainty which neither offends nor violates our reason," or even that the Jewish faith he presents is "a rational and responsible option."[38]

In the first chapter of *God in Search of Man*, Heschel makes unambiguous statements about the philosophic enterprise. He rejects the notion of a universal perennial philosophy but defends philosophy as "the human attempt to attain a synoptic view of things" (12). Later in the same chapter he speaks out against "the worship of reason" and cites the examples of Plato, Schelling, William James, and Bergson to illustrate the difference between rationalism and philosophy: in his view, all of these thinkers engaged in the latter without slavish adherence to the former.[39]

Abraham Joshua Heschel was a philosopher if by that term is meant a lover of wisdom who takes philosophical questions seriously and who knows a good deal about the Western philosophical tradition. He was not

33. Kaplan, "Philosopher," 1–14.

34. "In suggesting that abstinence freed a man's energies for spiritual pursuits, the Kotzker anticipated in a way Sigmund Freud's view of sublimation" in Heschel, *Passion*, 222. See references to the Freudian school in *Die Prophetie*, 1, 9, 45, and 47; see particularly Chapter 21 of Heschel, *Alone*.

35. Goldman, "Metapsychology, 106–12; Barnard, "Attitude," 26–43.

36. Cohen, *Natural*, 244.

37. Ben-Horin, "Via Mystica," 249–58; Ben-Horin, "Ineffable," 321–54; Ben-Horin, "Space," 28–32; Olan, Review, 180–82.

38. Fox, Review, 78. Rothschild, "Varieties," 102.

39. Heschel, *Search*, 18. For Heschel's understanding of the relationship between reason and faith, see "Reason and Revelation," 404–8 and the 1953 essay "Toward an Understanding of Halakhah," 127–45.

a philosopher if by that term is meant a thinker whose first commitment is to the unbridled pursuit of philosophic truth. Nor yet did he submit himself to the strictures of a particular philosophical method or system, although there can be little doubt that he found in the phenomenology of his teachers in Berlin an approach most congenial to his own enterprise. Heschel's most fundamental commitments predated his exposure to philosophy and outlasted his commitment to it. He was in a sense both more and less than a philosopher. Future discussions of Heschel the philosopher may include a transposition of a question asked about Maimonides in another context: did he "seek to make what exists conform to his ideas, or his ideas conform to what exists?"[40]

HESCHEL THE THEOLOGIAN OF THE DEED

An important essay by Arnold Eisen considers "Heschel's strategy for accomplishing his readers' teshuva—their return to God and mitzvot."[41] This approach allows for a consideration not only of Heschel's religious enterprise, but also of the techniques used to persuade his readers to take a step on the "ladder of observance." Major parts of the third section of *God in Search of Man*, for example, are devoted to promoting such an approach to Jewish observance.

For Will Herberg, Heschel's "theology of the act" was one of the two key aspects of the Heschelian theological enterprise.[42] Hartman believes that Heschel "attempted to guide Jews back to Halakhah by way of the prophets," implying that behind Heschel's evocative prose lies the intention to persuade his readers to undertake a traditional life of Jewish piety.[43]

It is perhaps not surprising that both Reform and Orthodox critics were uncertain about the efficacy of his approach to Jewish practice. Marvin Fox finds that Heschel "places too little value on the ordinary routine of piety," while Eugene Borowitz finds that Heschel "stands with those many post-moderns whose religiosity manifests a form of fundamentalism."[44]

40. Harvey, "Why Maimonides," 109.
41. Eisen, "Re-reading Heschel," 4. See also Eisen, "Seeing," 70–72.
42. Herberg, "Jewish Theology, 366.
43. Hartman, "Heroic Witness," 175. See also Hartman's "Heschel's Religious Passion," 173–83.
44. Fox, "Heschel, Intuition," 10. Compare this remark with Heschel's statement in "The White Man on Trial," 102: "The teaching of Judaism is the *theology of the common deed*."
Borowitz, *Covenant*, 29. See Borowitz's other references to Heschel, particularly *New Jewish Theology*, 147–73; *Choices*, 167–184; *Judaism After Modernity*, 343–60. Borowitz

There does appear to be a certain ambivalence on Heschel's part to traditional observance. On the one hand, he is genuinely committed to what he calls "living in a holy dimension, in a spiritual order."[45] On the other hand, he is convinced that in the contemporary context, simple reliance on the way of Halakhah is both insufficient and impracticable.[46]

As Breslauer has shown, Heschel's understanding of the sacred deed was extended beyond its traditional Halakhic context and came to refer to deeds performed for the betterment of society and the advancement of justice.[47] Finding inspiration and justification from the precedents of the prophets, Maimonides, Abarvanel, and others, Heschel increasingly threw himself into a variety of causes. Even Neusner, who is critical of the political effect of these activities, judges that his actions in support of the struggle for civil rights "were expressions of his religious faith no less than his putting on of tefillin in the morning and reciting the creed."[48]

Opinions differ on the question of Heschel's argument for an *a priori* commitment to Halakhah. There is little doubt that he was personally committed, but in turning to a largely nontraditional American readership, his defense of Halakhic conformity is open to interpretation. Chapter 34 of *God in Search of Man*, on "The Meaning of Observance," seems to reject the notion that mitzvot should be chosen and discarded according to some notion of the "original intentions of the law." Susannah Heschel is right to observe that her father was engaged in "a subtle critique of liberal theology."[49] On the other hand, Heschel does offer an argument for observance sharply distinct from approaches characteristic of Soloveitchik, Leibovitz, or other theoreticians of Halakhah.[50]

---

did much to promote Heschel's thought among students of the Hebrew Union College from the 1950s and regarded himself as a disciple, albeit with significant theological reservations. For evidence of the impact of Heschel on HUC students, see Liebman, "Training," 84–85.

45. Heschel, "Am, Eretz, Medinah," 121.

46. An important but problematic exposition of Heschel's views on the subject can be found in Dresner, *Heschel, Hasidism,*" particularly 84–123.

47. Breslauer, *Impact,* 47–48.

48. Neusner, "Heschel: The Man," 10–11.

49. Susannah Heschel, "Social Justice—The Theme of Heschel," 37. On A. J. Heschel's ambivalent view of modernity, see "Am, Eretz, Medinah," 119–20.

50. Rosenak, *Roads,* 267, argues that for Heschel, we can only be addressed with commandments when God's search for us has, as it were, been successful. Halakhic conformity is predicated on the success of a process beginning in wonder and moving to observance. Implicitly, then, he reads the three sections of *Search* as proposing a process towards observance. See also Hartman, "Heroic Witness," 178; Hyman, "Meaningfulness," 84–99. Magid believes that Heschel offers "a highly untraditional defense of

The ambivalence is not simply the result of disagreement among scholars and critics: it is present in Heschel's own writing on this question. Common to the different statements and interpretations is Heschel's abiding concern to promote sacred action, both ritual and political.

HESCHEL THE MYSTIC, HESCHEL THE HASID

Was Heschel a mystic? Opinions are sharply divided. Glatzer, Herberg, and Peli, for example, have stated unambiguously that he was not.[51] Others declare with equal certainty that he was.[53] Arthur Green discusses this question, and answers clearly if qualifiedly in the affirmative: "If by 'mystic' we mean one who sees inner experience of God as the true core of religious life, I have no difficulty in placing Heschel within that camp."[52]

Eliezer Schweid has pointed to the difficulty of judging whether thinkers such as Kook, Gordon, Zeitlin, Birnbaum, Buber, Rosenzweig, Breuer, Baeck, and Heschel should be classified as "authentic Jewish mystics of a modern type," and concludes that "[i]n the final analysis, it is the mystic who defines himself as belonging within the mystical tradition or outside of it.[53] Since there is almost no part of Jewish tradition from which Heschel distances himself, and since the mystical tradition itself is characterized by a certain degree of circumspection, even this criterion provides scant help in the search for an answer to this conundrum. The fact that Heschel did not present himself as a mystic has not stopped some from branding him as such.[54]

To judge from the last paragraph of his 1949 essay on "The Mystical Element in Judaism," Jewish mysticism is understood to assume "that there is an inner life in God and that the existence of man ought to revolve in a spiritual dynamic course around the life of God."[55] In this broad understanding, Heschel can be seen as an enthusiastic devotee of the mystical approach. However, Gordon Tucker has set out the salient characteristics of the Heschelian approach in a measured way, noting that: "Heschel sets

---

tradition" (Magid, "Heschel and Merton," 112–25).

51. Glatzer, "Review," 284–85; Herberg, "Jewish Theology," 366, in response to Cohen's critique; Peli, "Heschel and the Ḥasidic Tradition," 79. See also Bridges, *American Mysticism*, 60. See, for example, Graeber, "Heschel," 49.

52. Green, "Three Warsaw Mystics," 51.

53. Schweid, "Prophetic Mysticism," 139.

54. Kaplan, *Holiness*, 70, where he refers consistently to Heschel's mysticism "despite the author's admonitions." See also Kaplan, "Mysticism," 33–47. Even-Chen, "Mysticism," 359–70, is a trenchant argument for seeing Heschel as a mystic.

55. Heschel, "Mystical Element," 184.

out for us what he sees as the ambivalent nature of Jewish tradition when it comes to mystical speculation . . . mystical speculation has potentially great value, and that value is at the same time counterbalanced by the dangers that it poses.[56]

It is clear to Green and other sensitive readers of Heschel that his mysticism, indeed his approach to Judaism as a whole, is seen through the prism of the Hasidism into which he was born. A number of essays and articles have considered aspects of Heschel's Hasidic roots and identity.[57]

Even though the earliest discussions of Heschel in terms of Hasidism were undertaken during his lifetime, a shift of emphasis is discernible over the last few years. It is perhaps less necessary to engage in a defense of Heschel's philosophical seriousness or rigor than it was a generation ago. Heschel the German-trained philosopher has been joined by Heschel the Polish-born Hasid.

HESCHEL THE SCHOLAR

In the original Hebrew edition of his *The Sages*, E. E. Urbach cites Heschel's *Torah min Hashamayim* as an example of the neglect of rudimentary scholarly techniques. Urbach states that the book is nothing more than a translation of Heschel's own theological views as encountered in *God in Search of Man*, with the addition of a garment comprised of quotations woven from across the generations, in a neo-Hasidic style.[58]

The suspicion that Heschel's scholarship was in the service of his own theological agenda, or was inaccurate, or too broad-ranging and consequently superficial, seems to have been shared by such giants of modern Jewish scholarship as Saul Lieberman and Gershom Scholem.[59] Others hold

56. Heschel, *Heavenly Torah*, 279.

57. Borodowski, "Hasidic Sources," 36–47; Dresner, *Heschel, Hasidism*," 36–83; Green, "Recasting Hasidism," 63–69; Horowitz, "Heschel on Prayer," 293–310; Kaplan and Dresner, *Prophetic Witness*, vii–72; Katz, "Heschel and Hasidism," 82–104; Kaufman, "Heschel, Hasidic Prayer"; Klein, "Universal Hasidism," 255–65; Lookstein, "Neo-Hasidism of Heschel," 248–55; Peli, "Heschel and the Hasidic"; Schachter, "Hasidism and Neo-Hasidism," 216–21. An important essay by a student of Heschel contributes much to an understanding of the Kabbalistic provenance of a key Heschelian concept, while only mentioning Heschel once, and then in passing. See Faierstein, "God's Needs," 45–59.

58. Urbach, *The Sages*, 14. The comment is not to be found in the English translation of the work. According to the late Shmuel Avidor Hacohen, Urbach apologized to Heschel for the comment—but he did not take it out of the Hebrew edition.

59. Anecdotal evidence for the disregard in which Heschel was held by these scholars is to be found in the Heschel Archive at the Jewish Theological Seminary Library in

a very different view. Seymour Siegel describes the very work disparaged by Urbach as "an achievement of great significance on the history of Jewish thought."[60] Gerson Cohen concludes that "Heschel was what he purported not to be, a textual scholar," and Neusner concurs, acknowledging the magnitude of his scholarly achievement while criticizing what he regards as deficiencies of method.[61]

To what extent is Heschel taken seriously as a scholar today? His works still appear frequently on course bibliographies in Jewish Studies courses in a variety of fields, but usually as theology, not scholarship. Katz applauds "his uncovering of hitherto unknown original sources" in the area of Hasidism, and scholars of the Hasidic movement still cite Heschel, although not universally with approval.[62]

Heschel's achievements in the field of scholarship have been defended against the accusation of dilettantism, but none would suggest that Heschel functioned primarily as a conventional textual scholar. The interrelationship between his scholarship and theology has been explored by Siegel and Neusner, and summarized thus by Rothschild: "Heschel, the research scholar, explored the documents of the past in order to make certain that Heschel, the creative thinker, could make his message true and authentic."[63]

HESCHEL THE PROPHET OF PATHOS

Eliezer Schweid has described A. J. Heschel as a prophet of prophecy.[64] At the heart of his theory of prophecy lies the notion of divine pathos, described by Friedman as "one of the most significant original contributions

---

New York. More tangible evidence can be adduced from excerpts from the correspondence between Lieberman and Scholem. See Hacohen, "Schlemiel," 1.

60. Siegel, "Heschel's Contributions," 72–85.

61. Cohen, "Interpreter," 110. Neusner, "Review," 66–73; Neusner's "Intellectual Achievement," 13–22.

62. Katz, "Heschel and Hasidism," 89. For examples of a positive if nuanced reception of Heschel's Studies of Hasidism, see Rapoport-Albert, "Hasidism after 1772," 90; Schatz-Uffenheimer, *Hasidism as Mysticism*, 51. See, however, 231 and particularly 235. For a critique of his work on Nachman of Kossov, see Piekarz, *Beginning of Hasidism*, 26–31. See also Shapiro, "Scholars," 109–10. In a 1954 letter to Atlas, Weinberg writes: "I am concerned that Dr. Heschel is wasting his time and strength in 'scientific study,' producing a detailed and boring study of the life of R. Gershon Kotover. People make use of the scholarly approach for insignificant matters."

63. Rothschild, "Architect," 55. On Heschel and Biblical Scholarship, see Levenson, "Religious Affirmation," 25–44. On Heschel's Rabbinic scholarship, see Kolberg, "From Research," 65–82.

64. Schweid, *Prophets*, 234–254. See also Schweid "Prophetic Mysticism," 139–74.

to biblical thought in our times."⁶⁵ Understandings of the provenance of this key Heschelian conception differ: for Perlman, this (like everything else) can only be understood in phenomenological terms. Indeed, "the attempt to understand pathos without its phenomenological context is either self-contradictory or ignorant of Heschel's theological purpose."⁶⁶

In the category of self-contradictory readings of Heschel's theology of pathos Perlman places a long essay by Eliezer Berkovits devoted to this theme. Berkovits does indeed offer a reading of the theory of pathos and sympathy with no recourse to the phenomenological context, and concludes that the theology of pathos, "(w)hile it is utterly unknown to Judaism . . . has a long history in Christian thought."⁶⁷ Katz has taken issue with this reading and attempted to demonstrate that it is based on a deficient understanding of Heschel.⁶⁸

Others have also read Heschel's theology of pathos without placing the phenomenological perspective at the forefront. Particularly notable in this context is the judgment by Susannah Heschel that her father's "central category of divine pathos was derived from Hasidic thought and constituted his modernized version of the traditional kabbalistic term, *tzorekh gavoha*, divine need."⁶⁹

The provenance of pathos may be open to discussion. That it constituted a central part of Heschel's worldview is not. One example of the impact of this insight on an aspect of Heschel's thought is in the question of prayer. His insistence on seeing God as the subject and humanity as the object of His attention is a response to what he considered to be the narcissistic implications of the opposite view.⁷⁰ It is also an application and extension of the concept with which Heschel was concerned for over forty years: divine pathos.

A corollary to this emphasis on the urge of God to be revealed and experienced is a profound concern with Revelation in its various manifestations. Much of Heschel's work is concerned with one or other aspect of the question of Revelation, at Sinai or in an intimate moment. The implications

---

65. Friedman, "Review." See also Siegel, "Divine Pathos," 70–74. See Chester, *Divine Pathos*," 279–338.

66. Perlman, *Revelation*, 92.

67. Berkovits, "Pathos," 98.

68. Katz, "Eliezer Berkovits," especially 125–133.

69. Heschel, "Theological Affinities," 133. Perlman plays down the Hasidic dimension and prefers to credit the literature of the Tannaim in Perlman, *Idea*, 125.

70. See Hartman, "Prayer," 105–25, especially 119–20. See also Jeanrond, *Hermeneutics*, 129. Heschel's insistence on the subject-object distinction is also significant in understanding his relations with Buber, discussed below.

of this discussion bear an impact on his notions of prophecy, the Bible, the sanctity of the moment, the pre-theological foundation of religious experience, epistemology, and more.

It is rare for Edward Kaplan to express criticism or reservation about the subject of much of his scholarly efforts of the last several years. When he does, the comment merits special attention. In a recent essay, he writes, "The strength of Heschel's procedure is also its basic handicap: the assumption that all human beings have at least once in their lives experienced the momentous reality of God—and have forgotten it."[71]

One of the most widespread criticisms of Heschel relates to his lack of sympathy for a lack of belief. Some of his most trenchant critics, as well as his more supportive readers, regard this as a major weakness of the Heschelian worldview.[72] Heschel rarely denies his dismissal of the validity of an agnostic or atheistic position. True, in a 1958 letter to David Ben Gurion he professes full understanding of "those who in good faith find themselves unable to proclaim themselves Jews in the religious sense," but it is clear from the substance of his remarks that they are directed at the specific case of the Israeli secular Jew, and even then with major reservations.[73]

More typical is a comment written just two years earlier, on the Biblical view of reality: "In the spirit of biblical tradition, we must speak not of the foolishness of faith but rather of the foolishness of unbelief, of the scandal of indifference to God. What is called in the English language an atheist, the language of the Bible calls a fool."[74]

The theology of pathos argues for a Divine voice always available to be heard, and a prophetic impulse present in each human being which can be triggered and activated. It is this view which makes Heschel so open to interreligious dialogue, and so skeptical of the legitimacy of the principled unbeliever. If Heschel were to be credited with only one theological insight, one leitmotif throughout his work—it would be the notion of divine pathos.

---

71. Kaplan, "Philosopher," 1.

72. See Cohen, *Natural*, 251–53; Fackenheim, Review of *Alone*, 86; Olan, Review of *Quest*, 180; Peri, *Education*, 139.

73. Heschel, *Moral Grandeur*, 44.

74. Heschel, *Moral Grandeur*, 365 and page 271, where Heschel argues that Saadiah demonstrated that "agnosticism is absurd and cannot even be made a topic of discussion."

HESCHEL THE POET AND STYLIST

Heschel is sometimes criticized for his lack of clarity, just as he is praised for his rich use of language and imagery.[75] A serious of articles on the theme of Heschel's poetics culminated in a 1996 work by Edward Kaplan on the theme, and it represents an attempt to analyze the ways in which Heschel employs literary and other devices in the advancement of his theological enterprise.[76] In recent years attention has been paid to Heschel's early Yiddish poetry, and a translated edition has been published.[77]

Considerations of Heschel's writing style extend further than an analysis of his poetry, or even of his poetics. Borowitz has considered the structure of Heschel's thought as part of a study of form in Jewish theology, and others have noted the use of a typological structure in much of his work.[78] This structure is most dominant in *Torah min Hashamayim*, where an attempt is made to organize an immense amount of tradition according to a central organizing principle, namely the contrast between Rabbi Akiba and Rabbi Ishmael.[79]

There is ample evidence to suggest that Heschel saw himself drawn to each of these polar opposites, identifying with each pole and ultimately with both. In a private conversation with Maurice Friedman, Heschel is quoted as saying:

> What underlies my thinking is something I proved and demonstrated extensively in the two Hebrew volumes of *Torah min Hashamayim* . . . Jewish thinking moves along two paths, that of critical reasoning and that of imaginative intuition—Maimonides and Judah Ha-Levi, the Baal Shem Tov and Moses

---

75. See, for example, Ben-Horin, "New Space," 28–29; a more positive critique, but one which also emphasizes those elements of Heschel's system which are "at times incoherent or self-contradictory," can be found in Levenson, "Contradictions," 34–38.

76. Kaplan, *Holiness in Words*.

77. Heschel, *Ineffable*. This poetry is discussed in Green; "Three Warsaw Mystics," 38–44, and in Kaplan and Dresner, *Prophetic Witness*, 87–96. See also two letters of encouragement from Bialik, in Bialik, *Collected Letters*, 184, 415. (I am most grateful to Professor Avraham Shapira for his help tracing these and other materials.)

78. This article can be found in Borowitz, *Studies*, 117–19. Shapira's structural consideration of Buber is most suggestive as a comparison, and it includes an interesting footnote about Heschel. See Shapira, *Between Spirit and Reality*, 39. See also Peri, *Education*, 66–68. Heschel himself stated on numerous occasions his understanding of Judaism in terms of "a polarity of two principles." See, for example, Heschel, *Moral Grandeur*, 161, 277, 384–5.

79. See Schorsch, "Hermeneutics," 301–8; Tucker, "Heschel's Torah," 48–55; Levin, "Heschel's Homage," 56–66.

Mendelssohn. I am both . . . I live these two trends. I am neither a rationalist nor an irrationalist."[80]

Not only the substance of Heschel's distinctions but the way in which he presents them deserves serious attention. By considering Heschel as poet and stylist, questions of language, style, and structure provide a way of touching upon his self-understanding, and the core of his life's work.[81] If once calling Heschel a poet was a way of dismissing him, today his poetics have become a legitimate way of understanding him better.

HESCHEL AS TWENTIETH CENTURY SYMBOL

There is an irony, if not a downright contradiction, in the way Abraham Joshua Heschel related to the dimension of time and the reality of contemporaneity. It is possible to point to aspects of his thought which prefers eternity over the here and now. It is by no means trivial or incidental that his book about Israel bears the title *Israel: An Echo of Eternity*. How Heschel came to terms with the political reality of the State of Israel, and even more controversially, his response to the Holocaust have been the subject of debate.[82]

Fackenheim states that "Martin Buber and Abraham J. Heschel said little about the Holocaust—and that little with great reticence," but it is clear from the continuation of his remarks that he does not level criticism against them, rather against those "current Jewish writers [who] invoke two great Jewish thinkers, both no longer alive, in order to justify their own escapism."[83] Heschel's reticence may not necessarily indicate that he found the subject irrelevant. Indeed, given his biography such a conclusion is implausible. Rather, it appears that Heschel was incapable or unwilling to give

---

80. Friedman, "Divine Need," 67. For an example of the impact of this distinction beyond the confines of Rabbinic theology, see Green, "Reply," 206.

81. See Shandler, "Heschel and Yiddish," 245–99.

82. See Rosenberg, "Time," 103–4. A letter from Heschel to Dresner in May 1967 in the Israel box of the Heschel archive at JTS, includes the following: "I do hope and pray that Israel would *not* initiate action. *Havlagah* (self-restraint) is what is demanded. We are hopeful and waiting for a *Yeshuah* (salvation)."
See Eisen, "Rabbinic Theology," 211–225; Faierstein, "Heschel," 255–75.

83. Fackenheim, *To Mend*, 194–5. In a footnote, Fackenheim clarifies that he has Jacob Neusner in mind. See Neusner, *Stranger*, especially 82–91. It is a remarkable and not incidental fact that having mentioned Heschel and Buber together, Fackenheim goes on to discuss the case of Buber at length, and Heschel is not mentioned again. It is also significant that in Fackenheim, Review of *Alone*, 9, Fackenheim comments that Heschel "says hardly a word about history."

vent to the feelings he kept pent up. These feelings may have informed his writings and public activities, as Byron Sherwin suggests: "Though Heschel has been criticized for having failed to allow the Holocaust to influence his thinking, such is not the case. Memory of the lost Atlantis of European Jewry was always with him. It was a motivating force behind his words and deeds."[84]

As in so many aspects of the search for Heschel, just as there are those who imply that Heschel paid scant regard to the Holocaust in his thought, others have argued that it had a profound and clearly discernible effect impact. Goldberg is convinced that despite the paucity of explicit references, the Holocaust "had generated a Copernican revolution in Heschel's perspective; the reversal animated all that he wrote after 1944, date of his highly compressed essay 'The Meaning of This War.'"[85] This is a spurious claim, since the essay he cites was in fact written in large measure in February 1938—dark days indeed, but before the Final Solution nonetheless.[86]

Goldberg's mistaken sense of a new post-Holocaust sensibility speaks to a broader issue—the extent to which Heschel's thought changes and progresses through the decades and the extraordinary events to which he was witness in his lifetime. Katz finds it significant that at the end of his life Heschel was working on the dark and complex figure of the Kotzker, and speculates that "Heschel came to the conclusion that *our* time favors the way of Kotzk."[87] It may be true that a combination of Heschel's advancing years and the changing mood after the Six-Day War gave rise to a new sensitivity to the darker side of life, but the evidence for such a change is at best tenuous and speculative. It is in fact remarkable how little Heschel's theological program changes during his life, considering the epoch-making events which dissected it.

Alongside this purported self-distancing from the central events of the modern Jewish experience, we find Heschel increasingly and passionately involved in the most controversial campaigns in post-War America, as well as pioneering interreligious dialogue and spearheading efforts for the sake of Soviet Jews. Heschel appears both beyond and within the confines of his time.[88]

Another way, then, of searching for the elusive Heschel is to attempt to understand him in the context of his life and times, examining both his

---

84. Sherwin, *Maker*, 47. See also Davies, "Conscience," 213. For three examples of significant references to the Holocaust, see Heschel, "*Pikuah Neshamah*," 66; "The Plight of Russian Jews," 214; and most particularly "On Jews in the Soviet Union," 267.

85. Goldberg, *From Berlin*, 127.

86. See Kaplan and Dresner, *Prophetic Witness*, 259–62, 349–50.

87. Katz, "Hasidism," 95.

88. See Breslauer, "Theology."

views on history and his actions within history.[89] He seems to have reacted to the cultural and religious potential of life in post-War America with a mixture of excitement and horror, and these two approaches co-exist from the moment he arrives in the United States.[90] Already in 1948 he had bemoaned "the banalization of Judaism . . . the tumult of arrogant not-knowing and not wanting to know."[91] In unpublished remarks made in 1955, Heschel is recorded as having excoriated much of what he saw in Jewish life in post-War America, and said: "Had I grown up in the modern, American synagogue, I probably would not have remained."[92] In what appears to be a contradiction, in the same period we find Heschel praising the current mood of interest in matters of the spirit, and claiming that such a renaissance of interest only occurs once in two centuries.[93]

Breslauer has pointed out that Heschel would have greatly disliked being termed a "symbolic leader"—but he did indeed fulfill such a role.[94] The combination of his learning and activism, the European accent and even the white beard; the march with King and the stand against the Vietnam War—these and other factors have contributed to Heschel's iconic status in some sectors of Liberal Jewish America.

A key aspect of this iconic standing is Heschel's role in interreligious dialogue, and much has been written on this topic. Indeed, there have been times when the impact of popularity of Heschel among Christian audiences outstripped that achieved amongst Jews.[95] Systematic expositions of Heschel's thought have been written by Christian scholars, and some important discussions of his ecumenical activities are also a significant part of the Heschel literature.[96] His willingness to seek meaningful religious encounter

---

89. See Goldberg, "Heschel"; Goldy, *Emergence*; on Heschel and the history of the Theological Seminary, see Goldberg, "Becoming History," 355–437. See Heschel's 1944 essay "Faith," 332: "We must not idolize history. This world is more frequently subject to the power of man than to the love of God."

90. See Kaplan, "American Mission," 335–74.

91. Faierstein, "Holocaust," 269.

92. Heschel Archive, Jewish Theological Seminary, Box 1: American Judaism.

93. Heschel, "Teaching Religion," 148. He makes the same point in 1962 and 1965. See "Prophetic Inspiration," 66; "Existence and Celebration," 27.

94. Breslauer, *Impact*, 118.

95. In a private conversation, Morton Leifman recalls Heschel bemoaning the fact that he could be assured of a more enthusiastic reception among students of the Union Theological Seminary than could be expected at JTS.

96. The most significant example is the work of John Merkle, whose analyses of Heschel's theology represent a major contribution to Heschel studies. See especially Merkle, *Genesis*, and Moore, *Human*. See also McBride, *Transcendental*.
See for example Banks, "Heschel," 100–11; Blumenthal, "Heschel," 249–53; Chester:

while not settling for an anodyne consensus, his declaration that "I think it is the will of God that there should be religious pluralism," his role in negotiations with the Vatican, his openness to religions of the East—all this and more contributed to Heschel's unique position in the cultural and religious life of post-War America.[97]

HESCHEL AND INFLUENCE

In 1930 the young Heschel, not yet thirty, was asked if his recently published poems had been influenced by Rainer Maria Rilke. Heschel's response was both prickly and informative: "I didn't have to study in Rilke's *heder* to recognize that there is a God in the world. I had other teachers, other paths, other images."[98]

Almost forty years later, Heschel was asked in an interview if he had been greatly influenced by Martin Buber. His reply is reminiscent of his previous response: "I would not say so. I consider the important insights in Buber to be derived from Hasidic tradition, and these I knew before I met him."[99] In both cases, when asked explicitly, Heschel states that the most important influences were exerted upon him at an early stage of his development.

During his life and since his death, numerous attempts have been made to understand Heschel in terms of one or other thinker or school. The question of his relationship to Martin Buber has been raised often, despite Heschel's answer to the interviewer's question. Indeed, his earliest poetry includes a work entitled *Ich und Du*, "initiating his lifelong debate (mostly implicit) with the thought, and soon the person, of Martin Buber."[100]

Despite his response to the interviewer, and notwithstanding the paucity of direct references to Buber in Heschel's work, there is little doubt that such a debate with Buber is a recurrent theme in Heschel's life and work.[101]

"Heschel," 246–70; Kasimow and Sherwin, *Island*; Kimelman, "Rabbis," 251–71; Sanders, "Apostle," 61–63.

97. Heschel, *Moral Grandeur*, 405. See Heschel, *Search*, 15.

98. Kaplan and Dresner, *Prophetic Witness*, 145.

99. Heschel, *Moral Grandeur*, 384.

100. Kaplan, "Readiness," 25. Kaplan has dedicated an essay to the relationship between the two thinkers. See Kaplan, "Sacred," 213–231. A work which promises such a comparison but fails to deliver is Wolok, *Meeting*. Heschel is not mentioned for the first 200 pages, and at no point are the major disagreements and influences discussed, beyond the possibility of God (235) and the different place given to Kant in each of their systems (285).

101. See Klein, "Heschel," 201. For a rare but significant example of Heschel's

Some of Heschel's defenders have claimed his superiority over Buber, particularly in his presentation of Hasidism and his understanding of Rabbinic literature.[102] Others have avoided the tendency to rank—it hardly seems necessary to decide who is more significant between these two giants of modern Jewish thought-and dwelt instead on comparing and contrasting their approaches.

Some have attributed to Heschel a dialogical approach, but there seems little warrant for such a conclusion from Heschel's work and self-understanding. Friedman's claim that "Heschel's understanding of prayer is, in his own special sense, that of dialogue" is hard to reconcile with the following passage from *Man's Quest for God*:[103]

> Prayer is not a soliloquy. But is it a dialogue with God? Does man address Him as person to person? It is incorrect to describe prayer by analogy with human conversation; we do not communicate with God. We only make ourselves communicable to Him. Prayer is an emanation of what is most precious in us toward Him, the outpouring of the heart before Him. It is not a relationship between person and person, between subject and subject, but an endeavor to become the object of His thought.[104]

This and other passages demonstrate both that categories made famous by Buber were important to Heschel, and that the latter did not simply adopt the approach of the former. Buber for his part appears to have had reservations about certain aspects of Heschel's theology. Uffenheimer has pointed out that Buber does not provide an exposition of religious or prophetic experience, since for him it is in essence no different from regular human experience.[105] This insistence that there is nothing essentially different about the prophetic experience gives rise to the only mention by name of Heschel in Buber's own work on prophesy, published some six years after *Die Prophetie*. Buber rejects the notion (which he ascribes to Heschel) that the prophet sympathizes with Divine suffering and insists that the prophet

---

explicit polemic with Buber, see Heschel, *Truth*, 292–293. More typical is the kind of implicit allusion to be found, for example, in Heschel's 1941 Hebrew essay on "The Essence of Prayer," see also Heschel, *Alone*, 14; Heschel, *Quest*, 45; See the chapter on Buber and Heschel in Hyman, *Alienation*, 130–48.

102. For an example of the claim of superiority, see Schachter, "Hasidism," 217.

103. Friedman, "Heschel," 304–5. For another dialogical reading of Heschel, see Cohen, "Torah," 174–83.

104. Heschel, *Quest*, 10. See also Heschel, *Insecurity*, 255; Sherman, *Promise*, 101.

105. Uffenheimer, "Buber," 199.

experiences his own human emotions.[106] There were, then, significant differences between the two men.

Just as Heschel has been compared with Buber in search of influence and divergence, studies have also been devoted to the comparison of Heschel with other thinkers. The ways in which Heschel reads and is influenced by Maimonides, Spinoza, Mendelssohn, Kaplan, Scholem, and Buber himself, as well as Kant and Tillich, have been the subject of scholarly attention.[107] As will be shown, each of these has been considered as an inspiration or an opponent—and sometimes both.

Other figures of Jewish and Christian thought have been linked with Heschel. A dissertation has been written comparing Heschel with Viktor Frankl, and others have suggested connections with figures as diverse as Hillel Zeitlin, Gabriel Marcel, Thomas Merton, and others.[108] The figure of Karl Barth also deserves further enquiry: evidence can be adduced for mutual influence, and certain aspects of Barth's thought, particularly the emphasis on God's search for man, have clear Heschelian overtones.[109]

As Heschel's defensive comments about Rilke and Buber indicate, it is probable that Heschel considered the sources of traditional Judaism to be

---

106. Buber, *Torat*, 105.

107. For a further example, see Zuesse, "Heschel, Buber and Soloveitchik," 121–49. The third thinker in this triad is compared with Heschel from a wholly different perspective in "Rabbi Joseph B. Soloveitchik"; see also Sacks, *Tradition*, 53. See Marmur, "Rhetoric," where these figures are discussed. For discussions of the connections between Heschel and other thinkers not mentioned elsewhere in this article, see Breslauer, "Spinoza," 19–26; Breslauer, "Three Approaches," 234–53; Galli, "Transmissibility of the Ineffable."

108. Klapper, *Human*. Green, "Three," 4, speculates that the two would have met in Warsaw, and Kaplan and Dresner have taken up this theme, arguing that "Zeitlin's transformation was a prototype for Heschel's own journey" in Kaplan and Dresner, *Prophetic Witness*, 62–63. Green comments elsewhere that in his view the interpretations of Hasidism presented by Zeitlin and Heschel are most important for an understanding of "the *Gestalt* of Hasidic piety." See Green, "Early Hasidism," 445. Descriptions of Zeitlin's sense of his own mission are very suggestive of Heschel's own path. See Bar-Sela, "Yahaduto," 109–24; Holtz, "Hillel," 50–65. Gillman, "Tensions," 81–82. Magid, "Heschel," 112–25.

109. Fleischer, "Heschel's Significance," 159, notes the suggestion that Barth's *The Humanity of God* was influenced by *God in Search of Man*. The claim of such influence seems implausible since Barth is speaking in terms of the Divine search decades earlier. In view of later events, it is informative to read the 1949 essay of Martin Luther King, Jr. entitled "The Place of Reason and Experience on Finding God" (available in the Stanford University On-Line King Archive), where King takes issue with aspects of Barth's theology of search. See also Jeanrond, *Hermeneutics*, especially 129, where Barth's insistence on God as the subject is highly reminiscent of Heschel. See also Hunsinger, *Barth*. For a discussion of a connection to another Christian theologian, see Jaeger, "Heschel," 167–79.

the major influence on his thought. The image of Heschel as an "authentic" Jewish thinker continues to be the subject of attention.

All Heschel's biographical works are to some extent exercises in autobiography. When, in his 1937 monograph on Abravanel, he describes his subject as being at home in all fields of religious literature, in Halakhah, Aggadah, in religious philosophy and exegesis, as well as in Christian theology and Islamic philosophy, he is describing the range of his own learning and interests.[110] Neusner, contrasting the depths of Heschel's Jewish knowledge with that of Buber and Rosenzweig, concludes that "Heschel knew everything he had to know to do what he wanted to do," and Peli attests that Heschel, "more than anyone else I know in recent generations, represented the totality of what Judaism is."[111]

Not all readers of Heschel have seen in his work the epitome of Jewish thought. A number of his critics, both from the Liberal and Orthodox wings of Judaism, have implied or stated directly that his central theological tenets are Christian in essence, or at least betray a heavy Christian influence.[112] Fackenheim was "left speechless" by such claims, as Heschel himself no doubt was.[113] Indeed, in a talk to Jewish educators in 1969 Heschel addressed explicitly the issue of non-Jewish influence on contemporary Judaism:

> We are essentially trained in a non-Jewish world. This is where we obtain our general training. We are inclined to think in non-Jewish terms. I am not discouraging exposure to the non-Jewish world. I am merely indicating that it is not biblical thinking. It is not rabbinic thinking. It is not Hasidic thinking. It is non-Jewish thinking. A non-Jewish philosophy is fine. But we would also like to have in our thinking a Jewish view of things. We would like to apply the Bible and *hazal* and they are often incongruent. If you take biblical passages, or biblical documents or Rabbinic statements, and submit them to a Greek mind, they often are absurd. They make no sense. But we do want to educate Jews. We wish to maintain Judaism. What can we do about it? May I say to you personally, this has been my major challenge, ever

---

110. Heschel, *Don Jizchak Abravanel*, 6.
111. Neusner, "Heschel: The Man," 8. Peli, "Heschel," 84.
112. See Olan, "Review of *Quest*," 181; Berkovits, "Pathos."
113. Fackenheim, "Review of *Search*," 50. For an interesting discussion of the integration of non-Jewish sources into a "quintessentially Jewish" philosophy, see Freidenreich, "Islamic Sources," 353–95, especially 394. Saadiah was one of the medieval figures to whom Heschel devoted an extended monograph.

since I began working on my dissertation, that is: How to think in a Jewish way of thinking?[114]

Repeatedly Heschel speaks of the desired goal of a Jew being able to identify and engage with the great figures of Jewish history.[115] Here, then, another way of understanding Heschel is presented: Heschel in terms of the influences—classical and modern, Jewish and non-Jewish— which were exerted upon him, and by him.

SUMMARIZING AND EXEMPLIFYING THE EIGHT PERSPECTIVES: THE CASE OF THE SYMBOL

This list of eight different approaches to Heschel is not exhaustive—other dimensions of his life and work have been considered in various publications.[116] Nonetheless, in this summary of the leading questions raised in the scholarly and popular literature about Abraham Joshua Heschel, these perspectives predominate: philosopher; theologian of the deed; mystic/Hasid; scholar; prophet of pathos; poet and stylist; twentieth-century symbol; and Heschel in the context of influence.

In most cases, these varying perspectives offer complementary insights, and each serves to sharpen the focus in which Heschel can be most clearly seen. Occasionally, however, they cannot be reconciled.

In order to demonstrate this clash of perspectives, it is instructive to consider one of the most puzzling aspects of Heschel's thought—his critique of symbolism. In the fifth chapter of *Man's Quest for God* we find in concentrated form what can be discerned throughout his writings more

---

114. Heschel, *Moral Grandeur*, 156.

115. This theme recurs throughout his post-War career. In a 1946 essay on "The Eastern European Era," he declares (101) that "If Isaiah were to rise from his grave and were enter to the home of a Jew, the two would easily understand one another." This is by any criteria an extraordinary claim. In 1951 we find a prescriptive statement rather than a description. In "To Be a Jew: What Is It?" (9), we find the following: "Our way of life must remain to some degree intelligible to Isaiah and Rabbi Yoḥanan ben Zakkai, to Maimonides and the Baal Shem." In an unpublished talk to HUC students in Cincinnati in the early 1950s (a recording of which can be found at the American Jewish Archives in Cincinnati), Heschel expresses his fear of what he calls spiritual assimilation, and asks if he would really be understandable to Yoḥanan ben Zakkai. See "Existence and Celebration," 27; "A Time for Renewal," 47, where Rabbi Akiva is invoked.

116. See, for example, Holtz, "Heschel," 27–39. A number of works have related to educational dimensions of Heschel's work. See McBride, *Heschel*. Schremer's important article on Heschel's rhetoric is particularly worthy of note. See Schremer, "Heschel," 95–105. See also Meir, "Ahava," 141–49.

diffusely—a rejection of all forms of symbolism, and a barely-concealed animosity toward the unnamed source of such notions.

Heschel's view of the symbol is distinctive and remarkable. What is its source, and against whom does he wage his polemic? Various attempts to shed light on this question might be offered, and they exemplify some of the perspectives outlined above. For Perlman, Heschel's "repudiation of the symbolic content of revelation . . . fits Heschel's encompassing phenomenological strategy."[117]

Moshe Idel proposes a quite different explanation of Heschelian anti-symbolism. In his view, against the backdrop of Hasidism "the generally negative attitude to symbolism in Judaism, expressed by Abraham Joshua Heschel, is easily understandable."[118] Perlman refutes this reading, stressing that only through phenomenology can Heschel be understood.[119]

Aaron Mackler affirms that Heschel's "strong repudiation of religious symbolism presents a puzzle," and concludes that "it is Heschel's vehement opposition to a Tillichian use of symbol that causes him rhetorically to attack symbolism by presenting it in caricatured form."[120] Mackler suggests that it is Tillich's conception of God which Heschel cannot accept, because it leaves no place for the pathos so central to his own theology.

Kaplan provides an interesting description of "Heschel's (somewhat quixotic) campaign against 'symbolism,'" and claims that a "biographical incursion uncovers the original context of Heschel's surprisingly harsh opposition to symbolism." He suggests that it is the philosophical anthropology of Dilthey, as Heschel encountered it in the thought of Martin Buber, which lies at the heart of his polemic. A 1935 correspondence between the Heschel and Buber sets out the distinct directions of their thought.[121]

---

117. Perlman, *Idea*, 107. It is interesting in this context to note Scheler's call for "a continuous *de-symbolization* of the world," quoted in Staude, *Scheler*, 22.

118. Idel, *Kabbalah*, 377, note 21. It is interesting to note that the term "symbol" is used intensively in Heschel's essay on "The Mystical Idea in Judaism."

119. Perlman, "Report," 33.

120. Mackler, "Symbols," 290–300. Heschel's works of the early 1950s would have been written in response to Volume I of *Systematic Theology*, published in 1951. See Heschel, *Search*, 127. It is interesting to speculate that Tillich's defense of his conception of the symbol in his *Dynamics of Faith* is written with some of Heschel's criticisms in mind. I believe that Adina Davidovich's work on the thread connecting Kant with Otto and Tillich with regards to the symbol could help unlock the mystery of Heschel's anti-symbolic stance. See Davidovich, *Religion*.

121. Kaplan, *Holiness*, 75–89. This is a re-working of Kaplan's "Sacred versus Symbolic Religion: Abraham Joshua Heschel and Martin Buber." See also Kaplan and Dresner, *Prophetic Witness*, 220–25. Harvey has suggested to me that Heschel's resistance to the notion of the symbol may also be directed against Gershom Scholem.

Further possible readings of Heschel's anti-symbolic stance can be suggested. He writes of the Kotzker: "Reb Mendl had scorn for things symbolic, for ceremonious feasts, for faith become ostentatious."[122] This implies an opposition to the symbolic on the grounds of simplicity and modesty. In *Search* he writes: "To maintain that the exodus from Egypt is a symbol only, that the essential point is the general idea of liberty which the story signifies is to disregard the heart of Jewish faith."[123] Here, it is his wish to defend the events of Jewish history from evisceration which motivates his view.

The debate about the provenance of Heschel's anti-symbolic stance exemplifies the range of opinions concerning Abraham Joshua Heschel. It is perhaps the case that any significant thinker or leader is understood in a variety of ways. In the case of Heschel, this variety extends from philosophy to social activism, from theology to poetry. Somewhere behind these categories or beyond them, the life and thought of Abraham Joshua Heschel remains a challenge and an inspiration. The search for Heschel continues.

---

122. Heschel, *Truth*, 314.
123. Heschel, *Search*, 201.

3

God's Omnipotence and Presence in Abraham Joshua Heschel's Philosophy

ALEXANDER EVEN-CHEN

SCHECHTER INSTITUTE FOR JEWISH
STUDIES JERUSALEM

In this essay I will address Heschel's reflections on the presence and the power of God, as they appear in his different writings: in his poems, his articles and his books. It was Heschel's belief that a man's works are "windows allowing us to view the author's soul."[1] Heschel's writings attest to the deep inner struggle in his soul, as he considers the almightiness and presence of God. I will examine how historical events shaped Heschel's spiritual insights and brought on new conceptions, new in the sense that they represent renewed spiritual discoveries for Heschel. I will then attempt to analyze Heschel's changing perspectives on the matters of the almightiness and of the potency of God throughout his lifetime.

1. Heschel, *Search*, 6.

EVIL AND THE PRESENCE OF GOD

Heschel published his book of poetry in Warsaw in 1933. His poetry attests to the profound expectations he has of God and to the deep suffering of the soul when these are not fulfilled. In his famous poem "I-Thou" Heschel points to the immense closeness between God and man. It has been pointed out that the title of the poem is related to the basis of Buber's philosophy of dialogue.[2] Unlike Buber, though, Heschel describes a relationship akin to mystical unity. Despite this unity man does not relinquish his personality like a drop disappearing in an ocean.[3] The poem refers to the mutual dependence between God and man. The metaphors used are physical rather than spiritual or abstract: "When a need pains you, alarm me!/When You miss a human being/Tear open my door!/You live in Yourself, You live in me.[4]

The appeal to God is fraught with pain and terror. Heschel's God is in pain and Heschel rushes to His aid. The gates of the world may have closed before God, but Heschel leaves his personal door open and demands that God enter. There is a deep prophetic ring to this call, and the prophet is Heschel himself. The concept of divine pathos is one of the main precepts in Heschel's thought, and God is described as having deep feelings for his sons.[5] Heschel counters divine pathos with his human pathos. The poem attests to deep fear of the possible destruction of the spiritual as well as the physical world, but it is also a manifest of the belief that what has been damaged may be repaired. The aspiration to set the world right leads Heschel to state that his heart and soul are His dwelling place. God is indeed in exile, but his exile is not absolute; He still resides in the hearts of a few souls.

In the poem "Millions of Eyes, Clogged" Heschel makes an explicit demand of God to repair the world, and if He is not prepared to do so, to allow Heschel to complete the task: "God, pass me Your weapons!/Let me slash through the Gordian knots/Of that idolatrous embroidery of people's star-shaped fate!

The poem escalates in specific demands of God to prevent the slaughter of his children and ends: I am responsible for You too/And demand of you—feel!/Like us, like me. If not, I'll wander all around and scream/That God has forgotten his heart with me."[6] Reading these lines, we cannot ig-

---

2. On the distinctions between Heschel's theology and Buber's philosophy, see Kaplan, "Sacred," 213–31.

3. Even-Chen, "Prophecy," 359–70.

4. Heschel, *Ineffable*, 31.

5. Siegel says: "The God of the Bible is no unmoved mover a la Aristotle. He is the most moved mover." Siegel, "Divine Pathos," 71. See also Rothschild, *Between*, 24.

6. Heschel, *Ineffable*, 35.

nore the gravity of Heschel's rebellion and his disappointment with God's conduct. These are not words of heresy. I mentioned before that one of the innovative concepts of Heschel's thought is divine pathos. Here Heschel protests God's apathy and demands that He announce that he is indifferent to his sons. Heschel is aghast at the fact that God has forgotten him and the bond between His heart and Heschel's heart. Heschel feels that the partnership between man and God is no more. Is it possible that it had never really existed?

Heschel's desperate cry is clearly heard in the poem "Help":[7]

> Set me at the head of all the dying
> With a greeting, a message from you.
> The desolate call to You, and You don't come.
> So send me, and any others You might choose.
>
> I cannot curse as justly as did Jeremiah.
> People are poor, weak; and it seems to me
> That their guilt is Yours; their sins, Your crimes.
>
> You are meant to help here, Oh God!
> But You are silent, while needs shriek.
> So help me to help! I'll fulfill Your duty, pay Your debts.
>
> Let me always feel, suffer,
> When human hands in peril
> Reach for the emergency brakes of Your world
> Which You have forgotten to set up!
>
> And come like a slave at their call
> And quench all suffering with my help;
> To help each stone, each flower
> To serve each man, each worm.
> Help me to help!

Heschel is aware of the reality of destruction. Many are dead, many more are dying. Some are aware they are dying; others are not. Heschel approaches God to bestow hope and salvation to the dying, who have called to Him to no avail. Heschel's words are harsh; they are born of a deep sense of frustration. According to Heschel's theology God was expected to appear in the world, to make amends to His sons and to punish the wicked. The poem expresses the desperation at unfulfilled expectations and ends with the prophetic demand: "So send me, and any others You might choose." Heschel

---

7. Heschel, *Ineffable*, 33.

irreverently addresses God and is adamant: if you do not fulfill Your role in this world, let me and others do it.

In the second stanza of the poem Heschel opposes the traditional conception of reward and punishment. In times of grave distress man may transgress. The responsibility for man's wrongdoing is such instances is God's. Having let his sons reach the abyss and made their lives hellish, He has made their sins His own. He cannot judge his sons by standards that no longer rule the world. In the horrible reality in which man exists, the boundaries between right and wrong, holy and unholy, are no longer clear. Man strives to survive in any way possible, even if this entails violation of previously acknowledged norms of behavior.

The third stanza commences with a direct appeal to God, evidencing the enormous gulf between the believer's expectation and reality unveiling before him: "You are meant to help here, Oh God!" Instead of divine revelation, ringing clear with the voice of a God unwilling to allow the suffering of his sons, there is silence. This silence is awful because it is the silence of God. Heschel does not claim that God is dead, as Nietzsche does. Rather, he believes that God lives, and his silence is therefore painfully cruel.

Heschel's proposal to take over God's duties is not in the spirit of his later writings, which pertain to man motivated by God to act. This is not an allusion to a cooperation between God and man. Young Heschel's heart is torn because he believes God can come to the rescue but refrains from doing so. Thus, in the fourth stanza Heschel reproaches God with not completing the art of creation. Creation does not attest to His greatness: "Reach for the emergency brakes of Your world/Which You have forgotten to set up!"

God has apparently forgotten to install an emergency brake system in His world, one that should operate during a time of great crisis, such as the one unfolding before Heschel's eyes. No reasons are given for God's deplorable behavior in neglecting to rush to his sons' aid "[A]nd come like a slave at their call." Heschel reverses the conventional state of relationship between God and his people. They are no longer God's slaves; it is the other way around. A deep sense of urgency compels Heschel to contest the God who has abandoned His sons, and he goes as far as to say: "And forgive our sins/As we forgive You Yours."[8]

As we said, God is not dead, but the living God has to contend with serious accusations. In yet another of his poems Heschel writes: "God, answer us—we long for You!/Overcome Your silence, Lord of all words!/The downcast of a thousand years beg you—reveal Yourself!"[9]

8. Heschel, *Ineffable*, 201.
9. Heschel, *Ineffable*, 195.

Heschel stands before God and demands that He understand that it is His absence that is the source of our sins: "Truly, You hide from our craving for You. Oh, see:/Our lustful passions disguise our need for You,/Our sins—a desperate thirst for You,/And Your silence—*gehinnom*, Hell on earth."[10]

Our sins and passions are but manifestations of our continuous search for the hiding God. Man can no longer bear the awful divine silence and is led to unburden himself in impious ways. Therefore, according to Heschel, God himself is our prosecutor.[11] This is based on the belief that God approves of events on earth, else He, the Almighty, would intervene. It is therefore His decision to abstain from intervention. Heschel expects him at least to commiserate: "Why does not God say:/I'm sorry!"[12] Man thirsts for contact with the divine and finds none. Heschel asks: "Why do you tease our trust in You?"[13]

Heschel follows in Abraham's footsteps. Abraham was the first to challenge God and argue for Sodom and Gomorrah, saying: "Will not the Judge of all the earth do right" (Genesis 18:25). Heschel refers to possible answers to similar questions raised by his predecessors: "Spare us word plays on enigmas./Show us goodness, not craft; joy not magic."[14] Mysticism does not offer an acceptable answer. Heschel does not address angels or partial divinities or "Spheres." He takes issue with God himself.

In the poem "Brother God," Heschel claims: "God is fettered in jail,/In labyrinths of infinity."[15]

Has God willingly incarcerated Himself? Or does Heschel claim that God may be subject to mystical or natural laws beyond His control? The poem goes on to describe God's flight from his prison: "You escape and go through all the streets. /But Your divinity masks you, God."

Who is God fleeing from? From Himself? From us? Is he trying to escape his duty? Heschel tells God that it is impossible for him to escape. He cannot flee from His divinity nor shirk His responsibilities in managing this world. In the second stanza we read: "You are not only Lord and Almighty, no!/You can also be poor and sorrowful./Sometimes You behave like a child,/As if I were the bigger boy." God is almighty; therefore, his incarceration is self-imposed. God is seeking to escape the rules He Himself

---

10. Heschel, *Ineffable*, 195.
11. Heschel, *Ineffable*, 195.
12. Heschel, *Ineffable*, 199.
13. Heschel, *Ineffable*, 199.
14. Heschel, *Ineffable*, 199.
15. Heschel, *Ineffable*, 65.

has created, but this is no longer possible. The system shall continue to exist even if He does not administer it.

In the second stanza Heschel refers to God's behavior as childish. He acts as though He has not managed to win a game and huffily exits the room. Heschel, cast in the role of God's elder brother, seeks to restore His self-confidence and call Him back into the room: "Our brother God!/From the last, endless height/Bend down to us, tenderly/And kiss every creature;/Kiss us soft and clear." Heschel's God resides in His heavens, at an enormous distance from man and his world. Divinity is transcendental to the point of severance of any contact between God and His sons. Heschel asks God to return to this world and to reveal Himself. Revelation is not forced; it is akin to a Godly kiss. This soft kiss symbolizes the love of God for all his creatures. Heschel asks that this kiss be "clear," distancing himself from mystical explanations which obscure rather than clarify the relationship between God and Man.

The spiritual conflict in a difficult reality drives Heschel to pose the question: "Who is real, I or God? /Let's be clear: enthusiasm or mockery!"[16] Heschel is well aware of the Medieval discussions of the question of God's existence vis-à-vis the existence of other creatures. He is familiar with Maimonides' contention that only God's existence is obligated because His being is dependent only on Himself. Other creatures' existence is contingent on many different circumstances and barring the fulfillment of all these conditions they would cease to exist. Having said that, it is not apparent how Heschel could pose his question but pose it he did. Who does Heschel address when he boldly calls "enthusiasm or mockery"? Is it himself? God? His people? It is difficult to say. The second line of the poem may refer to the first line. It commences with the demand for clarity. Is Heschel calling to God to quit hiding and to reveal Himself clearly? Why does he oppose enthusiasm and mockery? Who is mocking whom? Is God mocking man? Or is it the other way around? Or is it mutual mockery? Whose enthusiasm is Heschel commanding? Can enthusiasm deter mockery? It may be that this is what Heschel was driving at. It may be that he feels the question he asked in the first line is ridiculous for a believer. Indeed, it is both ridiculous and serious. Heschel's heart shouts out that God cannot but be real, but somehow reality proves otherwise.

---

16. Heschel, *Ineffable*, 193.

BEFORE AND AFTER THE HOLOCAUST

In 1936 Heschel published "The Meaning of Repentance" in Berlin. The article deals with the Days of Awe. It begins, "When we pray, we fulfill a sacred function. At stake is the sovereignty and the judgment of God."[17] This sentence surprises the reader because we are used to seeing the praying individual as the one who stands trial. What is Heschel's intention? Does he mean to say that divine rule and power are at peril? Are these concepts up for judgment?

Heschel answers these questions by addressing the nature of the relationship between the Creator and his creation. The Eternal God existed before creation, and indeed creation reflects His will: "Sovereignty can exist only in a relationship. Without subordinates this honor is abstract. God desired kingship and from that will creation emerged. But now the kingly dignity of God depends on us."[18] This is a somewhat startling assertion. God wants to rule, and the world was created to satisfy this desire. Had he wanted to, Heschel could have turned to Saadya Gaon, with whom he was very familiar, who described the creation of the world and man as reflections of divine love. Heschel chose a different path. He focused on the symbols of domination of divine rule, envisaged as the interaction between the ruler and the ruled. This is also a source of weakness: God's rule is dependent on human recognition. Man may revolt and "overthrow" God's rule, in which case God shall no longer be "King." In reference to his own times Heschel says: "The establishment or destruction of the kingly dignity of God occurs now, and in the present, through and in us. In all that happens in the world, in thought, conversation, actions, the kingdom of God is at stake."[19]

Heschel alludes to the immense power held by man. This is not an abstract philosophical thought. Heschel writes this amid an era of dire antisemitism, which casts doubt over the reign of God. Yet in the rage of these terrible times the people of Israel assume the divine rule. Although Heschel does not address the question of God's absolute power directly, it seems that in creating the world God willingly chose to minimize His own power. Heschel's short article is written in the form of a sermon and does not deal with questions such as whether the creation of the world indeed reflects divine will or whether it was in fact a foregone conclusion. Heschel considers these issues in other writings. In this article it was imperative for him to express his deep anxiety: "The deepest human longing is to be a thought in God's

---

17. Heschel, "Repentance," 68.
18. Heschel, "Repentance," 68.
19. Heschel, "Repentance," 68.

mind, to be the object of His attention. He may punish, and discipline me, only let Him not forget me, not abandon me."[20] Heschel sees God's power waning before his eyes, yet he begs God as the Ruler who holds the power to punish. Heschel is willing to accept any punishment but God's abandonment. The article begins with an unemotional academic study. Yet suddenly emotions erupt, and fear of abandonment takes over. I will not attempt to analyze the psychological process which led Heschel down this path, but simply state that these sudden passages reflect the depth of Heschel's belief and the deep doubts he had to contend with in face of the unholy horrors brought on by the Nazis.

In 1942 Heschel published "An Analysis of Piety."[21] Here Heschel presents a phenomenological analysis of piety. This is no discussion of God's objective existence, nor of the manifestation of God's will through "verifiable" revelation. Heschel, rather, wishes to examine the religious experience, avoiding the questions posed by philosophers up to Edmund Husserl.[22]

Heschel is interested in the way the pious individual understands divine will and wishes to implement it. In order to do so he distinguishes between faith and piety: "Faith is a sense for the reality of the transcendent; piety is the taking of an attitude toward it. Faith is vision, knowledge, belief; piety is relation, adjustment, an answer to a call, a mode of life."[23] Piety addresses the realities of life; it seeks to translate the sense of a transcendental God to actual existence. Heschel does not claim that God is indeed present in the world, but rather that the pious individual feels him to be so: "The pious man is possessed by his awareness of the presence and nearness of God. Everywhere and at all times he lives as in His sight He feels embraced by God's mercy as a vast encircling space."[24] The pious individual is so deeply aware of God's existence that he feels Him to be present even in his hour of anguish.

I must admit that in this case I find it difficult to find the voice of Heschel's soul in these words, which seem so detached. Writing in 1942 Heschel says:

> The pious man needs no miraculous communication to make him aware of God's presence, nor is a crisis necessary to awaken him to the meaning and appeal of that presence. His awareness

20. Heschel, "Repentance," 69.
21. Heschel, "Analysis of Piety," 305–17.
22. See Perlman, *Idea*.
23. Perlman, *Idea*, 310.
24. Perlman, *Idea*, 310.

may momentarily be overlaid or concealed by some violent shift in consciousness, but it never fades away.[25]

Heschel claims that the pious man does not require miracles to confirm his belief. There is no discussion of whether miracles are indeed possible in God's world or not. It would have been interesting to learn what the younger Heschel, who was introduced through his poems, would have thought of this.

Heschel also claims that the pious man lives in constant search for signs of the divine dimension of this world. He is forever trying to live his life in accordance with divine will and is therefore in search of signs of this will. Here again Heschel touches on the fear of loneliness and abandonment: "The world of God is as vital to him as air or food. He is never alone, never companionless, for God is within reach of his heart."[26]

It seems that Heschel is describing the many pious individuals who were present in his world during his younger days. God is sealed in their hearts yet does not manifest His presence in the outside world. The pious individual is willing to sacrifice anything which might come between him and the religious experience: "Purpose of sacrifice does not lie in pauperization as such but in the yielding of all aspirations to God, thus creating space for Him in the heart."[27]

In surrendering private wishes and aspirations, the pious individual allows God into his heart. This is an extreme manifestation of "spiritualization" of divine presence. He adds a sentence born no doubt in face of the extremes brought on by the Holocaust: "For the pious man it is a privilege to die."[28]

Heschel finds it important to emphasize that the pious man is in no way divorced from reality: "He would feel wretched and lost without the certainty that his life, insignificant though it be, is of some purpose in the great plan."[29]

The pious individual considers all his actions to be destined to fulfill divine will and therefore sees himself as assisting God to execute His plan. There is, however, a basic difference between the pious individual and the prophet. Heschel says thus of the pious: "In promoting the right, he is directing things toward His will, in which all aims must terminate. Ascending by this ladder, the pious man reaches the state of self-forgetfulness, sacrificing

25. Heschel, "Analysis of Piety," 311.
26. Heschel, "Analysis of Piety," 311.
27. Heschel, "Analysis of Piety," 316.
28. Heschel, "Analysis of Piety," 317.
29. Heschel, "Analysis of Piety," 317.

not only his desires but also his will, for he realizes that it is the will of God that matters and not his own perfection and salvation."[30] As we shall see further on, the prophet does not negate his own self.

We should also make the distinction between the pious and the mystic. Unlike the mystic, the pious does not aspire to abandon this world in order to unite with God. Rather he strives to deepen divine presence in our own world. This is not a direct presence, but rather one which is dependent on human will: "Thus the glory of man's devotion to the good becomes a treasure of God on earth."[31] God is then present in the world in the soul and will of the pious individual.

In 1944 Heschel published "The Meaning of This War."[32] Heschel expresses his anger and rage at the God who allowed the slaughter of six million Jews and asks: "Who is responsible?" "Where is God?" And the most difficult question of all: "Why dost Thou not halt the trains loaded with Jews being led to slaughter? It is so hard to rear a child, to nourish and to educate. Why dost Thou make it so easy to kill?"[33]

No explanation, mystic or otherwise, can account for God's absence when He was so needed.[34] No academic reasoning can address the murder of so many millions and so many children amongst them.[35] This of course assumes that God had the power and capability to intervene, and chose not to do so. Heschel follows with: "Like Moses, we hide our face; for we are afraid to look upon Elohim, upon His power of judgment."[36] This sentence lays the responsibility for the Holocaust directly with Divine judgment.

We could of course say that man's disturbance of the balance between *Gevurah* (might) and *Chesed* (love) through his transgressions unleashes the Satanic power. When might is not tempered by love the destructive power of the left side of the tree may indeed be demonic. If this is indeed Heschel's intent, then the responsibility for destruction is man's own undoing. This could not satisfy Heschel, because in his mind God is the Creator of the universe, including spheres, angels, and other heavenly creatures. If God's might is responsible for the Holocaust, then this is a deity to be feared and avoided.

---

30. Heschel, "Analysis of Piety," 317.
31. Heschel, "Analysis of Piety," 317.
32. Heschel, "Meaning of This War," 209.
33. Heschel, "Meaning of This War," 210.
34. Kaplan, "Confronting."
35. Kaplan, "Confronting," 130.
36. Heschel, "Meaning of This War," 210.

I believe that this is the turning point in Heschel's theology. The conception that God could have the ability to save his sons and would choose not to do so could undermine Heschel's belief in Him. Heschel therefore begins to stress that God is not almighty, and that man bears responsibility for this world. Heschel turns to examine humanity and tries to understand how it has become "a pit of snakes." He states that God was exiled from this world by man: "God will return to us when we are willing to let Him in— into our banks and factories, into our Congress and clubs, into our homes and theaters. For God is everywhere or nowhere."[37] Heschel addresses his words to his American readership. Having vested mankind with moral responsibility, he presents the pillars of the public and moral activity to which he then dedicated his life. God shall return to our world when we have made it worthy of Him. Heschel claims totality: either God is everywhere, or He is nowhere to be found. One could ask why Heschel should pose such an impossible demand, which seems doomed to failure. It is as if God could only reappear in the days of the Messiah!

Heschel then proceeds to make the following important assertion: "Only in His Presence shall we learn that the glory of man is not in his will to power but in his power of compassion."[38] These words pertain to man, but they also apply to God. The greatness of God and Man reveals itself in the capacity of mercy, and not in the power to rule.

In 1945 Heschel addressed a forum organized by the Yiddish Scientific Institute. He described the uniqueness of Eastern European Jewry, which the Nazis sought to destroy. This speech would later serve as the basis for his book The Earth is the Lord's. He emphasizes God's exile from the world: "People who at midnight lamented the glory of God that is in exile They [The Hasidim] knew that the Jews were in exile, that the world was unredeemed."[39] Heschel no longer demands that God intervene to save his sons, as he did in his youth. He now comprehends God's lack of ability to miraculously change the world. Heschel does not explain the concept of divine exile, which plays a major role in his later theological writings, and how it is realized. He does, however, make the connection between the exile of God and the exile of the people of Israel. He explains that according to Hasidic thought this dual exile was a manifestation of the fact that the world had not yet reached *Geula* (redemption). This Hasidic line of thought undoubtedly influenced Heschel's later ideas.

37. Heschel, "Meaning of This War," 211.
38. Heschel, "Meaning of This War," 211.
39. Heschel, *Earth*," 96.

Heschel presents the notions of the Kabbalists, who greatly influenced Eastern European Jewry. Here we encounter the ideas which would become central to Heschel's thought. As Heschel writes of the Kabbalists: "Inspired by the idea that not only is God necessary to man, but that man is also necessary to God, that man's actions are vital to all worlds and affect the course of transcendent events It became a matter of popular conviction that what takes place 'above' in the upper sphere, depends upon man 'below.'"[40] Man carries an enormous burden of responsibility. Man needs God and God needs man. Man may influence the divine world. God is in exile because man has banished him from his world. Man can let God back in. The Rabbi of Kotzk was asked: "Where is God?" His answer was: "Wherever man lets Him in."

This view takes strong root in Heschel's thought. Theologically, this reasoning relieves God of responsibility for this world. The difficult questions generated by the Holocaust should now be directed to man, who is sovereign of this world. Man can choose to love and construct, but he may adversely prefer to kill, thieve, and destroy. The burden of the Holocaust rests with man.[41] Heschel claims that in their darkest moments the Jews of Eastern Europe felt the presence of God. This was not a hope-inspiring presence, based on belief in miraculous salvation, but rather a deep feeling within their hearts. Indeed, this was a unity of suffering forged between the divinity and the people of Israel: "The feeling of the presence of the Shechinah in human suffering became indelibly engraved in the consciousness of the East European Jews. To bring about the restitution of the universe was the goal of all efforts. The meaning of man's life lies in his perfecting the universe."[42]

The exiled, suffering God cannot offer redemption. "The highest heavens belong to the Lord, but the earth He has given to man" (Psalms 115:16). In light of Heschel's words, the verse distinguishes between the realm of the rule of God and that of the rule of Man. Heschel asserts that this led the Kabbalists to treat all human deeds as having bearing on the possibility of mending this world. Man holds the keys to the gates of redemption.[43] He cannot shirk his responsibility for this world. He must choose: "Mankind

---

40. Heschel, *Earth*, 71.

41. Of course some would consider this an attempt on Heschel's behalf to shirk casting responsibility upon God.

42. Heschel, *Earth*, 72.

43. Heschel, *Earth*.

does not have the choice of religion and neutrality We are either the ministers of the sacred or slaves of evil."[44]

GOD IS NOT A POWER BUT A FATHER (1951–1957)[45]

In 1951 Heschel published *Man is Not Alone*. The title raises many questions: Why is man not alone? How do we know that he is not alone? Does God make contact with man? Who is God? Who is man? Is God present in this world? What meaning can we attribute to God's presence? These are just some of the questions raised in Heschel's book. One of the differences between this book and the previous ones is in Heschel's way of treating existential questions. Here he presents a cognitive theory, which is the basis for his analysis. Based on this cognitive theory we can understand Heschel's conception of God's presence, as well as the meaning he accords to His might and power. Heschel says: "His Power is His Love. His justice is His mercy."[46]

This should probably be read considering the mystic views Heschel inherited from his forefathers. As we mentioned above, in the Kabbalistic Tree of Sefirot, *Chesed* (love) is opposed to *Gevura* (might). These need to be balanced in order to allow the flow of Divine Emanation into this world. Once the balance is disturbed both the upper and the lower worlds may be destroyed. Heschel unites these powers and sees God's love as his might and the powers of judgment as the powers of mercy. This definition negates the typical interpretation of God's power. God is completely disarmed and cannot fight the battles of this world. In one of his youthful poems Heschel turned to God and asked Him to vest him with His arms so that he could continue battling in this world. Now we see that these arms are nonexistent. God has only His mercy and love. These are inspiring qualities, but in the battlefield Heschel and the prophets would have to tap their own resources. Prophets do not aspire to transcend this world in order to unite with God, they work to allow God and holiness back into this world.[47]

The first part of Heschel's book is titled "The Problem of God." We soon become aware that this part deals with "The Problem of Man." Heschel argues that God is present in this world, but man is not aware of Him. To the question "Where is God?" Heschel replies, "Where is He not?"[48] Hes-

---

44. Heschel, *Earth*, 107–8.
45. Heschel, *Search*, 68.
46. Heschel, *Alone*.
47. Heschel, *Alone*, 281.
48. Heschel, *Alone*, 70.

chel goes on to clarify that man must acquire special spiritual sensitivity to become aware of His presence. In reference to man's original sin Heschel says: "Man was the first to hide himself from God, after having eaten of the forbidden fruit, and is still hiding. The will of God is to be here, manifest and near; but when the doors of this world are slammed on Him, His truth betrayed, His will defied, He withdraws, leaving man to himself. God did not depart of His own volition; He was expelled. God is in exile."[49]

God is not present in this world because man banished Him. How can we continue to claim that he is ever-present? I believe Heschel meant to say that man exiled God from his inner world. God may be present in the hearts of His children, but only if they let Him in.

Heschel claims that original sin occurs time and again every day and that the gates of this world remain sealed to God. Having been exiled from the hearts of men, God can no longer influence the life of mankind. This is central to Heschel's theology. Heschel is aware of the problematics of this theory and comments:

His need is a self-imposed concern. God is now in need of man, because He freely made him His partner in His enterprise, a "partner in the work of creation."[50]

This is a very unusual assertion. It is the only reference of this type which I found in Heschel's body of writings. It is lacking in *God in Search of Man*, which is devoted to the topic of the divine quest of man. Heschel claims that there is no limit on divine power, but rather it is God Himself who has chosen to need man.

Theologically speaking, this is in line with the conception which is the basis of many of Heschel's texts: Man cannot fathom God, and therefore cannot determine that God has a need (intrinsic or extrinsic) of man. We can take this further and claim that Heschel is following Maimonides, who states that man cannot understand God, but may become acquainted with His ways.

We are back to the basic tenet that it is God's choice not to intervene in this world. This may set us back to the criticism leveled at God by the younger Heschel, who demanded that God exercise His power to aid his tortured and murdered sons. We should note, however, that the idea that God has independently chosen to be in need of man is not consistent with the rest of Heschel's book. We have already seen that in discussing God's exile Heschel says:

---

49. Heschel, *Alone*, 153.
50. Heschel, *Alone*, 243.

God did not depart of His own volition; He was expelled. God is in exile.[51]

God's exile is not described as an act of free choice. It was imposed by man. How can we settle this apparent contradiction? We could claim that there is a distinction between God's free choice to need man and His exile. The former makes the latter possible. Man has been made sovereign of this world, and therefore may abolish God from it.

The first part of the book deals with cognition, or the ability of an "to sense the presence of God." The problem of modern man is that he no longer has this capacity. Heschel says: A sensitive person knows that the intrinsic, the most essential, is never expressed."[52] A sensitive man would be aware of the mystery of this world and comprehend man's inability to understand everything. Furthermore: "The awareness of the unknown is earlier than the awareness of the known. The tree of knowledge grows upon the soil of mystery."[53] This is the basis for Heschel's discussion of the premise that "man is not alone":

The awareness of the ineffable is that with which our search must begin. Philosophy, enticed by the promise of the known, has often surrendered the treasures of higher incomprehension to poets and mystics, although without the sense of the ineffable there are no metaphysical problems, no awareness of being as being, of value as value.[54]

In Heschel's mind, we can approach the world in one of two ways: either through reason or through feelings of wonder. Heschel believes that "wonder is, and must be, the root of knowledge."[55] We must sense the mystery of this world to feel the presence of God. The chapter dealing with His presence commences thus: "The sense of the ineffable introduces the soul to the divine aspect of the universe, to a reality higher than the universe."[56]

It is in this divine aspect that "[w]e possess an intuition of a divine presence."[57] There is a substantial difference between what is said in the above paragraph and what is expressed in Heschel's earlier writings. Here Heschel may claim that the question of God's presence is one of cognition. Man cannot sense God through reason. For this purpose, he must rise

---

51. Heschel, *Alone*, 153.
52. Heschel, *Alone*, 4.
53. Heschel, *Alone*, 7.
54. Heschel, *Alone*, 8.
55. Heschel, *Alone*, 11.
56. Heschel, *Alone*, 67.
57. Heschel, *Alone*, 67.

beyond it and attain an intuitive sense of God's presence.[58] Of course, this is no answer for the younger Heschel. This is not a representation of a God who can redress the state of things in face of the suffering of the pious and the rejoicing of the impious. We could be led to the Maimonidean interpretation of the book of Job (undoubtedly known to Heschel).[59]

Maimonides claims that Job's suffering was a result of his lack of wisdom. Had he been wise he could have distinguished between real and unreal happiness. It is this understanding which allows Job, at the end of the book, to know that suffering in the material world has no effect on true happiness, which is attained through spiritual and mental nearness to God. Job reaches the perception that suffering and pain no longer have meaning in this world. Heschel could not accept such a mystical view. He would probably reject the Maimonidean perception on the basis that it would lead us to conclude that real happiness could only be attained if we abandon the material world. Contrary to mystical conceptions, which differentiate between the material and the transcendental-divine worlds, Heschel speaks of one unified world. The distinction between the material aspect and the divine one is in the eye of the beholder. While many may consider this world to be materialistic and devoid of spirituality, the spiritually sensitive would not consider it to be so. Heschel considers the prophets to have attained a spiritual level which bestows them with a divine viewpoint of the world. This endows them with the vigor to try to mend this world. Once mended, the world shall be both human and divine.

In the chapter titled "In the Presence of God" Heschel further clarifies: "Once our bare soul is exposed to the omnipresence of the ineffable, we cannot bid it cease to shatter us with its urging wonder."[60] Through use of the term "omnipresence" Heschel elucidates God's full presence in this world. From the spiritual viewpoint of most of humanity, however, God's presence is obscure. According to Heschel, man's soul is at times awakened to the fact that sources of mystery may eclipse our ruled and orderly vision of the world. The term "omnipresence" signifies the limitations of human reasoning. Despite these limitations man may intuitively become conscious of the immanence of God: "In the realm of the ineffable, where our own presence is incredible, we don't ask: Where is God? We can only exclaim: Where is He not? Where are we? How is our presence possible?"[61]

58. Merkle clarifies: "By beholding the sublime and mysterious dimension of this world, one may find a way to an awareness of God who is beyond, yet present in, this world." See Merkle, "Sublime," 366.
59. Maimonides, *The Guide of the Perplexed*, part III, chapters 22–23.
60. Heschel, *Alone*, 68.
61. Heschel, *Alone*, 70.

Thus, the question we should address is not whether God exists or whether He is present, but rather what this presence signifies for us. Towards the end of the chapter Heschel describes an experience of the emergence of divine presence in all its splendor, illuminating the deep meaning of awareness of the divine:

But, then, a moment comes like a thunderbolt, in which a flash of the undisclosed rends our dark apathy asunder. It is full of overpowering brilliance. The ineffable has shuddered itself into the soul. It has entered our consciousness like a ray of light passing into a lake. . . . We are penetrated by His insight.[62]

In this experience the individual becomes overwhelmingly aware of divine presence. Arthur Green claims that Heschel is describing a very personal experience.[63] This is a very interesting remark because the experience described is a prophetic one.[64] If we accept Green's supposition, then we may conclude that Heschel considered his experience prophetic, at least in the sense described by Maimonides, an experience characterized by divine lightning illuminating man's mind. These moments are prophetic, yet very short. When the light subsides, man returns to his prior mental state. According to Maimonides, Moses was the only one to enjoy continuous enlightenment.[65] No doubt Heschel, conversant in Maimonidean thought, saw himself enjoying a momentary flash of prophetic enlightenment. In these moments divine presence manifested itself in all its brilliance:

We cannot think any more as if He were there and we here. He is both there and here. He is not a being but being in and beyond all beings.[66]

At the moment of this outstanding spiritual experience all obstacles barring God from this world were dropped, and Man came closer to understanding the concept of "omnipresence."

Heschel proceeds to discuss the concept of divine unity, and argues that this unity implies being at one with the material world: "Unity of God is power for unity of God with all things. He is one in Himself and striving to be one with the world."[67]

---

62. Heschel, *Alone*, 78.

63. See Green, "Three," 53–54.

64. Kaplan says that a completely transformed vision of reality arises from depression and from the *death* of the old self: "Apathy turns to splendor unawares." Kaplan turns our attention to the fact that in describing a mystical-prophetic experience Heschel is in fact using the same terms he referred to when defining the Kabbalist. See Kaplan, "Mysticism," 40.

65. Maimonides, *The Guide of the Perplexed*, part 1, Introduction.

66. Heschel, *Alone*, 78.

67. Heschel, *Alone*, 123.

God cannot achieve unity while "in exile." He wishes to reunite with this world and to be present in the hearts of His sons. Man therefore affects the unity of God. Unity is not a physical concept: "The unity of God is a concern for the unity of the world."[68]

This may be a difficult idea to grasp because Judaism considers "unity" to be an intrinsic attribute of God, while "concern" is an incidental attribute. Heschel sees things differently. He considers the unity of God to imply concern for his creations. "Concern" is therefore an inherent attribute, while unity is incidental because it is contingent on the will of Man.

In 1951 Heschel published The Sabbath. In it he presents a new definition of divine presence. He contends that if we limit ourselves to regarding created "things," we may lose sight of their Creator. However: "Time is the presence of God in the world of space, and it is within time that we are able to sense the unity of all beings."[69]

If we contemplate the continued renewal of creation, we gain the sense of the living God. Heschel recognizes God in the everlasting process of change, as opposed to the Greeks, who believed that divinity exists forever in its infinite perfection. Perfection implies a lack of will, a lack of emotion. Transformation may be understood as a threat to unity because earlier stages give way to later ones. Heschel argues that contrary to this, continued transformation entails coexistence of past, present, and future. This is not a physical unity or a unity of will, but rather mutual responsibility assumed by all beings. All beings interact, whether man is aware of it or not. We may become conscious of this interaction over time, because in the dimension of time we witness the changes effected in creatures through other creatures. This may be a destructive type of interaction, but if this interaction mirrors the will of God, we may say that He is again present in this world.

In 1954 Heschel published *Man's Quest for God*. In it we read that prayer is the manifestation of the feeling of divine presence. It is this feeling which urges a man to pray.[70] Heschel goes on to say that prayer is invoked by divine presence, but also serves to strengthen it:

To pray, then, means to bring God back into the world Great is the power of prayer. For to worship is to expand the presence of God in the world. God is transcendent, but our worship makes Him immanent. This is implied in the idea that God is in need of man: His being immanent depends upon us.[71]

---

68. Heschel, *Alone*.
69. Heschel, *Sabbath*, 100.
70. Heschel, *Quest*, 59.
71. Heschel, *Quest*, 62.

Heschel states again that divine presence is contingent on man, but we are led to ask whether this presence is manifest only in the hearts of those praying. This would not conform with Heschel's opinions, nor with his intent to discover divine presence in the world. It would seem Heschel assumed that the person who had sensed divine presence in his heart would then proceed to try to improve this world. Prayer can awaken new understandings in the heart of Man, and these would motivate him to act. Thus, prayer serves to spread divine presence.

One could also maintain that prayer reveals the presence of the transcendental God in this world, thus affirming His immanence. This idea is consistent with the notion of divine presence introduced in *Man Is Not Alone*. Divine presence manifests itself when the individual reaches a state of spiritual relation. This relation is attained through sensual rather than mental capacities. Prayer may arouse the senses and allow the individual to feel divine presence. Prayer allows the individual to overcome the boundaries of human comprehension:

> The art of awareness of God, the art of sensing His presence in our daily lives, cannot be learned off-hand. God's grace resounds in our lives like a staccato. Only by retaining the seemingly disconnected notes comes the ability to grasp the theme.[72]

The musical metaphor suggests a dissonant and disunited world assembled together in one melody. The musical symbol may also point to the interaction between God's unity and the unity of all His creations. This unity is achieved while the praying individual reaches a powerful spiritual uplifting. Here, as in *Man is not Alone*, we are introduced to a forceful experience of divine presence. God was banished from man's spiritual world, but the power of prayer may unveil His presence and allow us to sense Him. The spiritualization of divine presence is essential to Heschel's notion of prayer. Prayer is not intended to beseech God to assist man, because such intervention is not within His power.

In 1955 Heschel published *God in Search of Man*. It can be considered a continuation of *Man Is Not Alone*. Heschel analyzes the revelation of divine presence in terms of a process taking place in the human mind: "'Lift up your eyes on high and see: Who created these' (Isaiah 40:26) One must rise to a higher plane of thinking in order to see, in order to sense the allusions, the glory, the presence."[73]

In order to "see" and to "sense" divine presence man must rise above the normal stages of consciousness. At the beginning of the book Heschel

---

72. Heschel, *Quest*, 60.
73. Heschel, *Search*, 118.

presents three ways of sensing divine presence: "The first is the way of sensing the presence of God in the world, in things; the second is the way of sensing His presence in the Bible; the third is the way of sensing His presence in sacred deeds."[74]

Only an individual endowed with spiritual sensitivity may feel the divine presence. Simply put, divine presence is not evident to all. People of special sensitivity may only experience it at special moments, not constantly.

Heschel then characterizes the mitzvot as stimulating feelings of holiness. The mitzvot may "let Him [God] enter our daily deeds, in which we coin our thoughts in the mint of eternity."[75] Heschel devotes several chapters to the meaning and to the role of the mitzvot. What makes the mitzvot special is the devotion of human beings to God's will, and God's will is to mend the world. Hence, the immense importance of the mitzvot in Heschel's thought. Heschel remarks:

It is more meaningful for us to believe in the immanence of God in deeds than in the immanence of God in nature.[76]

Considering his book on the Sabbath, Heschel explains that the man who performs the mitzvot draws closer to God in the dimension of time. Time is the living dynamic relation between man and God, as opposed to the static relation between things in the spatial dimension. Although Heschel does not claim that God does not exist within nature, it is sometimes difficult to sense his presence there. Man has not gained control over natural catastrophes, but he does exercise mastery over the enactment of the mitzvot. Heschel refers to the conception that man has absolute responsibility over the immanence of God, and clarifies: "We do not meet Him in the way in which we meet things of space. To meet Him means to come upon an inner certainty of His realness upon an awareness of His will. Such meeting, such presence, we experience in deeds."[77]

The performance of the mitzvot allows man to experience the certainty of divine presence in his heart. Heschel speaks of a "meeting," hence there is no distance between man and God, and the contact is direct.

In order to comprehend the biblical religious experience Heschel points out the central import of the scriptures:

This is what Israel discovered: The God of nature is the God of history, and the way to know Him is to do His will.[78]

---

74. Heschel, *Search*, 31.
75. Heschel, *Search*, 312.
76. Heschel, *Search*, 311–12.
77. Heschel, *Search*, 312.
78. Heschel, *Search*, 31.

This task is next to impossible. God does not appear as the Lord of History. This ideal has not been realized yet. Heschel considers the biblical aspiration as an ideal which must strive to achieve. We should not be surprised that the book carries little reference to the concept of "miracle." A "miracle" would imply direct divine intervention in this world. Heschel refers to this concept in one sole paragraph, and even then, it is to a "hidden" miracle, not apparent to those who gaze at reality.[79]

At this stage of his work, Heschel has already concluded that God is in exile, and therefore not omnipotent. The discussion of the hidden miracle, based on Nachmanides, deals with the religious experience of "wonder." Man is astounded by the mystery of reality, is moved to sense divine presence, and his belief in God is awakened.

In a chapter titled "An Ontological Presupposition" Heschel presents his theory of cognition. As the name of the chapter denotes, Heschel believes that we cannot prove the existence of God in rational ways; it is a presupposition. This assumption is an "insight," which bears absolute certainty:

The living encounter with reality takes places on a level that is responsive, immediate, preconceptual, and pre-symbolic. Theory, speculation, generalization, and hypothesis are efforts to clarify and to validate the insights which preconceptual experience provides.[80]

Heschel speaks of a level of cognition which is prior to conceptualization. It is on this level that man's direct encounter with God awakens these "insights." Merkle said of this experience that:

Only an ultimate presence can be ultimately meaningful to the personal reality of man.[81]

Like Merkle, Heschel considers that God is a challenge rather than a notion.[82] Rothschild maintains that God's pathos is a response to changing human actions, and therefore in itself is not constant but evolving.[83] Heschel defined the concepts of "creation" and "revelation" as ongoing transformations. I believe we should therefore read Heschel's concept of divine presence as a process of discovery of God's presence. Man can influence the process and expedite it, but he can also bring it to a halt.

Heschel draws a distinction between Jewish theology and what he terms "theology of fate." He goes on to present two differing notions of the relations between man and God:

---

79. Heschel, *Search*, 51.
80. Heschel, *Search*, 115.
81. Merkle, "Sublime," 372.
82. Merkle, "Sublime, 170.
83. Rothschild, *Between*, 25.

The theology of fate knows only a one-sided dependence upon the ultimate power. That power has neither concern for man nor need of him. History runs its course as a monologue. To Jewish religion, on the other hand, history is determined by the covenant: God is in need of man. The ultimate is not law but a Judge, not a power but a father.[84]

We should note that the theology of fate, which is based on the idea that God is the sole determinant of all that happens, is described in Heschel's other writings as Islamic theology. Jewish theology, in contrast, is based on a dialogue between man and God. God does not operate on the basis of predetermined laws and principles, regardless of his subjects. He judges His sons with empathy. The relation between God and mankind is based on a paternal affinity, not on authority.

One of Heschel's most central and famous notions deals with the partnership between God and man. Heschel says: "The destiny of man is to be a partner of God and a mitzvah is an act in which man is present, an act of participation; while sin is an act in which God is alone; an act of alienation."[85] The image of God is not of an active deity struggling to vest this world with holiness. This is man's task.

In 1957 Heschel wrote the article "Sacred Image of Man," in which he states: "The Paradise we have built may turn out to be a vast camp, for the extermination of man."[86]

This comment highlights the fact that the Holocaust was ever present in Heschel's mind. He believed that man may choose to unleash the satanic demons in his soul and to bring on the destruction of humanity. It is this conviction which led him to devote himself to the struggle for human rights. This was Heschel's response to the Holocaust.

THE MISSION OF THE PROPHETS: TO READMIT GOD INTO THIS WORLD

In the introduction to the English edition of his book on the prophets, Heschel asserts that one can only understand prophecy if one identifies with it.[87]

84. Heschel, *Search*, 68.
85. Heschel, *Search*, 312.
86. Heschel, "Sacred Image of Man," 165.
87. Heschel wrote his Ph.D. thesis at the University of Berlin. It was published in 1936 in Warsaw. The English version is not a translation of the original German. It expands on his theological notions of the prophets, which were influenced by his work on writings which preceded the English version of *The Prophets*. See Heschel, *Prophets*, ii. First published in 1962. As is stated by the publisher, "Some paragraphs in this volume are taken from *God in Search of Man*."

Heschel feels such an identification.[88] He therefore attempts to renew the prophetic struggle to make this world a Kingdom of God. Heschel dedicates his book to those deceased in WWII, because it is the role of the prophets to uproot the evil which made the Nazi monstrosities possible.

The prophet's unique religious experience drives him to strive to redress this world. Heschel characterizes the prophet as a "Homo Sympathetikus."[89] His experience of the divine, like Heschel's is a *"unio sympathetica"* rather than a *"unio mystica."*[90]

Unlike the mystic's religious experience, which voids his own existence, the prophet's divine encounter is a meeting of wills, whereby he is empowered.[91] A prophet may attain a perspective of reality similar to God's, as his grasp of reality has been changed through his religious experience.[92] Heschel describes it thus: "The pathos of God is upon him. It moves him. It breaks out in him like a storm in the soul overwhelming his inner life, his thoughts, feelings, wishes and hopes. It takes possession of his heart and mind, giving him the courage to act against the world."[93]

Their complete identification with God leads the prophets to an uncompromising stance regarding this world. They are willing to contend against any obstacles hindering salvation.[94]

Heschel reiterates the distinction he has made in *God in Search of Man*, between the Jewish God and the omnipotent God:[95] "The God of pathos may be contrasted with the God of Islam. For all the belief in divine mercy, Allah is essentially thought of as unqualified Omnipotence."[96] The God of the prophets relies on the struggle led by His children.

---

88. Rotenstreich notes: "We find in Heschel the awareness of his indebtedness to phenomenology when he explicitly says that he is concerned with the description of the essence of prophetic assertions and not with their truth." See Rotenstreich, "Consciousness," 186.

89. Rothschild says: "The sympathetic union must be clearly distinguished from the view of speculative theology which sees the culmination of the quest for the divine in a *knowledge of God*." Rothschild, *Between*, 25.

90. Heschel, *Prophets II*, 99.

91. See also my article "Mysticism," 359–70.

92. Heschel, *Prophets II*, xvi.

93. Heschel, *Prophets II*, 88.

94. Kaplan says: "The prophets and Heschel extend divine involvement in history by combining a concern for self and for others with consciousness of *God's eternal presence*" (Kaplan, "Spiritual Radicalism, 44).

95. This is an Islamic notion presented by Maimonides in *Guide of the Perplexed*, part 3, chapter 17.

96. Heschel, *Prophets II*, 21.

THE TORAH OF THE SHEKHINA AND GOD'S POWER IN THE THOUGHT OF THE SAGES

In 1952 the first volume of *Heavenly Torah—As Refracted through the Generations* was published. Heschel dedicates part of this book to a discussion of divine presence in this world. This was the same year Heschel published *The Prophets*, and we may discern the influence of the theology attributed by Heschel to the prophets to the one attributed to the sages.

Heschel begins his discussion with a presentation of the concept of divine pathos. God identifies with the fate of His children. Here Heschel demonstrates through various midrashim that God and man are partners not only in strife, but also in redemption. As an example he cites the midrash that when the people of Israel are redeemed, God is redeemed as well.[97] He notes that this was a revolutionary concept, because redemption is perceived not only as a human need but as a divine need also.[98] This could lead us to conclude that God's concern for man is basically egotistic, but this is not Heschel's intent. Redemption refers to God's return to this world.

Heschel continues by examining the question of God's might and greatness. How can we continue to call him "the great almighty God"?[99] If he is so great, how is his greatness apparent? How can we attribute these characteristics to a God who allows His sons to be butchered, tortured and raped? These questions were asked by the rabbis in a very problematic age. They saw the destruction of the Temple, the profanation of God's name, and the humiliation of the house of Israel and ask: "If there is Mercy, there surely is no power; and if there is power, there surely is no mercy! For could one maintain that the Holy and Blessed One empathizes well but does not carry through?"[100]

These questions are asked with pain. Heschel says that "Rabbi Akiva and his cohorts believed that it is better to limit belief in God's power than to dampen faith in God's mercy."[101] Heschel's own opinion follows Rabbi Akiva.

This is one of the strongest of Heschel's theological ideas. Heschel abandons the classical concept of the divine omnipotence. He is aware of the theological danger of his conception and asks: "Does not this doctrine diminish our image of the divine and limit our belief in the creator's

---

97. Heschel, *Heavenly Torah*, 115.
98. Heschel, *Heavenly Torah*, 107.
99. B. Talmud, Yomah 69:a.
100. Heschel, *Heavenly Torah*, 118.
101. Heschel, *Heavenly Torah*, 119.

omnipotence?"¹⁰² As we saw earlier, he chooses to regard the notion of an almighty God as non-Jewish. He, like sages before him, prefers the conception that God is not omnipotent.

REDUCTION? DID GOD CHOOSE TO REDUCE HIS POWER AND PRESENCE?

In 1965 Heschel published Who Is Man.¹⁰³ This book is largely dedicated to contemplation of the essence of man, but in Heschel's thought that cannot be divorced from the relation of God and man. Heschel therefore turns again to the issue of divine presence:

Being is both presence and absence. God had to conceal His presence in order to bring the world into being. He had to make His absence possible in order to make room for the world's presence. Coming into being brought along denial and defiance, absence, oblivion, and resistance.¹⁰⁴

In this paragraph Heschel assumes the mystical conception of an infinite God reducing Himself in order to create space for the creation of this world. It is this very reduction which allows man to defy God, to negate His existence and to act in independent ways which may be sinful. We should note the distinction between God and His honor. In our daily prayers we repeat thrice: *Kadosh, Kadosh, Kadosh* (Holy, Holy Holy). Heschel claims that this repetition is designed to emphasize divine transcendence. God's Honor is present in the world, indeed is immanent. Nevertheless, this presence is hidden, and few are aware of it.

THE STATE OF ISRAEL: GOD IS NO LONGER IN EXILE

Following the Six-Day War, Heschel arrived in Israel with a group of rabbis. They joined Israeli thinkers for a seminar in Beit Berl, where Heschel addressed them in Hebrew. Later he expanded this lecture into a book, under the title *Israel: An Echo of Eternity*. Pinhas Peli translated it into Hebrew and added an introduction, citing parts of Heschel's speech.¹⁰⁵ The speech is very impassioned. Heschel returns to the conceptions which ruled his poems in younger days and to his disillusionment with a God who fails to come to the

---

102. Heschel, *Heavenly Torah*, 118.

103. Heschel, *Who Is Man?* 90. First published 1965. This book comprises lectures delivered in May 1963 at Stanford University.

104. Heschel, *Who Is Man?* 90.

105. Heschel, *Israel*, 17. Foreword: *Israel* (Heb.).

aid of His sons. The victory in the war led Heschel to the renewed belief in a God of history. Before victory was attained his feelings were very different.

Heschel begins his book with the Holocaust: "In 1945 our souls were ruins Those of us who were not asphyxiated continued to cling to Thee. "Though he slay me, yet I will to trust in him" (Job 13:15)."[106]

At the end of the book of Job, Job is blissful again, and none of the mishaps which affected him can cloud his happiness. He understands that all that happened was for the best and that God is a God of mercy. Heschel chooses not to quote these passages. His chosen reference states clearly that God inexplicably butchers His sons. This is a return to Heschel's theology in his poems, blaming God for not intervening miraculously to save the people of Israel.

As a survivor of the Second World War Heschel was mortified at the prospect of the destruction of the state of Israel: "Will God permit our people to perish? Will there be another Auschwitz, another Dachau, another Treblinka?"[107]

Does this wording signify a change in Heschel's theology, or is it just a literary twist? I believe this exclamation was born of deep spiritual contemplation. It is reminiscent of Heschel's earlier poem, but in this case, he does not wonder why God had not prevented the first massacre but implores Him to prevent a second one. Heschel does not hesitate to say: "Some of us felt that those were days of judgment for the Holy One of Israel. Will He desert us? Will He hide His face again?"[108]

It is then God who stands trial. Will God be sentenced to death if He deserts His people again?

Further on in the book Heschel recants and reiterates the notion that God is indeed powerless, because His sons have exiled him from this world. Then he goes on to announce: "We of this generation stand face to face with events of vast magnitude. The Lord of history does not slumber nor sleep."[109]

Our generation, says Heschel, has undergone a deep spiritual experience: God is present in our world again! Tremendous events attest to this presence: The Six-Day War affirms that God has awakened, and he is fully empowered again, He is once more God of history. Heschel writes exuberantly. His poetic and literary talents climax; he is almost messianic.

106. Heschel, *Israel*, 17. Foreword: *Israel* (Eng.).
107. Heschel, *Israel* (Eng.), 197.
108. Heschel, *Israel* (Eng.), 197.
109. Heschel, *Israel* (Eng.), 48.

Heschel describes the days of exhilaration with immense emotion. After the victory, the השמים ארובות, which had previously closed, re-opened.[110] With a feeling of elation Heschel proclaims that the Torah and prophecy are rejuvenated and that new chapters are being written in our days: "The Bible, we discovered, is not a book sealed and completed; the Bible lives on, always being written, continuously proclaimed. The Bible, we discovered, lives within us, reverberates in our anxiety. Our involvement with it continues. Almost suddenly it dawned upon many of us that Biblical history is alive, that chapters of the Bible are being written.[111] Heschel claims: "It is a Renaissance of biblical events that we witness in our days.[112]

At this uplifting hour, the bond between God and man is renewed and they are close again. The Jew hears the call again: Where art thou? And replies: Here I am.[113] The Shekhina, which was banished from our world in the days of darkness, returns and addresses man directly. In prophetic pathos Heschel adds: "To the religious consciousness of the Jews the people being in exile means also God's being in exile and the return of the people to the land is also experienced as God's return to the Land."[114]

The English title of this book is slightly different than the Hebrew one. In the Hebrew edition, published one year after his death, the main title remains "Israel," but in Hebrew this is followed by "Present and Eternity," while in the English version it is "An Echo of Eternity." I do not know whether this change was made by Pinhas Peli, who translated the book, of his own choice, or whether he had discussed it with Heschel. The Hebrew title seems more appropriate because the book does not refer to victory as a faint echo, but rather as a triumph of divine presence.

GOD IN EXILE AGAIN—1969

Two years after the victory Heschel published an article about Jewish theology in which he restates the limits of God's might.[115] He is explicit:

The whole conception of God's Omnipotence, I suspect, was taken over from Islam. God is almighty, and powerful. Man has nothing to say and nothing to do except to keep quiet and to accept. But God needs man's cooperation. There will be no redemption without the cooperation of man.

---

110. Heschel, *Israel* (Heb.), 22–23.
111. Heschel, *Israel* (Eng.), 49.
112. Heschel, *Israel* (Eng.), 49.
113. Heschel, *Israel* (Eng.), 20.
114. Heschel, *Israel* (Eng.), 25–26.
115. Heschel, "Jewish Theology," 154–63.

Omnipotence as such will not work. God cannot function in the world without the help of man.[116]

Heschel cites Maimonides, who had to contend with Islamic influence and considered that God was not omnipotent.[117] Indeed, in his Guide of the Perplexed Maimonides asserts that God cannot deviate from the eternal rules of logic.[118] Heschel adds: "So in a sense he [Maimonides] fought the exaggerated conceptions of omnipotence. But he did not go far enough. I tell you that the idea of divine omnipotence, meaning, holding God responsible for everything, expecting Him to do the impossible, to defy human freedom, is a non-Jewish Idea."[119]

The People of Israel let God back in this world in June 1967, but they have exiled him again. God is still waiting for us to reopen the gates.

---

116. Heschel, "Jewish Theology," 159.

117. Maimonides, *The Guide of the Perplexed*, part III, chapter 15.

118. I believe Maimonides also intends to say that God may not deviate from physical and metaphysical rules.

119. Heschel, "Jewish Theology," 160.

4

No Religion Is an Island

Following the Trail Blazer

ALON GOSHEN-GOTTSTEIN

**THE ELIJAH INTERFAITH INSTITUTE
(JERUSALEM, ISRAEL)**

> This may be compared to a thicket of reeds which no man could enter, for whoever entered therein lost his way. What did a certain clever man do? He cut down [some reeds] and entered, then cut down more and penetrated further; thus he entered through the clearing and went out; then all began to enter through his clearing.[1]

Through a rereading of Heschel's essay "No Religion Is an Island," I will highlight his conceptual and methodological contribution, as well as address the issue of Heschel's legacy and how it continues to challenge us. As one who follows in Heschel's footsteps I shall move between a description

---

1. Genesis Rabba 12:1 in Freedman and Simon, *Midrash Rabbah*, 87.

of Heschel and his theoretical contribution and the realities, challenges, and work that lies ahead of us, now and in the future.[2]

INTRODUCTION

The Midrashic parable quoted above, applied in some traditions to the figure of Solomon, whose parables break a path of understanding in the Torah, provides an apt description for the accomplishments of Abraham Joshua Heschel in the field of interreligious dialogue.[3] Heschel was a path breaker. While Jews and Christians have been in some form of exchange ever since the younger religion grew out of the older, something novel characterizes the historical situation in which Heschel operated, the relationships he enjoyed, and the theological and spiritual challenges he faced. I believe it is fair to say that Heschel was the first Jewish thinker to have consciously grappled with the question of the meaning of interfaith (or interreligious) dialogue and to have suggested some of the psychological, intellectual, and spiritual moves it requires.[4] In other words, he was Judaism's first theoretician of interreligious relations.[5]

Heschel was a trail blazer. Many of the important voices that have been sounded over the forty years are in some way indebted to Heschel, or at

---

2. I am presently involved in a project of developing a contemporary Jewish theology of world religions, a project that is very close in spirit to Heschel's work. The theoretical foundations of this research and education project, carried out under the auspices of the Elijah Interfaith Institute, are spelled out in the Hebrew article, "Theology of Interreligious Dialogue: An Initial Mapping," *Akdamot* (2006) and in the English article, " Towards a Jewish Theology of World Religions: Meeting the Challenges of Interreligious Pluralism," to be published in a volume prepared at Georgetown University.

3. See Song of Songs Rabba 1:8.

4. On Heschel's originality, see Kasimow, "Heschel," 423–34.

5. A comparison with Buber is helpful. Buber was a philosophical theoretician of dialogue, as well as an important exponent of Judaism to Christians, who engaged issues of Jewish-Christian interest seriously. Yet, the relational paradigm that governed Buber's relations with Christian thinkers and with Christianity represents an earlier era in Jewish-Christian relations. Buber was engaged in the fight for the legitimacy of Judaism as a religious form in the face of Christianity. Accordingly, his efforts were devoted to distinguishing Judaism from Christianity and to legitimating the former. See Rodin, "Two Types of Faith," 131–69; and Stegemann, "Introduction," 111–21. The general climate under which Buber operated is well described, in relation to Franz Rosenzweig, by Rivka Horowitz. See Horowitz, "Jewish-Christian Dialogue," 241–69. Both Buber and Rosenzweig are contrasted with the present climate. The reigning paradigm of mission and polemic has given way to an alternative paradigm of dialogue. Heschel's contribution to the Second Vatican Council took place when Buber was dying. Heschel operated at a crucial moment in time and played a crucial role in ushering in the new relational paradigm.

least cognizant of his significance for interfaith relations.[6] Trail blazers create new paths in the thicket of the wood. Broadening the path, paving it, and tidying it is left to those who follow the path breaking clever man. My own reflections are of this nature. I seek to follow Heschel by clarifying the moves and positions taken by him, by considering their application today, and by suggesting ways in which we might either broaden the path or take it deeper into the forest. I shall attempt these tasks through a rereading of Heschel's most significant writing in the field of interreligious dialogue, his 1966 essay "No Religion Is an Island."[7] The essay itself is short, compact, and dense. It does many things within the scope of one short essay. The moves it makes are often rapid and at times take place through leaps in the argument and presentation. I think it is fair to say that many of its readers were impressed by the depth and pathos of the argument, without following the intricacies of Heschel's arguments and the multiple moves he makes.[8] It would have taken a book length presentation, in which each of the arguments is carefully unpacked, to drive home the full wealth of Heschel's contribution. Such a fuller and more systematic presentation does, in fact, remain a desideratum. Moreover, it may well be that only a reader who is equipped with sensibilities similar to those that informed Heschel's work and who can appreciate Heschel's contribution against the background of earlier Jewish sources can offer a fuller appreciation of the originality and depth of Heschel's essay.

NO RELIGION IS AN ISLAND: PRELIMINARY OBSERVATIONS

"No Religion Is an Island" is a powerful essay. It is full of passion, inspiration, and deep conviction. It is hard to remain neutral in the face of the powerful message that Heschel delivers. The essay, like most of Heschel's writing, operates on the emotional, no less than the cognitive level. The emotional component is an important one in effecting the kind of attitudinal change for which the essay calls. The area of interreligious relations is fraught with

---

6. One thinker, in particular, who is aware of Heschel's importance and who draws heavily upon his premises is David Hartman. See Hartman "Heroic Witness," 169–92. See further Meir, "Hartman," 262–73.

7. Published originally in *Union Theological Seminary Quarterly Review*, Vol. 21 (1966). The essay is quoted from its reprint in Kasimow and Sherwin, *Island*, 3–22.

8. A reader-response perspective to Heschel's essay is offered by the essays collected in the Kasimow-Sherwin volume. All readers relate to only a portion of Heschel's argument, often citing the same few passages as representative of his thought. No one I know has undertaken an analysis of Heschel's presentation in its entirety.

centuries and millennia-old emotional baggage. It is therefore both fitting and necessary that new conceptual developments be accompanied by their own emotional weight.

Heschel as a person, theologian, and theoretician of interreligious relations is a figure that touches. This touch has a healing and transformative effect. It is this very "Heschel-touch" that provides the essay with its depth and power. As already suggested, many of the essay's readers were touched by Heschel, at times at the expense of engagement with his ideas.[9] I too am in deep sympathy with Heschel's tone and spirit and identify myself very much with the existential and experiential basis that informs his own reflections. The pioneering inspiration of Heschel has remained a guiding light that few have been able to follow fully. I consider the coming together of heart, mind, and spirit in the process of engagement with other religions, as exemplified by Heschel, to be a paradigm worth following. I therefore express the hope that my own focus on the ideas, maneuvers, and strategies that Heschel employs will enhance our view of Heschel the trail blazer and make us more fully aware of the road he invites us to walk.

A key question that must inform the reading of "No Religion Is an Island" is that of the audience for which it was composed. Most readers of the essay assume that it was written for both a Jewish and a Christian audience. Indeed, this is borne out by the fact that Heschel speaks both of the attitudes that Jews must adopt and the attitudes that Christians must adopt.[10] Nevertheless, it seems to me that the essay is more directed at a Christian audience than it is at a Jewish audience; perhaps it is even primarily addressed to Christians.[11] The context would, of course, account for this. This essay was Heschel's inaugural lecture as a visiting professor at Union Theological Seminary. Heschel also published it in the seminary's review and not in a Jewish publication or in a scientific publication regularly read

---

9. The voices collected by Kasimow and Sherwin seem to resonate with Heschel and his interreligious experience. Opposition to Heschel is itself ultimately based on experiential grounds. Thus, the great alternative to Heschel's views are those posed by Rabbi Soloveitchik. Underlying Soloveitchik's views is the recognition of the singularity of Jewish religious experience and of the impossibility of communicating religious experience. See Meir, "Hartman," 262–273. For a systematic exposition of the views of the two thinkers, in the context of their actual contacts with Church hierarchs and the interreligious politics of the time, see Kimelman, "Rabbis," 251–71. While not explicitly stated, Kimelman's essay attempts to narrow the commonly perceived divide between the two figures by pointing out their commonalities, the involvement of Soloveitchik in dialogue, alongside and independently of Heschel, and by suggesting conditions for dialogue to which Soloveitchik would probably not, in the author's view, be opposed.

10. Heschel, "No Religion," 12.

11. Hartman, "Heschel," 184, seems to be of the same opinion, even though later in his article he refers to Heschel's message to a Jewish audience (186–7).

by both Jews and Christians. Recognition of the context in which Heschel is addressing Christians will go a long way towards clarifying some of the questions the essay poses. The choice of sources, the structure of the argument, what is included and what is omitted from his discussion—all cohere with the primarily Christian context of the essay's delivery. The emphasis placed on giving up missionary work in relation to the Jews and even the lengthy review of Jewish attitudes towards Christianity all make sense in the context in which Christians are the primary audience and Jews are secondary.[12]

That "No Religion Is an Island" was framed particularly with a Christian audience in mind finds confirmation from a comparison of this essay to one printed a year later, based on Heschel's address to the Rabbinical Assembly. The essay entitled "From Mission to Dialogue?" cannibalizes large parts of "No Religion Is an Island," while adding some passages that are particular to the present essay.[13] The comparison is illuminating. What Heschel presents to his Jewish audience amounts to a primer in recent ecumenical developments and a call to arise to the challenges of the present moment, when Jews are expected to share their treasures with Christians. It highlights changes in the Catholic Church and offers Heschel's' reading of the significance of the moment. However, as the closing passage suggests: "We may not be ready for a dialogue in depth, so few are qualified. Yet the time has come for studying together on the highest academic level in an honest search for mutual understanding and for ways to lead us out of the moral and spiritual predicament affecting all of humanity."[14] Students familiar with the lecture offered by Rabbi Soloveitchik to the parallel Orthodox rabbinic convention will be struck by the similarity of some of the

---

12. On the face of it, the disproportionately lengthy presentation on pages 18–22 should be read as addressing a Jewish audience, encouraging them to be accepting of Christians, in a reciprocal movement to the earlier affirmation of the importance of the continuing survival of the Jewish people as Jews (16–18). However, upon close reading one realizes that the message that Christians ought to be accepted, based on historical precedent, is never really drawn from the sources. In context, the argument reads more like offering Jewish acceptance of Christianity, as legitimate in and of itself without need of conversion to Judaism, as a model for Christians to adopt in relation to Judaism. See the opening paragraph on page 19. It should be noted that these final pages of the essay are its weakest part. Heschel the historian has cobbled historical precedents together. We no longer hear the prophetic or inspired Heschel, but rather the scholarly and erudite sage. The entire section is almost an addendum to the powerful essay, and may have indeed been composed later, or at least under the pressure of time. The multiple possibilities of intended audiences may thus be the outcome of weak writing, rather than of express intention.

13. Heschel, "From Mission to Dialogue," 1–11.

14. Heschel, "From Mission to Dialogue," 11.

warnings and concerns.¹⁵ Concern for successful dialogue and care for the quality of exchange seem to push both leaders to positions that fall short of their own high points of contact with members of other traditions. In Heschel's case, the comparison with "No Religion Is an Island" is important precisely for what is omitted from his rabbinical address. Gone are much of the pathos and the spiritual highs. Gone are the daring commentaries and the theological breakthroughs. Gone is the personal encounter. In short, the great highlights of the essay did not make it into the "Jewish" presentation. Practical collaboration—yes. Openness to self-transformation through the encounter with the other, the mutual spiritual help of two religions—of that we no longer hear. Based on our later presentation of the impulses that underlie "No Religion Is an Island," we may safely claim that Heschel only brought a part of himself and a part of his insight to his Jewish listeners. Those who are sufficiently attuned to Heschel's spiritual message would have to hear it in a context where Heschel could be more fully himself, in front of a Christian audience.

What this means is that Heschel may have never intended, and could therefore never achieve, an adequate treatment of the theme of interreligious relations from a purely Jewish perspective within this essay. While much of what Heschel has to say on the subject may be relevant to a Jewish, no less than a Christian audience, it still leaves important gaps in relation to the needs of a Jewish audience. If its primary readership is Christian, we should not expect Heschel to be doing all the work of developing a Jewish attitude, or as it is known today, a Jewish theology of world religions. Some of the questions, procedures and methods that would be required by the Jewish reader will be found lacking in Heschel's essay. This does not detract from the significance of the essay for a Jewish audience. That so many Jewish readers could have been influenced by it is testimony to the universality of Heschel's religious understanding. Having couched his ideas within his own native idioms and ways of thinking, Heschel's work would certainly be of interest to a Jewish audience. And we cannot exclude Jewish listeners from Heschel's intended audience completely, if only because it is obvious that some of his Jewish colleagues from across the street at the Jewish Theological Seminary were in the audience, along with the primarily Christian public. But we should not be surprised if Heschel's treatment leaves gaps, from the Jewish perspective. A contemporary inquiry that sets to construct a Jewish theology of other religions will find in Heschel a foundation and

---

15. See above note 265.

an inspiration, but also many gaps that have not been addressed. Those who follow the trail blazer are called to fill these gaps.

HESCHEL'S AUTHORITY

As a trail blazer, Heschel had to articulate what he saw as the appropriate response to the new situation presented by contemporary interreligious relations and to the possibilities it contains. The ability to articulate such a response draws upon and raises the question of the authority by which Heschel was able to state his position. The question of authority is particularly relevant when we consider Heschel's reception as well as the challenges that Heschel places before present-day readers. Overall, Heschel has had little impact within Jewish Orthodox circles.[16] He has had huge impact within non-Orthodox circles, and perhaps even more so within non-Jewish circles.[17] These facts touch directly upon the question of the sources of Heschel's authority.

Heschel was a scholar of Judaism. His historical and philosophical knowledge thus provide the foundation for any statement made by him. We can identify in "No Religion Is an Island" traces of Heschel's scholarly and theological work.[18] However, Heschel's authority draws on much more than his erudition and theological acumen. There are two factors that I would regard as sources of authority.

The first is the personal friendships and the shared spiritual experience that Heschel enjoyed with leading Christian theologians and men of religion, both Catholic and Protestant. Heschel offers testimony to those relationships in our essay, and they are presented as a model that the reader is implicitly invited to emulate.[19] I believe the particular sensibilities that Heschel expresses could not be developed outside the matrix of strong

---

16. Those who engage in dialogue are informed in part by Rabbi Soloveitchik's position and in part by the social and political forces that afford interreligious dialogue an increasingly prominent role.

17. The essays in the Kasimow-Sherwin volume bear witness to the extent and quality of reception, even if they express the conceptual design of the editors, who invited the particular essays.

18. For example, the reference on page 15 to Rabbi Ishmael's statement, "The Torah speaks in the language of man," draws heavily on Heschel's reflection on the themes of language and revelation, as expressed in his *Heavenly Torah: As Refracted through the Generations*. His reflections on revelation also echo his work in *The Prophets*. Obviously, his unique theological voice, expressed in his classical works, finds expression also in this article.

19. See Heschel "No Religion," 10 and 17. I believe his personal experience also informs statements such as those found at the top of page 9.

friendships and powerful relationships and the sharing they make possible. It is thus not an accident that Heschel begins his reflections on the meaning of encountering a person of a different faith by reflecting upon the meaning of the very meeting of another human being. Interreligious relations are thus an expression of interpersonal relations, and their success and depth are a function of the depth of the latter.

It seems to me that one of the essay's main insights also grows in the hotbed of trusting and profound relations between people of different religions. Heschel makes the striking statement that God is greater than religion and that religion is a means, not an end.[20] While such a statement can grow from abstract reflection, it seems to me that it is strongly indebted to the perspective which is discovered when God's reality is shared or mutually recognized through friendship and communion between members of different religions. It is then that God, not the particular form of a religion, is discovered as the deeper common ground and ultimate end. Heschel thus assumes that people of different religions may share religious experience in recognizing the common God and his effects upon the human person in ways that transcend the details and particulars of their religions. Because God precedes religion, people of different religions can share in meaningful ways their relationship with God.

Heschel's personal experiences and attitudes also help account for various details that one would have a difficult time accounting for in traditional terms. Thus, he describes the appropriate attitude between members of different religions as reverence.[21] The demand for reverence far exceeds the conventional demand for respect or tolerance. Heschel does not provide a basis for making that demand. The history of relations between Judaism and other religions would not equip him to make such a demand. One can only assume that this demand is itself a carryover from his personal relations and a fruit of the lessons he himself learned as a pioneer of interreligious relations.

The second component that informs Heschel's essay and that must be recognized as a source of authority is what might be called a prophetic perspective or prophetic vision. It obviously draws upon Heschel's work on the subject. While formally prophecy has been out of reach for Jews for close to 2,500 years, it seems Heschel's self-awareness was nevertheless heavily infused with prophetic self-consciousness.[22] While never claiming

20. Heschel "No Religion," 13. See further Heschel, *Insecurity*, 181.
21. See Heschel "No Religion," 11.
22. See Schweid, *Prophets*, 239–54 [Hebrew]; Eisen, "Prophecy as Vocation," 835–50 [Hebrew]. Heschel's interest in the enduring presence of the holy spirit throughout the ages offers further support to Schweid's and Eisen's analyses. See his Hebrew study

prophetic status, there is clearly something prophetic in Heschel's stance. It is significant that the essay opens with a quote from Isaiah's vision of his dedication as a prophet.[23] It is also noteworthy that many of writers who speak of Heschel's work, refer to it by use of the adjective "prophetic."[24] I understand that this adjective denotes the ability to read the times and their signs and to recognize God's will, word, and mandate for the particular moment in time. The prophet is thus the interpreter of history who can carry forth God's will for the particular time and place. In this sense, Heschel found himself challenged by the historical moment, seeking to articulate the broader vision and the particular spirit appropriate for it. A statement such as: "In this aeon diversity of religions is the will of God" is nothing short of a prophetic statement.[25]

Heschel recognizes that humanity is moving towards new models in its communication and organization.[26] His reading of reality leads him to issue the call to extend collaboration to relations between religions. Recognition of the failures of the past is closely related to the call for new models of collaboration.[27] Heschel's reading of contemporary reality goes beyond the recognition of common challenges and regrouping to address them. His reading touches upon the heart of religion, its success and efficacy. It leads him to pass a verdict upon the failures of all religions. Heschel's reading of reality includes awareness of failure and crisis, as well as the recognition that the only way out of common crisis is through collaboration.[28] He recognizes that we are at a particular point in time and in the evolution of our religious traditions, and that this time affords us new possibilities, including the relinquishing of former models. Thus, he assumes that we can transcend both mission and polemic.[29] In the coming together of historical knowledge, personal experience and prophetic analysis of the moment we

---

on the holy spirit in the Jewish middle ages in Heschel, "On the Holy Spirit," 75–142.

23. Heschel "No Religion," 4. While the quote may be limited to an illustration of Heschel's fear that we may be deprived of the means of understanding God's word, it would seem from the full quote that he himself is receiving a calling to serve the people, in this connection.

24. Note the title of Kasimow's essay in *No Religion Is an Island*: "Heschel's Prophetic Vision of Religious Pluralism." It is telling that so many of the quotes, brought by Kasimow and by other writers (non-Jewish) in the volume, in which "prophetic" is used, are mouthed by non-Jews. Outside the Jewish tradition that shuns, or minimizes, prophetic expression, it is easier to refer to "prophetic" as a religious quality.

25. Heschel "No Religion," 14.
26. Heschel "No Religion," 11.
27. Heschel "No Religion," 14.
28. Heschel "No Religion," 5.
29. Heschel "No Religion," 17 ff.

have the ingredients that make up Heschel the person, the source of the vision expressed in "No Religion Is an Island." It seems to me that ultimately the appeal to authority cannot be external. The vision Heschel points to can neither be validated by means of historical precedent nor based upon pure halakhic reasoning. Precedent and halakhic ruling are second-order activities that ground a primary understanding and that translate it to the community at large. There is something self-validating in the perspective that Heschel offers. Heschel's vision draws upon his own view of reality and the particular vantage point, formed by knowledge, experience, and understanding, from which it is expressed. Heschel speaks as someone who recognizes a dimension of religion—we would today say spirituality—that transcends the particular forms of religion. A dual perspective of being human beyond, or before, being religious and of being religious before, or beyond, being religious in a particular sense, informs his spiritual horizon. This is the meaning of Heschel's important distinction between theology and depth-theology. Heschel's authority ultimately draws upon his ability to be situated within this horizon and to report to others how reality is viewed from there.

There is thus full justification in citing Heschel as an authority. The various components—knowledge, experience and more—that have brought him to see spiritual reality and interreligious relations in the way he does have situated him within certain horizons of vision. Ultimately, his authority draws from his ability to see, and later translate, from that high vantage point. The rest is commentary, or more correctly, translation.

This has several consequences. The first is that not all will recognize Heschel as an authority or accept the horizons from which he speaks as providing a superior vantage point. A self-validating spiritual authority is delicately balanced between the subjective perspective of the authority and the objective canons by means of which a community recognizes and endows with authority. Hence, Heschel may be recognized as an authority by some, while for others he may represent little beyond the objective knowledge he possesses.

The second is that a reading of Heschel and a critique of his work must maintain awareness of the dual levels of proof, justification, and validation. If Heschel's insights do not grow out of the proofs he brings, but from the vision gained from within his own spiritual and existential horizons, they cannot be undermined through alternative readings. Even if Heschel's proofs and the translation of his insights into the traditional language of sources and their interpretation are judged weak, this does not undermine the basic insights he conveys. Also, the type of translation work needed in the transition from personal spiritual insight to communal policy, education, and ruling may need to be developed significantly beyond the work done by Heschel. Heschel would not claim to have exhausted the translation work in this short essay. However, all future translation work would ultimately amount to quantitative improvement upon Heschel's work. It would remain ancillary to the fundamental spiritual insights that transcend the realms of law and hermeneutics.

Finally, this analysis places before us the greatest of all challenges. Heschel recognizes that dialogue with other religions is an activity for the elite.[30] It calls for the same kind of profound engagement that Heschel brought to it. It cannot be justified simply by appeal to the precedent or the insight of one individual. Therefore, must not everyone who seeks genuine interreligious understanding undergo a process like the one Heschel underwent? Can one rely on Heschel's experiences and on his own reading of the historical moment or must these be continually rediscovered by every serious practitioner of dialogue? Surely, to some extent one may be able to rely on others, Heschel included. However, Heschel challenges us not only to follow him, but to become like him. The horizons of vision we will discover may be the same as his, or different in various ways. The important point, however, is that one cannot simply engage other religions without the full emotional and spiritual engagement that Heschel brought with him, through study, friendship and shared experience. Heschel would have discouraged his epigones. He would have sought first-hand answers, drawn from first-hand spiritual experiences. In this he continues to challenge us.[31]

THE LEVELS OF DIALOGUE

A starting point for Heschel's discussion is that there are things concerning which different religions cannot and will not agree. Faith includes reference to tenets of faith and dogmas concerning which religions must agree to disagree and consequently to leave beyond the pale of discussion.[32] Heschel's entire argument is based upon the premise that certain areas must be excluded from dialogue and upon the need to search for the common ground

---

30. Heschel "No Religion," 11.

31. I am sure Heschel would have approved of the broader coexistence-driven dialogue that is common nowadays, provided basic conditions of clarity and security of identity were maintained. However, this type of broader dialogue should be recognized as distinct from and derivative of the theological and spiritual dialogue that Heschel himself practiced.

32. Heschel "No Religion," 8–9.

regardless of these exclusions. Throughout the essay, Heschel appeals to different types, or different levels, of dialogue. Because of how the essay is written, the distinction between the different types is not always clear enough. Nevertheless, one notes a transition within the essay. The earlier part discusses one type of dialogue, the latter another. The first emphasizes collaboration in the face of common challenges. Collaboration itself has varying shades—some more practical, some more religious. Heschel reads the times as indicating that religions must collaborate today. We can no longer afford the luxury of remaining divided, because we are challenged and threatened in similar ways. The legacy of Nazism and nihilism forces us to unite against common threats in the face of common dangers and crises.[33]

This first dimension of dialogue is quite like that accepted by Orthodox Jewish participants in interreligious dialogue in light of the views, or rulings, of Rabbi Soloveitchik.[34] Theological dialogue is avoided, while practical cooperation is encouraged.[35] It is noteworthy that the catchy phrase that gave the article its title appears in this part of the essay.[36] That no religion is an island thus means that no religion is isolated from the problems we all face, and therefore religions must collaborate in addressing those problems.

But Heschel goes beyond this initial sense of dialogue. He assumes that beyond having common enemies, people of different religions can meet in a common religious domain. That domain is where religion, or God, touch or influence the human being. The distinction between God Himself and his effects upon human consciousness opens for Heschel a broad arena for contact with other religions. All that concerns the human encounter with God, listening to God's word, and the Divine impression upon the soul falls within the purview of encounter with other religions.

This distinction draws upon the centrality of the human person to Heschel's interreligious understanding and upon the centrality of the spiritual dimension to Heschel's understanding of the human person. To be religious is part of the human experience and the human condition. Heschel would resist any distinction between being human, as being limited to the moral domain, and being religious.

Heschel does not limit himself to the recognition of similar responses in the human psyche to the religious phenomenon as a basis for human commonality. The common human basis and the similar response to the

33. Heschel "No Religion," 4 ff.

34. See Soloveitchik, "Confrontation." It is available electronically, along with a panel discussion on the continuing relevance of Soloveitchik's position.

35. Heschel himself never uses the term "theological dialogue."

36. Heschel "No Religion," 6.

divine allow him to conclude that it is in fact the same divine reality that is touching believers in different religions.[37] Consequently, while ignoring the rituals and dogmas of the religions, all religions are validated as vehicles through which the same divine reality is contacted and through which it makes its impression upon humanity.[38]

It is interesting to compare a classical statement regarding Christianity that Heschel brings towards the end of the essay with his own way of describing Christians. Heschel cites Rabbi Israel of Danzig (1782–1860) who refers to the Christians as "our brethren, the gentiles, who acknowledge the one God and revere His Torah which they deem divine and observe, as is required of them, the seven commandments of Noah."[39] This reference highlights creed and observance, the objective expressions of the Christian faith, on account of which it is recognized as legitimate by this Jewish writer. Contrast Heschel's own description: "What unites us? A commitment to the Hebrew Bible as Holy Scripture. Faith in the Creator, the God of Abraham, commitment to many of His commandments, to justice and mercy, a sense of contrition, sensitivity to the sanctity of life and to the involvement of God in history, the conviction that without the holy the good will be defeated, prayer that history may not end before the end of days, and so much more."[40] Some of the classical objective yardsticks are echoed. However, reference to the one God has been nuanced by reference to the common God of creation and of Abraham, while the field of common commandment too has been broadened. But more significantly, an entire subjective domain has been opened. It contains reference to contrition, sensitivity, sanctity of life, and a common historical conviction. These are complemented by a common vision of social action and of contemporary concern that Jews and Christians share. The earlier statement is concerned with recognition and legitimation. Heschel's statement is concerned with common ground and

---

37. Heschel "No Religion," 9.

38. The question of religions and religious practices that are beyond the pale of legitimacy does not arise in Heschel's discussion, which is primarily aimed at Christians. One might conjecture that invalid (impure, satanic, etc.) religious experiences would leave different traces in the soul than would the genuine encounter with the God of Israel, common to Jews and Christians. Ritual and dogma are ignored, and the processes of the human psyche and the experiences of the human person are privileged. This could be a strategy for upholding dialogue in face of profound differences. It could, however, also express Heschel's own evaluation of the priority of elements within religion. The view that privileges the psychological and spiritual processes of the human soul over outward rituals and objective creeds may itself have been formed through Heschel's encounter with religious phenomena outside Judaism.

39. Heschel "No Religion," 21–22.

40. Heschel "No Religion," 9.

with sharing. It is therefore broader and more penetrating. It also tells us what about religion is important and how Jews and Christians share what is truly important.

While one may recognize two distinct levels of dialogue, there is a unifying factor, in the form of the purpose of dialogue. Unlike the purely practical dialogue, which seeks to help each other through addressing external problems common to both religions, Heschel suggests the purpose of dialogue is to help each other achieve our spiritual goals. Such help is needed in part in the face of common external challenges. But it seems to also be immanent to religious reality. Sharing and mutual support are thus fundamental to the identities of religious people. The essay's concluding paragraph is thoughtfully located to deliver this message as the summary of the entire essay.[41] What, then is the purpose of interreligious cooperation?

It is neither to flatter nor to refute one another, but to help one another; to share insight and learning, to cooperate in academic ventures on the highest scholarly level, and what is even more important to search in the wilderness for well-springs of devotion, for treasures of stillness, for the power of love and care for man. What is urgently needed are ways of helping one another in the terrible predicament of here and now by the courage to believe that the word of the Lord endures forever as well as here and now; to cooperate in trying to bring about a resurrection of sensitivity, a revival of conscience; to keep alive the divine sparks in our souls, to nurture openness to the spirit of the Psalms, reverence for the words of the prophets, and faithfulness to the Living God.[42]

Help is needed because we face similar challenges. We traverse the same desert. However, the depth of collaboration and mutual help far exceeds the social and public collaboration in projects of a practical nature. Jews and Christians share the same scriptures and they can help each other reach into the depths of those scriptures as resources for today. Faith, sensitivity, conscience, and ultimately the divine in our soul are common to Christians and Jews. We are called to help each other in growing and maintaining them.

One may characterize the two levels of dialogue as corresponding to the two sources of Heschel's interreligious vision. The prophetic drive calls

---

41. One notes this paragraph is disjointed from the argument of the previous pages. I have already commented that those pages are of a lesser quality than the bulk of the essay. This further highlights the importance of the concluding paragraph as the final chord of the entire essay, rather than as a conclusion of the immediately preceding argument.

42. Heschel "No Religion," 22. See further where Heschel speaks of help in overcoming hardness of heart, in cultivating a sense of wonder and of unlocking doors to holiness in time.

for an assessment of what must be done here and now and corresponds to the call for practical collaboration. Collaboration is, as Heschel points out, a sign of the times and must be extended to the field of religion. The second dimension of dialogue highlights the influence of God upon the human psyche and the ways in which religious people of different traditions are called to help each other. Is this not a precise image of the kind of relations Heschel himself enjoyed with prominent Christian religious figures?

BETWEEN COMMON GROUND AND COMMON LANGUAGE

Heschel assumes that Jews, Christians, and others can recognize traces of the same God in their lives and souls. This assumes a range of common responses to encounter with the divine as well as communicability of those responses.[43] Thus mutual recognition of experience points to mutual recognition of the religions.

However, experience cannot be communicated directly. It relies upon language as a means of communication. A sense of commonality in experience, and consequently in the ultimate source and referent of religious experience, is thus founded upon shared religious language. An examination of Heschel's language reveals that in communicating the very notion of the communicability of experience, the language employed is not traditional Jewish language. At times the language is neutral, at times it has affinities with the thought of Christian thinkers. This may be simply a consequence of the essay being addressed primarily to Christians. Or it may suggest that there is no absolutely neutral common ground and that Heschel was able to share with Christians because he was able or willing, to a certain degree, to frame his religious experiences in terms that echo Christian conceptualization of religion.[44] Some examples follow.

---

43. Incommunicability constitutes the basis for Soloveitchik's rejection of dialogue.

44. Breslauer,"Theology," 81–86, has pointed to the problematics of drawing a firm distinction between religious psychology, the common religious experience that Heschel also terms depth-theology, and religious sociology, which governs the social institutions and creeds into which the assumed primary religious experience is translated. Breslauer's critique would be strengthened if we realize that the language by means of which Heschel conceptualizes the assumed common religious experience is itself derived from one particular tradition. Kimelman, "Rabbis," n. 60, quotes Dr. Twersky as accounting for Rabbi Soloveitchik's fear of engagement in interreligious dialogue due also to the concern that Judaism and Christianity share theological terms without sharing their meanings. The dialogue is therefore prone to misunderstanding. While the domain of experience could have provided shelter from these concerns, it may itself be subject to these very misunderstandings, inasmuch as its communication depends on language, and hence on the

In distinguishing between the religious path and its effects upon the human person, Heschel writes: "We may disagree about the ways of achieving fear and trembling, but the fear and trembling are the same."[45] The Jewish reader will, of course, recognize that certain rabbinic passages do refer to fear and trembling as appropriate attitudes that should accompany the study of Torah, following the precedent at Sinai.[46] Nevertheless, conceptualizing the primary religious experience as fear and trembling is almost alien to Jewish thought. The classical experiential articulation refers to "love and fear," rather than to fear and trembling.[47] "Fear and Trembling" is, of course, the title of Soren Kierkegaard's classical work. By framing religious experience in these terms, Heschel is, in fact, operating within his Christian host community's linguistic and conceptual realm.

Similarly, in addressing the thorny issue of Jewish rejection of Jesus, in the framework of the call for mutual acceptance between Christians and Jews, Heschel states: "None of us pretends to be God's accountant, and His design for history and redemption remains a mystery before which we must stand in awe."[48] Heschel's intended Christian audience could relate well to the concept and the language. The use of mystery language is typically Christian and is almost completely lacking in Jewish sources.[49]

A third moment relevant to the choice of language employed by Heschel is found when making a key argument for God transcending religion and hence for the need to suspend, maybe transcend, any exclusive truth claims of a given religion. Heschel states: "Does not the all-inclusiveness of

---

conceptual and cultural baggage that each tradition attaches to a particular term. For a response to Breslauer's concerns, see Merkle, "Heschel's Attitude," 102–4.

45. Heschel "No Religion," 9.

46. See, for example, Bavli Berachot 22a and Yoma 4b.

47. Reference to love and fear (or awe) is ubiquitous since the rabbinic period. A classical halachic articulation is found in Maimonides' *Laws of the Foundations of the Torah*, Chapter 2.

48. Heschel "No Religion," 17.

49. This is not to suggest that mystery language is absent from the history of Jewish thought. For discussions of "mystery" in the rabbinic period see Petuchowski, "Mystery," 141–52 and Bregman, "Mishnah and LXX," 333–42. More significantly, we should note the heavy reliance upon "mystery" language in Heschel's own philosophical work. The index of *God in Search of Man* suggests "mystery" is the most heavily used term in Heschel's religious vocabulary. There are more references under this term than under any other single term in the index! Most of these, however, use mystery as synonymous with wonder. The above quote is more in keeping with classical Christian usage. Thus, while mystery language is very much Heschelian language, it still seems to me that "mystery," in this context, will evoke a more familiar response from a Christian audience than from a traditional Jewish one.

God contradict the exclusiveness of any particular religion?"[50] The argument itself is not obvious from a traditional Jewish point of view. Whatever "all-inclusiveness" may mean; it may express itself by means of religious exclusivity. Or we may distinguish between the caring aspects of God, by means of which he provides sustenance to all creatures, and issues of ultimate religious truth. The problem really arises from the lack of clarity in the key term underlying the present argument. I would not know how to say "all-inclusiveness of God" in Hebrew. It is not a natural Jewish idiom and cannot easily constitute the basis of a theological argument. Unlike the previous examples, I am also not sure that the argument was formulated using proper Christian concepts. It seems Heschel expresses here an intuitive understanding that God could not have excluded some of his creatures from his design for salvation or for religious fulfillment. The issue itself has a venerable history in the context of Christian reflection and the challenges posed to Christianity by other religions. Heschel seems to be carrying forth this philosophical concern into a broader statement of the relativity, or at least lack of legitimate exclusivity, of all religions.[51]

Language itself cannot, so it seems, provide an adequate common denominator. It is too closely implicated in the conflicted history of Christians and Jews. For the Jewish audience further work would be needed to ascertain that it is indeed the same God whose touch is recognized in the souls of Jews and Christians. Translating Heschel's experientially based religious intuition would require historical and theological work, beyond that provided by Heschel himself. Heschel shares with us his experience and the view gained from his experiential and existential vantage point. In what way does he also suggest how to gain such a perspective? How can a Jewish audience identify with his intuitions without adequate grounding in the historical and theological resources of Judaism? How does the trail blazer lead people to follow in his steps?

Heschel seems to also suggest a pedagogy by means of which his vision can be realized by others. "No honest religious person can fail to admire the outpouring of the love of man and the love of God, the marvels of worship, the magnificence of spiritual insight, the piety, charity and

---

50. Heschel "No Religion," 11–12.

51. Hartman, "Heschel," 188, sees this as a carryover of Maimonidean negative theology, even though Heschel himself does not make that association explicitly. Reliance on Maimonidean negative theology would lead to the kind of extreme pluralistic position that Hartman seeks to establish. That Heschel does not rely on Maimonides could be due to the type of sources that he does and does not use, as discussed below. But it is just as likely that Heschel would not ground his case in such a philosophical understanding, precisely because he would wish to avoid the radical conclusions that Hartman seeks to establish, based on Heschel's foundations, as will be discussed below.

sanctity in the lives of countless men and women, manifested in the history of Christianity."[52] Heschel assumes that unbiased study and observation will lead to admiration. Open-mindedness and lack of prejudice thus emerge as preconditions for a genuine appreciation of Christianity (of any religion for that matter) on its own terms. The method employed relies in part on the neutral observations of the scientific study of religion. But Heschel seems to also call for a less neutral engagement with the spiritual lives of Christians and their potential testimony for Jews. His argument is made for the "honest religious person." Religious— having some sense of religious life and reality, that would make the person open to recognizing it in others. Honest—having removed preconceived notions that would impede recognition of the religious life of others. While the precondition of religiosity does, to a certain extent, already assume a certain type of religious personality, the overall import of the passage amounts to an instruction: Observation, knowledge, and genuineness are components of a spiritual program that would allow one to be touched by the religious life of the other.[53]

Heschel's argument here also suggests how we might shift attention from theology and focus it upon the lives of human beings, particularly of saints, as bridge builders who provide a testimony that can extend beyond the boundaries of the individual religion. The lives of men and women are the ultimate indication of the educational and spiritual success of a religion and they also provide the means for others to recognize the value inherent in each religion.

Heschel offers other helpful suggestions for how to enter the depth of experiential sharing with someone from another religion. Let us begin with his own testimony: "Gustave Weigel spent the last evening of his life in my study at the Jewish Theological Seminary. We opened our hearts to one another in prayer and contrition and spoke of our own deficiencies, failures, hopes."[54] The intense intimate moment that Heschel shares with us focuses upon confession, contrition, and awareness of imperfection. This gives a unique meaning to the term inter-confessionalism. By focusing upon our imperfection, we can highlight that which is human in us. Our humanity is our imperfection, and that imperfection is shared by all. As it is also part of our religious experience, it is our very weakness that provides a gateway to mutual understanding. As he states elsewhere in the essay: "I suggest that the most significant basis for meeting of men of different religious traditions is the level of fear and trembling, of humility and contrition, where

---

52. Heschel "No Religion," 12.

53. See further Heschel "No Religion," 7 on the need to get beyond the abyss of ignorance.

54. Heschel "No Religion," 17.

our individual moments of faith are mere waves in the endless ocean of mankind's reaching out for God.[55]

While stripped of pretension and conceit we sense the tragic insufficiency of human faith."[56] Heschel takes us beyond the previously problematized expression of "fear and trembling." He speaks of humility and contrition. Recognition of our own imperfection provides the foundation for a genuine spiritual self-awareness and hence of awareness of and communication with the other. Human faith is tragically insufficient. What room is there, then, for pride? What we share in the deepest sense is our own inadequacy.

Inadequacy leads to humility. This is as true for the individual believer reaching across the ocean of life to God as it is for the greater structures of religions. "We have all been defeated," claims Heschel.[57] There is no room for pride. "Humility and contrition seem to be absent where most required—in theology. But humility is the beginning and end of all religious thinking, the secret test of faith. There is no truth without humility, no certainty without contrition."[58] Humility thus provides the only sound epistemological foundation. The common experience based upon which members of different religions can truly share is thus not some mystical experience of the unity of all, but rather the common recognition of failure and the ensuing humility that opens the way to a proper perception of God and the other.[59]

---

55. Compare the use of the ocean metaphor amongst contemporary Hindu writers, with whom Heschel must have been familiar. Rather than express the plenitude of the divine, of which man's life is but a wave, the metaphor is harnessed to convey the huge distance across which humanity must strive in its reaching out for God. The ocean is what unites us not in the fullness of divine being, but in the infinity of distance and quest, born of human imperfection.

56. Heschel "No Religion," 9.

57. Heschel "No Religion," 7.

58. Heschel "No Religion," 15.

59. Heschel's emphasis upon contrition and confession lifts up one of the components of classical Jewish prayer and elevates it to a cognitive principle. Another component that is highlighted as part of the description of ideal relations and common spiritual experience is the praise of God. See page 10. I wonder to what extent Heschel was consciously applying categories of Jewish prayer to his epistemology. If gratitude is seen as an expression of praise, and if petition is taken for granted, then in fact Heschel utilizes two of the primary structuring notions of Jewish prayer to suggest the common experiential ground between Christians and Jews. Noticeably lacking is any reference to the Credo. Indeed, Jewish liturgy features credal statements only in a very secondary and historically late level in its evolution. Classical Jewish prayer may thus provide Heschel with some of the categories and the direction through which religious experience may be shared across traditions. Classical prayer suggests what is key in our religious experience. That which is key, according to this reconstructed argument, is also what can be shared between people of different religions. That which is not key, i.e., creeds,

What allows Heschel to be so open about the imperfection inherent in all religions, his own included? Several factors converge. First and foremost, intellectual honesty and integrity call for an honest assessment of the successes and failures of religions. His own recognition of other religious forms and of people of different religious paths must have surely conditioned him to greater self-awareness, including criticism of self and other. Finding a perfection in others that is lacking in oneself, and vice versa, enhances awareness of how imperfect we can all be. Heschel's own theological understanding, drawing as it does upon the Bible and rabbinic literature, does not shun imperfection as a quality of humans, as well as of the anthropomorphic God it represents. It may be that a theologian who grows out of this theological school may have an easier time recognizing the imperfection inherent in all our traditions. But it seems that ultimately what allows Heschel to be so open about imperfections in religion is his ability to distinguish between God and religion. God is perfect; religions are imperfect. We cannot know whether this distinction underlies his ability to openly recognize imperfection in religion, or whether it is a consequence of such recognition. One thing is clear: Perfection resides with God alone. We all share an imperfection that must lead us to humility and contrition and to a common search for crossing the ocean that separates our imperfection from the fullness of divine reality.

SEEDS OF A JEWISH THEOLOGY OF WORLD RELIGIONS

An important indication for the progress that has been made in interreligious relations since Heschel's days is the growth of the field of "theology of religions," especially among Christian thinkers of various denominations. "Theology of religions" describes the conversation and the quest for accounting for the place of other religions within the broader economy of the divine. It is the field of theological reflection that is concerned with making space and accounting, usually in positive terms, for the other. Any serious call for understanding between religions assumes some degree of involvement in such a theological exercise. Heschel is no exception. Because his essay is first and foremost an appeal, an appeal for understanding and cooperation, the "theology of religions" dimension of his work is secondary to its immediate purpose. But it is, nevertheless, an important component of the essay. Throughout the essay Heschel makes numerous moves that are expressive of his own theology of other religions. The insights are stated in terse and rudimentary form. Heschel's broader knowledge and erudition underlie these statements, but it is usually not made explicit, nor is the

---

should be left aside.

treatment of issues of a "theology of religions" undertaken in a systematic way. Heschel's insights deserve to be unpacked more fully and supported by the kind of corroborative analysis that history and theology can provide. They need systematic exposition, and they could benefit from a careful presentation considering the concerns of a "theology of religions." The following paragraphs seek to contribute towards these goals.

It may be fairly stated that Heschel, within the pages of this brief essay, tackled almost all the cardinal questions that are relevant to a Jewish consideration of other religions. Heschel is aware of the key issues and suggests his own strategies for dealing with them. This evaluation is made in light of my own analysis of issues that a Jewish theology of world religions must grapple with.[60] I note that with one important exception, Heschel addresses all major issues that would be of concern to a Jewish audience.[61] In light of my own analysis, I would like to point to three, out of four, major issues addressed by Heschel. I will not enter here into a full presentation of the scope of the issues and the challenge they present, as this has been done elsewhere. I shall only concentrate on Heschel's contributions to dealing with these issues.

The legitimacy of other religions, or put differently, the recognition of other religions. Heschel devotes much attention to these issues. His attempt to legitimate other religions, in fact, all religions, is one of the main thrusts of the essay and an important contribution to his role as a path breaker in interfaith relations. While Heschel focuses primarily on Christianity, his own logic extends beyond Christianity. While the latter part of the essay, devoted to historical precedents, is taken almost exclusively from the history of Jewish reflection upon Christianity, his own personal contributions, earlier in the essay, are as relevant to other religions as they are to Christianity.

Heschel legitimates other religions by employing a classical twofold strategy: argument from reason and argument from scripture. The argument from reason is part of his own reading of history and the place of different religions within it. It thus comes under what we earlier termed his "prophetic" vision. This "prophetic" perspective allows Heschel to frame the discussion not simply in terms of human logic or the needs of human society, but in terms of God's vision and will for humanity. "How can we be cured of bigotry, presumption, and the foolishness of believing that we

---

60. See above, note 264.

61. Most of these issues would be equally significant for a Christian audience. It seems to me that while speaking to a primarily Christian audience, Heschel, perhaps unconsciously, raises those issues that a Jew would be most concerned with in relation to other religions. As I will suggest below, speaking to a Christian audience would account for the great omission of *Avoda Zara* (idolatry) from the present discussion.

have been triumphant while we have all been defeated?"[62] Heschel's view of history in general and of the failure of all religions as its common denominator underlies this cry to go beyond triumphalism. Jews and Christians are called to recognize one another within a relationship that is framed in family terms. Heschel employs the metaphor of mother and daughter, suggesting that the full human, emotional, and legal weight of that relationship is relevant to Jewish-Christian relations.[63] But he also goes further. Beyond recognition and acceptance, Heschel raises diversity of religions to the level of a divine ideal. "Does not the task of preparing the kingdom of God require a diversity of talents, a variety of rituals, soul-searching as well as opposition? Perhaps it is the will of God that in this aeon there should be diversity in our forms of devotion and commitment to Him. In this aeon diversity of religions is the will of God."[64]

As all good theologians would do, Heschel corroborates his theological understanding by a reading of traditional sources. Heschel offers a very straightforward, yet radical, reading of at least two biblical sources that are indeed some of the most important biblical resources for thinking about other religions. The one is his reading of the prophecy of Micah 4.[65] The other is his interpretation of the following prophecy of Malachi. It is no accident that this is probably the most quoted passage of his essay.[66]

For from the rising of the sun to its setting My name is great among the nations, and in every place incense is offered to My name, and a pure offering; for My name is great among the nations, says the Lord of hosts (Mal. 1:11).

This statement refers undoubtedly to the contemporaries of the prophet. But who were these worshipers of One God? At the time of Malachi there was not a large number of proselytes. Yet the statement declares: All those who worship their gods do not know it, but they are really worshipping Me.

It seems that the prophet proclaims that men all over the world, though they confess different conceptions of God, are really worshipping One God, the Father of all men, though they may not be aware of it.[67]

This is a stunning passage. It sidesteps intention and the conscious awareness of believers and supplants them with a higher perspective that really belongs to God alone, through which they are recognized as worshipping

---

62. Heschel "No Religion," 7.
63. Heschel "No Religion," 12.
64. Heschel "No Religion," 14.
65. Heschel "No Religion," 19.
66. As witnessed in the Kasimow-Sherwin volume.
67. Heschel "No Religion," 14.

God, even though they may not be aware of it.[68] No religion can be critiqued or dismissed, then.[69] The educational dangers of dialogue and the threat to identity. This is a major concern of the essay. On one level, it finds expression in Heschel's call for dialogue to remain an elite activity, founded upon sound knowledge and firm identity.[70] But there is a second, no less important, dimension. While Heschel makes huge personal and theological strides in his approach towards other religions, he remains aware of the continuing efforts at mission, at rejection, and at undermining Jewish identity. Depending on how the argument is read, almost a third may be devoted to the attempt to uphold religious identity and in the case of Judaism to ward off mission and rejection of Judaism.[71] Judging by the proportion of the essay devoted to this issue, one may conjecture that not only did Heschel not see his engagement in interreligious dialogue as undermining his Jewish commitment, but he may have actually considered it an arena by means of which to strengthen Jewish communal identity in relation to other religious identities that sought to undermine it. Without in any way detracting from the sincerity of his open and dialogical engagement, it may be conjectured that Heschel's call for mutual acceptance constitutes more than a call for fair play and openness between religions. It may suggest the importance Heschel attached to interreligious dialogue as a means of upholding Jewish identity.[72]

The problem of truth. From the philosophical perspective, the issue of truth presents the biggest challenge. Religion preaches truth, and truth claims seem mutually exclusive. How, then, can one accept the legitimacy of another faith considering the inherent understanding of one's own tradition

---

68. Merkle, "Heschel's Attitude," 99, claims that Heschel does not develop a Jewish notion, analogous to Rahner's "anonymous Christianity." Some such similar anonymity must be acknowledged, however, as a means of relating the worship of other gods to the one true God.

69. An additional passage that Heschel evokes, from Malachi, is found on page 10, without reference to Malachi. The use of Malachi 2:10 is intuitive. I have heard it used in the same intuitive way by the present Sefardi Chief Rabbi of Israel, Rabbi Amar, in dialogue with a Spanish Cardinal.

70. Heschel "No Religion," 11.

71. See above, note 268.

72. The relations between genuine engagement with others and the pursuit of maintaining Jewish identity and validity may be considered the Jewish expression of the type of fundamental mixed motive that perhaps accompanies any involvement in interreligious dialogue. The mixed motive grows out of the dual impulses of upholding the community's needs and visions, while being open to and integrating the reality of the other. The complexity of Catholic upholding of the dual imperatives of dialogue and of mission is famous. Similar tensions can be pointed out in relation to the involvement of other religions in dialogue. My suggestion that the essay is intended primarily for a Christian audience lends further weight to the present point.

as possessing the truth? Heschel employs an entire battery of strategies in dealing with this issue. All of them are carried out through the application and interpretation of traditional Jewish sources. All of them contribute to some degree or another to relativizing the notion of religious truth.

One of the main strategies is the analogy drawn between religion and language. Language provides a model considering which religions are understood. Underlying this model is the understanding that in the same way that language enables communication, so too religion is a means of communication. It communicates absolute reality to the particular religious community. It can also, as Heschel's overall argument points out, enable communication between members of one religious community and another.

One interesting application of the analogy of religion and language is found in Heschel's appeal to the story of the tower of Babel.[73] It is found immediately following the recognition of religious diversity as the will of God and the proof from Malachi in favor of such an understanding. The move from religion to language is made as though the two domains were identical.[74] The suggestion that the use of one language only leads to rebellion is stretched to making a similar argument in favor of multiple religions. A further expression of the use of language to relativize religious truth is found further on:

The ultimate truth is not capable of being fully and adequately expressed in concepts and words. The ultimate truth is about the situation that pertains between God and man. "The Torah speaks in the language of man." Revelation is always an accommodation to the capacity of man. The voice of God reaches the spirit of man in a variety of ways, in a multiplicity of languages. One truth comes to expression in many ways of understanding.[75]

All religious truth is translation, accommodation. Because we cannot reach ultimate truth, every religion's approach is partial and hence never possesses the fullness of truth. All religions are alike in being impulses of translation by means of which God's voice reaches man's spirit. According to this formulation, there is nothing inherently truer about any religion, provided a genuine revelation is at its base. As Heschel the Jew is here addressing Christians who share the view of the Bible's sanctity, he need not be unduly concerned with the revelational validity of other religions. Nevertheless, Heschel's application of a linguistic model to understanding religion does suggest that ultimately all religions are ways of accommodating the one truth. The philosophical challenge of truth has pushed Heschel farther than

---

73. Heschel "No Religion," 14.

74. On page 20 Heschel quotes a passage from Maimonides where the future recognition of God by all peoples is couched in terms of language. Heschel does not use this as proof for his argument, but it certainly corroborates his suggestion.

75. Heschel "No Religion," 15.

either his prophetic impulse or his personal religious experience would have taken him. These were focused primarily on the Jewish-Christian relationship based upon the common revelation, to which Heschel makes repeated appeal throughout the essay. Considerations of religious truth and the analogy to language seem to stretch the notion of revelation and the validity of religion beyond biblical revelation and potentially remove any barrier in the recognition of the validity, perhaps even equal value, of all religions.[76] It may well be that the statement "no religion is an island," which initially referred to the inability to seal oneself off from the common challenges of the world, may take on a deeper meaning now that religions are examined in relation to ultimate truth. No religion is beyond the dynamics of translating the divine impulse into human categories. No religion can transcend the limits inherent in human language and in human categories. No religion is apart, and all religions share in the same predicament, approaching the divine through human language and understanding.

The historical view and the philosophical perspective merge in the next statement: "Human faith is never final, never an arrival, but rather an endless pilgrimage, a being on the way. We have no answers to all problems. Even some of our sacred answers are both emphatic and qualified, final and tentative; final within our own position in history, tentative because we can only speak in the tentative language of man."[77]

The historical argument becomes a metaphysical one when Heschel introduces the epistemology of humility, born of failure, into his argument: "Is the failure, the impotence of all religions, due exclusively to human transgression? Or perhaps to the mystery of God's withholding His grace, of His concealing even while revealing? Disclosing the fullness of His glory would be an impact that would surpass the power of human endurance. His thoughts are not our thoughts. Whatever is revealed is abundance compared

---

76. At this point Heschel comes close to certain Hindu theories of religion, as suggested by Sharma, "Hindu-Jewish Dialogue," 163–74. I would disagree, however, with Sharma's description of Heschel as presenting all religions as meeting at the top. This is a distinctly Hindu reading of Heschel and is not born out by Heschel's writing. Heschel's continued emphasis upon the human condition, failure, and humility do not allow us to recognize an experiential, mystical, or even philosophical high ground in which all religions meet and where all differences vanish. Rather, as part of his humility-based epistemology, Heschel recognizes the fundamental limitations of our understanding and the unbridgeable abyss that lies between our own religious understanding and the ultimate truth as God knows it. All our religions stand on the other side of the abyss and must therefore learn to accept each other. It is a commonality of impoverishment, in the face of divine perfection, not a commonality born of partaking of that divine perfection, as the Hindu model suggests.

77. Heschel "No Religion," 16.

with our soul and a pittance compared with His treasures. No word is God's last word, no word is God's ultimate word.[78]

We have encountered these arguments earlier in the call for collaboration. Now failure and impotence are part of a higher divine plan whose meaning can only be fathomed within the fundamental tension of divine reality and its human expression. By alluding to Isa. 55:8, Heschel lumps all expressions of religion under the category of human thought, as distinct from divine reality. The theological and interpretative audacity of extending the verse from reference to sinners to reference to all religions, Judaism included, may be justified through Heschel's appeal to a rabbinic passage. The midrash states that the Torah is but an un-ripened fruit of divine wisdom.[79] An internal mechanism of relativizing tradition in relation to the divine is thus extended to all expressions of religion. If divine wisdom and divine thoughts transcend human understanding, then not only the Torah but all forms of religion are but the human attempt to capture the divine impulse within their understanding.

But just how relative is the truth captured by a given religious tradition? Has Heschel here adopted a completely relativistic position? On what grounds would he then continue affirming his preference to have died at Auschwitz rather than convert to Christianity?[80] Harold Kasimow has struggled with this problem.[81] According to Kasimow, Heschel considers paradox an important component of his theological worldview. How all religions can be affirmed while upholding the truth claims of Judaism would be one further instance of paradoxical belief.[82] David Hartman too notes

78. Heschel "No Religion," 16.
79. See Genesis Rabba 44:17, paraphrased by Heschel on page 16.
80. See Kimelman, *Edah Journal*, 6.
81. See his *Heschel and Interreligious Dialogue*, page 430 ff.
82. We may be able to further flesh out the recognition of paradoxical thinking by considering the nature of Heschel's thought processes. The following questions may be considered: How situational, as opposed to systematic, was Heschel's thinking? To what extent did he function based on key intuitions, that in turn served the need of the context and the moment, rather than upon consistent positions? This is a typically Hasidic way of functioning, and Heschel would be in keeping with his native tradition. The ability to uphold multiple complementary intuitions and perspectives is less of a philosophical paradox, and more of an expression of spiritual agility that prefers appropriate spiritual response to the consistent and well-thought-out philosophical position. Thought should also be given to whether the distinction between theological truths in and of themselves and the effects of the encounter with the divine within the human realm might be helpful to resolving the tension. If, as suggested above, all religions are parallel responses to the encounter with the divine, one may uphold the validity of all responses qua responses, while privileging the actual content of one particular revelation. The complexity of the divine-human relationship may be such that it can accommodate both the validity of a

this tension in Heschel's thought.[83] On the one hand Heschel's thought tends to an epistemology of revelation that completely precludes absolutist truth claims. On the other hand, Heschel stops short of complete relativism by restricting complete diversity as God's will to the present aeon only. As a thinker concerned with undermining absolute truth claims and developing genuine pluralistic views of other religions, Hartman considers himself as one of those who, because they take Heschel's thought seriously, must be prepared to take his ideas further. Hartman would concentrate not only on what Heschel said, but also on what he suggested and intimated. For Hartman, Heschel's true agenda, to be followed by others, is arriving at a point where religious pluralism becomes a permanent feature of revelatory faith systems. Hartman sees his own role, therefore, not only in taking Heschel's thought to the next level, but in bringing to their fulfillment Heschel's own assumptions. Hartman must account for why Heschel himself was not explicit about his understanding of revelation in the terms in which Hartman himself considers proper. Hartman's answer is both political and pedagogical. Had Heschel suggested a radical relativization of all religious truth claims, he would have found himself outside traditional theological modes of discourse.[84] Heschel's method of speaking to religious communities was to speak to them in their own language. Without changing the vocabulary of their basic beliefs, Heschel tried to "work within" to justify a form of radical religious pluralism. Heschel therefore did not go the whole way, leaving it to others to do.

My own reading of Heschel is less extreme than Hartman's. It seems to me that his attitude on issues of absolute truth and conflicting truth claims is best understood in light of the two drives that shape the essay— a prophetic assessment of history and the impact of personal experience. The historical assessment leads to the realization that the tensions between conflicting truth claims have not yet, nor will they, be resolved. It is futile to come together at the level of dogmas and creeds. Focusing upon irreconcilable truth statements takes away from what religions could do for each other, were they to address each other through appropriate parameters. These parameters are known to Heschel through his own personal experience, and he seeks to shape continuing relations between religions in light of personal transformation that he experienced within his own relations.

---

given truth claim and the recognition that on another level all formulations share the nature of a response to a primordial recognition of the divine.

83. Hartman, "Heschel," 188–91.

84. There is thus an esoteric and an exoteric Heschel. This twofold presentation of Heschel fits well with the Maimonidean theological roots that Hartman sees as underlying Heschel's views. Negative theology is summoned to buttress Heschel's views, and Heschel is cast in light of Maimonides. See Hartman, "Heschel," 188.

The combination of these two drives leads to a split between different levels of the religious life: "In facing the claim and the dogma of the Church, Jews and Christians are strangers and stand in disagreement with one another. Yet there are levels of existence where Jews and Christians meet as sons and brothers."[85] One may argue that the distinction between these different levels of religion is more problematic than Heschel acknowledges and that the religious life cannot be so neatly divided.[86] Heschel, however, seems to have been able in his own personal life to discover a formula for interreligious exchange that he recommends to others. The meaning of this formula is not the relinquishing of absolute truth claims. They are, rather, bracketed as beyond the pale of meaningful exchange between believers and ultimately beyond the pale of history itself. Heschel, it seems to me, would continue to uphold in the privacy of his faith the classical beliefs of Judaism, and would expect his interlocutors to do the same.[87] The private faith zone may enrich religious experience, which itself may be shared. It can be shared because it no longer concerns the understanding of God proper but the effect of God's touch in the human soul.

The meaningful distinction thus seems to me to be not between the esoteric and the exoteric Heschel, but between those dimensions of faith that belong to the private world of the religious community and those that can be successfully shared with others. Heschel is therefore neither paradoxical, nor is he telling us only part of the truth. His is a pragmatic pluralism. He shares with us a working formula that he recommends to our attention, based on his own experience. Our challenge is both a theoretical and an experiential one. On the theoretical level, we must consider whether it is really possible to exclude parts of another's faith from the encounter.[88] On the experiential

85. Heschel, "No Religion," 10. The distinction is echoed in several other places in the essay.

86. This point has been made in relation to the distinction between theological dialogue and socially oriented cooperation associated with Rabbi Soloveitchik's position. See David Rosen's comments, Rosen, "Orthodox Judaism." Heschel's position is slightly more nuanced. It is not theology that is excluded, but the realm of dogma proper, where Jews and Christians cannot meet, that is bracketed from conversation.

87. I suspect that Heschel would consider a faith that opts for a completely relativistic epistemology a watered-down faith, having lost much intensity and zeal along with the loss of belief in absolute truth. Heschel would probably prefer to share in the experiential and human fruits of the full faith experience, even if its content contains errors.

88. Heschel's exclusion of dogma from the realm of dialogue may be seen as part of his broader campaign against Christian missionary attitudes and for upholding the continuing validity and legitimacy of Judaism. Exclusion functions here as a strategy for protection. Soloveitchik's avoidance of theological dialogue is framed in precisely these terms. One may consider whether forty years of advances in Jewish-Christian relations may make this strategy less urgent and whether areas of the dialogue that

level, we must explore whether we can realize his experiential strategy in broader ways by identifying a broader range of experiential zones in which Jews and members of other religions can meet. For Heschel, success would not be the arrival at some successful resolution of the philosophical tension of conflicting truth claims or the successful articulation of a theory of religious pluralism. Success would be measured in terms of personal transformation and the ability of religious communities to help each other grow spiritually. It is up to us to demonstrate whether and how this can indeed be accomplished.

THE QUESTION OF SOURCES

There is one important issue that defines Jewish attitudes to other religions, and to Christianity in particular, that is almost completely missing from Heschel's discussion. Anyone familiar with Jewish sources will know how central the issue of idolatry is to a Jewish view of other religions. The Hebrew term is Avoda Zara. Its literal translation is "foreign worship," and it encompasses a range of issues from compromising the strict unity of God to the worship of idols and other expressions of worship foreign to Jewish practice. The critique and the application of the halakhic category of Avoda Zara is relevant to Judaism's appreciation of all religions; and even Islam, which is conventionally considered a pure monotheism and therefore not subject to the laws of Avoda Zara, has been considered by various halakhic authorities over the generations as a form of Avoda Zara. Heschel's discussion completely ignores the issue of Avoda Zara. In other words, he sidesteps the hottest and most problematic issue from the perspective of a Jewish consideration of other religions.[89]

Moreover, in one place in the essay Heschel himself applies the category, in ways that are completely new to the Jewish tradition. "Religion is a means, not the end. It becomes idolatrous when regarded as an end in itself."[90] Thus, any religion can become idolatrous, Judaism included, when sight is lost of its ultimate purpose and when it becomes an end unto itself.

This reflection is a profound reflection. It suggests a completely new approach to idolatry that is qualitative and spiritual, rather than halakhic

---

needed to be excluded could be opened.

89. There is only one passing reference to idolatry. When presenting the view of Halevi, according to which Christianity and Islam have a role in the divine plan, Heschel acknowledges, in passing, that Halevi's recognition comes in spite of retaining relics of ancient idolatry. See Heschel, "No Religion," 18. That the issue of idolatry emerges in the context of a philosophical discussion of history and its purpose, rather than in the context of a halakhic consideration is telling.

90. Heschel, "No Religion," 13.

and formal. It cuts across different traditions, making all traditions susceptible to the inherent critique of idolatry, rather than allowing idolatry to function as the instrument by means of which one religion criticizes another. Here too Heschel has made a significant theological foray, one that requires much further consideration and development.

However, important as this contribution may be, we must also acknowledge that Heschel's presentation, as well as his application of the notion of idolatry, situates him outside conventional Jewish categories and methods, by means of which religions are appreciated. This may not be inappropriate for a trail blazer; whose task is also to redefine earlier categories and to establish new paradigms. However, this redefinition cannot be glossed over and it cannot find an echo in the traditional Jewish community in its present form. The reason is that Heschel completely ignores the constitutive language within which traditional discourse regarding other religions takes place—the Halakha, Jewish law. Even the catalogue of sources on Christianity that forms the final part of the essay relies completely on non-legal materials. Heschel almost consciously rejects the relevance of Halakha to his enterprise: "The supreme issue today is not the halacha for the Jew or the Church for the Christian—but the premise underlying both religions, namely, whether there is a pathos, a divine reality concerned with the destiny of man which mysteriously impinges upon history."[91]

Ignoring Halakha may be understood as a function of context. Halakha may not prove helpful or appropriate in an address to a Christian public. Perhaps had the essay been addressed primarily to a Jewish audience, Halakha would have played a more prominent role. But perhaps lack of acknowledgment of Halakha is also a function of Heschel's own religious personality and reflects his deeper theological preferences.[92] Either way, a serious Jewish consideration of other religions must take into account a range of sources and a methodology entirely ignored by Heschel. While

---

91. Heschel, "No Religion," 5.

92. The stronger the prophetic component, by means of which a moment in time is appreciated as a transition point, the weaker the reliance upon halachic categories formed under the "old order." If Heschel's reading of the meaning of the present moment in time is informed by a sense of failure of religion, this would further vitiate the relevance of halacha and its ability to guide the present moment in time. On the Halakha's importance for Heschel, see Dresner, *Heschel, Hasidism, and Halakha*. On Heschel and Halakha, conceptualized in terms of the dichotomy of halakha and aggadah, see Hartman, "Heschel," 174 ff. Hartman, page 183, suggests that Heschel's ability to discover common experiential ground with members of other faith communities stems precisely from his conceiving of Judaism in terms of Aggada (i.e., non Halakha), while Rabbi Soloveitchik's emphasis upon Halakha highlights the insurmountable differences to mutual understanding (page 180).

this is true to some extent for all streams of Judaism, it is obviously and powerfully the case with reference to Orthodox Judaism. Heschel's position cannot begin to be heard until it is complemented by careful attention to halakhic sources and to how they could be addressed, contextualized, and adapted to the broader spiritual view that informs Heschel's presentation.

To drive the point home: The distinction that Heschel makes between God and religion allows him to state: "[W]hile dogmas and forms of worship are divergent, God is the same."[93] The claim that "God is the same" is less obvious than one might think. It presumes having settled the problem of the status of Christianity as Avoda Zara.[94] It is likely that Heschel did not need to go through the appropriate halachic machinations. His prophetic, spiritual and personal experience taught him something that precedes halakhic discussion and that should inform and direct the halakhic discussion, rather than be informed by it.[95] But such a possible privileging of personal intuition over traditional halakhic discourse itself requires discussion, certainly if Heschel's testimony is to have any consequence for halakhically oriented Jews.

A second halakhic component that is virtually absent from his discussion is the halakhic category by means of which Judaism has traditionally framed its consideration of non-Jews and in light of which it has often assessed other religions. I refer to the seven Noahide commandments.[96] The essay only includes a passing reference to them. It is not Heschel's voice we hear, but that of Rabbi Lifschutz, quoted above, whom Heschel quotes as being favorable and accepting of Christianity. That Rabbi Lifschutz includes observance of the seven Noahide commandments as a basis for his positive view of Christianity, while Heschel himself remains mum on this subject, suggests that Heschel ignores this halakhic consideration as well. Again, it may be a function of the audience to whom the address is delivered, or it may reflect Heschel's appropriate sense of the inadequacy of the category

---

93. Heschel, "No Religion," 9, followed by reference to the God of Abraham. The notion of the God of Abraham as common ground gained currency around the time of the Second Vatican Council, in whose preparation Heschel participated, through the work of Louis Massignon. This statement seems to draw on Massignon's work, rather than on traditional Jewish conceptualization of the one God as the common God of Abraham. See Griffith, "Sharing," 193–210.

94. A similar issue arose recently with the publication of "Dabru Emet," a statement on Christianity by Jewish scholars and religious leaders. The first article in the statement affirmed that Jews and Christians worship the same God. This point was one of the issues to have come under critique. See Levenson, "Dialogue," 36–7.

95. One imagines that Heschel would have gravitated towards the appropriate halachic authorities in light of his intuitive and experiential understanding.

96. Their halachic status is explicated in Maimonides' *Laws of Kings*, Chapter 8:10 to Chapter 10:6.

as a means of addressing other religions. It is likely that Heschel felt that religions ought to be addressed on their own terms, rather than through the lens of an internal Jewish category such as the Noahide commandments. Regardless of how Heschel viewed the matter, it cannot go undiscussed if it is to form the basis of a serious Jewish view of other religions.

That Heschel completely sidesteps halakhic considerations raises a broader issue regarding the type of sources upon which he relies in making his presentation. If we bracket the final pages of the essay, which I have already suggested form an essay within an essay, and which constitute a historical catalogue of Jewish attitudes to Christianity, one notes that most of the sources crucial to Heschel's argument are biblical. Certainly, of all the textually grounded moments in the essay, those that engage biblical sources are the most inspiring ones. Reliance upon rabbinic sources is second to reliance on biblical sources, and sources from later Jewish writings are infrequent. This observation is interesting not only because it points to the sources that Heschel employs, but even more so because it brings to our awareness what sources were excluded from his purview. We lack any reference to the philosophical tradition, common to Jews, Christians, and Muslims, that could have provided bridges of understanding between the traditions. We lack any appeal to Kabbalistic doctrine and to the riches of Jewish mysticism. Even the Hasidic tradition, from which Heschel emerges, plays absolutely no role in "No Religion Is an Island." Perhaps these sources represent a Judaism that is less open to the outside world, and therefore Heschel could not identify in them principles that would be helpful to an emerging theory of interreligious relations. Still, his own creative interpretive abilities could have been brought to bear upon these sources, just as they were upon earlier materials. Perhaps herein lies the key. It is possible that the earlier sources are indeed more open to creative interpretation and recasting, given the literary and theological nature of biblical and Rabbinic materials, than the more structured articulations of Jewish identity found in later Jewish writings. In the same way that the halacha leaves, so it would seem, less room for creativity and new constructions, so certain kinds of writings provide more interpretative leverage than others. Heschel may therefore be operating with those Jewish sources that are more supple and pliant, from the creative interpreter's viewpoint.

Context may play here as decisive a role as does the question of hermeneutical flexibility. The essay is an address of a Jewish theologian to a primarily Christian audience. As stated explicitly several times in the essay, the Bible provides a common ground for Christians and Jews. It would therefore stand to reason that the primary scripture that Heschel would cite would be the Bible. Rabbinic traditions are recognized as the early stratum of Jewish interpretation and have as such also captured the attention of non-Jewish scholars.

A Christian audience would therefore still be comfortable with theological work done in light of Rabbinic sources. Later sources are less familiar and, in that sense, less appropriate for presentation to a Christian audience.[97]

Finally, the question of sources should be considered in the broader framework of Heschel's use of sources throughout his oeuvre. Eliezer Schweid has noted that in his philosophical works, Heschel relies upon biblical prophecy as the almost exclusive source. Whatever is brought from the works of rabbis, philosophers, and kabbalists is only brought in order to shed light on the nature of prophecy and upon the words of the prophets.[98] This astute observation highlights the place of prophecy in his view of Judaism and in his own experience of it. It may well be the case that Heschel's reliance on biblical, and in particular prophetic, materials is a broader phenomenon.[99]

Whether we account for the choice of sources by reference to Heschel's audience or by appeal to Heschel's personal spiritual disposition, a translation process, like the one that Heschel envisions as underlying any major revelation, is called for. Heschel's fundamental insights must be translated into other media and other traditional languages beyond the translations already offered by Heschel himself. These translations include the Halakha, the mystical tradition, and more generally a reading of Heschel against the background of problematic, yet authoritative, Jewish texts. For those readers for whom authority encompasses the Halakha, as well as the various masters, traditions and disciplines that emerged in later Judaism, one cannot simply cite Heschel as an authority, while sidestepping a rich and complicated tradition of reference to other religions. Heschel cannot supplant that tradition. He can challenge it with alternative insight and pose fundamental questions regarding its perspective, breadth of vision, accuracy of description of the other, and ultimate spiritual effectiveness. But this is already a dialogue. Such a dialogue between Heschel's perspective and that of traditional Judaism, in light of which sources are read, positions examined, and details negotiated, is a must if more people are to follow the trail opened up by Heschel's pioneering intuitions.

---

97. This statement reflects my sense of what the shared knowledge base between Christians and Jews would have permitted forty years ago. I suspect Heschel would have had a much harder time developing his ideas from a Hasidic platform because that literature was less well known and less accessible to audiences beyond those committed to the study and practice of that literature, even within Jewish circles. I believe much has changed in this respect in forty years, and we therefore have to imagine a different intellectual climate when we reflect upon the choice of sources Heschel could have comfortably used in such a context.

98. Schweid, *Prophets*, 234.

99. It is still worth noting, though, that the address to the Rabbinical Assembly lacked biblical prooftexts.

Part of such a dialogue is also the scholarly dialogue of revisiting Heschel's presentation of classical texts. It is understandable that the context of presenting ideas to a Christian audience will inevitably lead to highlighting certain features of a text, while ignoring others. But if those same texts are to be incorporated as part of a new internal attitude to other religions, they must be read in their entirety, and one must struggle with their difficult parts alongside what one finds inspiring. When we speak among ourselves, we cannot tolerate selective and partial citations. And that is precisely what Heschel does when he addresses his Christian listeners. An example of such partial citation is found in the way Maimonides is cited as making room within the divine economy of history for Christianity, while ignoring his unflattering remarks in that context, or more seriously: his view of Christianity as Avoda Zara.[100] Closer reading of some of his rabbinic sources raises serious doubts regarding how some of the texts were manipulated and whether Heschel was completely unaware of the radically new content he introduced into them.[101] The meaning of other sources is stretched, and this stretching requires further clarification and justification.[102]

Following the trail blazer is a rich process. We must follow his vision and his inspiration. We must also follow the track of his thoughts and scrutinize it. The outcome of such scrutiny will be the process of engaging the prophetic insight in relation to the rich history of interpretation, law, and philosophy. A rereading and reconsideration of these is the order of the day if the flash of prophetic inspiration is to become a steady light illuminating the path, a path to be followed by a broad section of Heschel's own brothers and sisters in faith.

100. Heschel, "No Religion," 20.

101. See Heschel, "No Religion," 8, for his reading of the Mekhilta to Exodus 17:6 (See Lauterbach, *Mekilta*, 133). The midrashic passage, in context, does not make a statement regarding the universal relationship of the human and the divine. Rather, it seeks to clarify how Moses would recognize God standing before him on the rock, as described in Ex. 17:6.

102. When Heschel, "No Religion," 18, quotes from Seder Eliyahu Rabba that the Holy Spirit can also rest upon a gentile, in consonance with his deeds, he is stretching the text from reference to the person and his deeds to acceptance of different religious forms. The original statement envisioned a good gentile acting in morally, or even spiritually, valiant ways, but not necessarily within the framework of alternative religious systems. To arrive at Heschel's reading requires exposing the hidden dialogue between Heschel and the text that led to the particular reading. I note that Heschel's discussion on pages 7–8 does not make a similar leap. His discussion of the image of God as the foundation upon which a meeting between members of different religions takes place does not slide into a legitimation of other religions, as manifestations of the image of God. The image of God is contained in the individual person, not in all fruits of humanity's spirit. I also note that I occasionally encounter accounts of how other religions ought to be accepted by appeal to the notion of the image of God. Heschel himself was not so radical in his application of the notion of the image of God.

THE CHALLENGE OF DIALOGUE TODAY: APPLYING HESCHEL'S LEGACY

Much has changed since the pioneering work of Heschel was given expression in "No Religion Is an Island." Dialogue is no longer a matter for the elite. It has become widespread. It has become popular, almost a social necessity, in a way one could not have imagined in Heschel's time. But it is precisely the spread of interfaith dialogue that poses the challenge of how it ought to be carried out and what Heschel's legacy is in this context. Can Heschel's vision be adapted to the various changes that have taken place since?

In addition to the spread in quantity, there have been significant qualitative advances. The players have changed. Interreligious dialogue is no longer a strictly, or primarily, Jewish-Christian affair. Everyone is in, with special place allotted to the dialogue with Islam, which is of concern to all who are engaged in dialogue. Dialogue with eastern religions is on the rise as well. Heschel probably never envisioned such a rise in interreligious dialogue.[103] It requires other foundations than the assumed commonality of scripture and God that underlies Heschel's engagement with Christianity.

That interfaith dialogue today is so much broader than anything Heschel could have imagined is further reason for paying careful attention to the range of issues pointed out above as insufficient on the legal, historical, and hermeneutical levels. Contact with multiple world religions in a changing world, in which the self-understanding and practice of religious communities and their attitudes to Judaism are in flux, requires constant and detailed work that exceeds by far the testimony of a forty-year-old inaugural lecture. Beyond the need to incorporate halacha and to pay closer attention to the meanings of texts and the history of their interpretation, especially problematic texts that are easily ignored but continue to inform the community of believers, there are other methodological advances that impact how dialogue may be carried out. In Heschel's day the study of "theology of religions" had not come into being as a form of self-standing theological discourse. Nor had the work in the area that has gained great prominence over the past decade which is referred to as "comparative theology."[104] Both disciplines allow us to deepen our view of other religions and to frame them in ways that go beyond the fundamental acceptance of otherness espoused

---

103. Kasimow and Sherwin already tackled this issue fifteen years ago by asking members of other religions to respond to Heschel, thereby creating a dialogue with him. It remains, however, a one-sided dialogue and cannot address the issue of the theoretical foundations for a Jewish engagement of those other religious traditions.

104. Francis Clooney, S.J., is a pioneering figure whose work in this area is gaining increasing recognition and providing a model for others.

by Heschel. Heschel excluded theological discussion from his encounter with other religions, emphasizing instead the human reaction, primarily human imperfection, in the face of the divine. The two newer disciplines challenge us to conduct meaningful conversations between believers of different faiths on those very fundamental issues excluded by Heschel. The dogma, the world of faith, that which is particular and unique to each religion, need not remain beyond our ability to explore it. We may not agree, but we may also try to understand what it is that the other is stating in their own theological language and what, if any, resonance this might have in our own theological worldview.[105] We may therefore dare think of carrying dialogue into zones explicitly excluded by Heschel.

Much of Heschel's work relies on the distinction between people and religions. He highlights the image of God as central to the encounter. He utilizes Jewish sources on gentiles and extrapolates from them regarding other religious traditions. He explicitly makes the distinction between Christians and Christianity.[106] Dialogue is only possible, according to this formulation, between the members of the religions, not between the religions themselves.[107] It is at this very juncture that we are called to consider whether forty years later the tools we have and the trust we have built could not allow us to go beyond that distinction, and whether meaningful dialogue between the religions, qua religions, is not indeed possible.

There are thus a variety of ways in which we can go beyond Heschel. In scope—in addressing multiple religions, as well as in extending the scope of the dialogue to broader strata of society. In depth—allowing ourselves to engage the faith of the other, and their vision of God and the spiritual life. In rigor—in filling in the blanks left open by Heschel, in all that concerns the translation of his insights into the language of the historical sources of tradition. In methodology—by adopting new methodologies that have developed in the academy, as well as by giving more serious attention to the classical methodology of halacha.

But in all this Heschel can remain a guiding force. His basic insights, and they are many, continue to inspire us, regardless of the translation work they still require. But more important than substance is the legacy of method. Heschel offers us an approach to interreligious relations, and it runs through the heart of the human experience. Heschel has taught us how to encounter

---

105. For an example of such an attempt in relation to Christian dogma, see my own reflections on the incarnation, in Goshen-Gottstein, "Judaisms," 219–47.

106. Heschel, "No Religion," 10.

107. Of course, dialogue is always only possible between people. The point is that dialogue is only possible about the "peopleness" of the believers, rather than their proper faith.

the common human experience that underlies our religious experience. Heschel illustrated for us a small section of what such common experience might consist of. But we can identify much more by way of common human experience, and it can be extended beyond the experience common to Christians and Jews. Heschel's legacy mandates encounter with all expressions of the human religious experience and its religious significance. This includes those experiences already recognized by Heschel as similar to our own as well as a range of other experiences we may have in common with members of different religions that await further sharing, experiencing, and reflection. The range of religiously significant experience may even transcend what for Heschel was the basis of commonality: the traces of God in our lives and souls. We also share suffering and the broader human condition. These too condition our religious life in significant ways. They can therefore provide further points of commonality and solidarity between religions.[108] They allow us to encounter members of traditions such as Buddhism, who share little of the theological and historical premises common to Christians and Jews. If the foundation for interreligious understanding is being human, then let all that is truly human condition our understanding of the religious other.[109]

If Heschel's work grows out of a "prophetic" reading of the moment and its challenges, one cannot rely on the forty-year-old reading. By its very nature, a "prophetic" approach cannot become stale. It must be restated time and again, with the changes in circumstances. Following Heschel, therefore, means much more than engaging in interreligious dialogue based on his ideas. It means developing the "prophetic" sense, in light of which a broader spiritual vision is formed, that encompasses other religions and that is appropriate for the moment. It must be as informed by personal transformative experiences as Heschel's views were. Personal experiences may differ, given the broad range of emotions and interior realities that comprise the spiritual life. Others may have encounters at different spiritual bandwidths than those developed by Heschel in his own encounters. These experiences in turn may generate different perspectives through which the broader philosophical, theological, and historical issues are dealt with. But underlying the variety in approaches and attitudes is the possibility of following a method fundamentally like that used by Heschel. Creating bases, multiple bases, of experience and prophetic, intuitive understanding of the reality between religions is Heschel's greatest legacy. If we seek to uphold the

---

108. See Fernando, "An Asian Perspective," 175–84.

109. This is the great benefit of not grounding understanding between religions upon mystical commonality. Even though Heschel comes out of a mystical tradition, he grounds our commonality in our humanity, thereby opening the door to the discovery of greater and greater commonalities, as our mutual knowledge deepens.

continuing relevance of his vision, we are called to discover these qualities at the basis of our interreligious activities.

"No Religion Is an Island" assumes we can help each other. It begins with helping each other face the challenges of the world. It concludes with helping each other in our spiritual lives. The former help grows out of a reading of the needs of the time. It has become widely practiced. The latter grows out of the personal experience of Heschel and his ability to find ways of sharing religious experience with religious people outside Judaism. That Heschel closes his essay with the call to help each other in our spiritual life suggests the importance of this calling. It also points the way forward. To follow Heschel is to be able to cultivate the space of heart and mind and those relationships by means of which we can really help each other address and fulfill our deepest spiritual yearnings. The range of religions in dialogue may now be broader and the range of experiences may be conceived as larger.[110] But the fundamental call remains the same. Not all will be able to answer this call. The dialogue of the masses, in service of society, will surely grow. But only those who are able to cultivate the depth of personal relations and of personal experience can explore new dimensions of what it means to share religious experience, of what it means to be truly human. Only those who can enter the thicket and create new paths within it deserve to be considered true followers of the trail blazer.

---

110. While Heschel engaged mainly in dialogue with Christianity, he may have already been aware of the potential help that may come to Judaism from engagement with eastern traditions. See Kasimow's paraphrase of Heschel's *God in Search of Man* in Kasimow, *Interreligious Dialogue*, 430.

5

I Am What I Do

Abraham Joshua Heschel Seen from Two Perspectives, Secular Jewish and Christian

> Each mortal thing does one thing and the same: Deals out that being indoors each one dwells; Selves—goes itself; *myself* it speaks and spells, Crying What I do is me: for that I came.
> (from "As Kingfishers Catch Fire" by Gerard Manley Hopkins)

Shoshana Ronen

A SECULAR JEWISH PERSPECTIVE

This article shows how a thoroughly religious thinker like Heschel can be relevant also for a secular way of thinking. Heschel believed in the inseparability of life and that intellectual and social activities go hand in hand. This belief, inspired by his study of the biblical prophets, was realized in his active social advocacy for human rights.

Heschel's analysis of religion and its weakness in modern times also appeals to secular thinking. He did not blame the secular world for the decline of religion, but looked directly into religion, which as he felt, had ceased to be a living entity, and became degenerated, petrified, frozen.

Heschel's God is merciful but not omnipotent. This concept is a religious answer for the difficulty to believe after Auschwitz. Using the Kabalistic term *tzimtzum*, Heschel recovers the idea of God I would first like to clarify what is meant by "secular Judaism." Judaism is more than just a religion, and being a Jew is more than just being a member of a religious community. Judaism, as Mordecai Kaplan defined it, is a whole civilization.[1] Judaism is a culture, a historical narrative of a group of people held together by a special attitude to a collection of texts and historical memories. Whether or not these texts or memories are entirely true is less important than the fact that they form a common ethos. Being a secular Jew doesn't mean simply that you were born Jewish but don't cleave to the God of Abraham, Isaac, and Jacob; secular Jews are those who have consciously chosen to identify themselves as a bead in a long chain of Jewish existence and creativity and yet are willing to look at Jewish tradition and history with a critical eye. Being a secular Jew does not necessarily mean being indifferent to the Hebrew Bible, to the Talmudic texts, to Jewish philosophy, or Jewish literature through the generations. My agnosticism does not mean I am blind to the mystery of existence, which can be defined by believers as divine, nor does it mean I believe that reason is the ultimate answer to all questions.

Heschel was a thoroughly religious thinker; he was the embodiment of a religious creative soul in constant dialogue with God. How then can a person like me, for whom God is a cultural construct of humankind, be fascinated by Heschel's thinking? Why do I see him as a challenge for my secular spirit? In short, what made me fall in love with him? We all know the saying that love is blind, so perhaps trying to rationalize that love is doomed to failure, but I will try my best.

LIFE AND THINKING

You might find my personal tone surprising, but I believe that when dealing with Heschel's thinking one cannot be detached or reserved. In his writing and philosophy, Heschel could not, and never tried to, separate his life from his thought. More than that, he suggested that writing and understanding without involvement are not valuable. He was wary of claims of impartiality. He thought that if we write about something that is relevant to us, then impartiality is only a pretense, and if the subject is irrelevant, why would we

---

1. "Judaism as otherness is thus, something far more comprehensive than Jewish religion. It includes that nexus of a history, literature, language, social organizations, folk sanctions, standards of conduct, social and spiritual ideals, esthetic values, which in their totality form a civilization" (Kaplan, *Judaism*, 178).

have dealt with it in the first place? Concerning the divine, which was the most significant and vital question for him, he wrote: "In asking about God, we examine our own selves: whether we are sensitive to the grandeur and supremacy of what we ask about, whether we are wholeheartedly concerned with what we ask about. Unless we are involved, we fail to sense the issue."[2]

I would like to refer to two philosophers who are very dear to me, Nietzsche and Wittgenstein. I wrote something about them that I think is very relevant to Heschel:

> In *Beyond Good and Evil* Nietzsche wrote: "It has gradually become clear to me what every great philosophy has hitherto been: a confession on the part of its author" (BGE #6). I would like to argue that Wittgenstein's philosophy does not differ from that Nietzschean way of looking at things. In *Culture and Value*, Wittgenstein wrote: "Working in philosophy is really a working on oneself. On one's own interpretation. On one's way of seeing things." Philosophy is not only something subjective and individual, a personal perspective and not a generalization, but also the conception of philosophy is dependent on interpretation and perspective. Philosophers are incapable of being indifferent towards their activity; they cannot separate their personality from it. . . . Philosophy is life.[3]

I wrote then that philosophy was not a mere profession for Nietzsche and Wittgenstein, but a consuming passion. The same I believe is true of Heschel. One's philosophy, according to Heschel, is a gate to one's self; life and thought cannot be separated: "In a profound sense, the philosopher is never a pure spectator. His wisdom is not a commodity that can be produced on demand. His books are not *responsa*. We should not regard them as mirrors, reflecting other people's problems, but rather as windows, allowing us to view the author's soul All philosophy is an *apologia pro vita sua*."[4]

This subjective way of looking, of perceiving soul and mind as indivisible, interweaving life and intellectual activity, is enormously appealing to my "Jewish" perspective, which looks at human beings as a unity of mind and body. My Jewish perspective does not consider those two aspects of human existence as parallel or separate; it does not see any hierarchal relation between them, because they are one entity.

Regarding the inseparability of life and thinking, Heschel's disciple Byron Sherwin wrote about him: "Heschel's philosophy of religion and his

---

2. Heschel, *Prophets II*, 46.
3. Ronen, *Nietzsche*, 9–10.
4. Heschel, *Search*, 6.

philosophy of Judaism are expressions of his own quest for self-understanding, for self-transcendence. They are crucial strokes in the artistic masterpiece that was his own life."[5] And Heschel's daughter added: "We can get to know my father by reading his books, because they are a window into his own soul, into the life he led and the kind of person he was."[6]

Heschel's ideas and thoughts were realized in the social sphere, in his active social advocacy for human rights, especially in the Civil Rights Movement led by Martin Luther King, Jr., and in his opposition to American involvement in the war in Vietnam. His interest in the preaching of the prophets of the Hebrew Bible was not mere intellectual curiosity, but the spark for a transformation in his life. Heschel admitted that his study of the prophets of ancient Israel was one of the main factors that changed his attitude towards political involvement and activity.

The more deeply immersed I became in the thinking of the prophets, the more powerfully it became clear to me what the lives of the prophets sought to convey: that morally speaking there is no limit to the concern one must feel for the suffering of human beings. It also became clear to me that regarding cruelties committed in the name of the free society some are guilty, while all are responsible And so I decided to change my mode of living and to become active in the cause of peace in Vietnam.[7]

His disciple Harold Kasimow wrote that Heschel's life was transformed by his study of the Hebrew prophets, and he adds, "part of Heschel's greatness stems from the fact that his life was in harmony with his works."[8]

So, what do I find so appealing in Heschel's thought? The fact that life and thought are not separated, that intellectual activity and social involvement go hand in hand. As he wrote in *God in Search of Man*, "unless we are involved, the problem is not present."[9]

THE ILLNESS OF RELIGION IN OUR TIME

The first essay which I read and was struck by was "The Religious Message" in *Religion in America: Original Essays on Religion in a Free Society*.[10] Stanislaw Obirek gave me this text about a year ago, and I will always be grateful to him for that. So, my encounter with Heschel is still fresh and quite new.

5. Sherwin, "My Master," 51.
6. Heschel, "My Father," 24.
7. Heschel, "Reasons," 225.
8. Kasimow, "Prophetic Vision," 89.
9. Heschel, *Search*, 5.
10. Heschel, "Religious Message," 244–71.

Upon that first encounter, I was very much impressed by Heschel's poetical language, by the fact that though this paper was written more than 40 years ago it is so relevant today. Above all I was so much impressed by his diagnosis. Finally, I had the pleasure to read a religious thinker who was not blaming the secular world for the decline of religion. At last I came across an honest attempt to find the roots for an illness, one that didn't try to accuse others but looked directly into one's own world. In that essay Heschel criticizes the relevance of religion for the modern man. "Little does religion ask of contemporary man. It is ready to offer comfort; it has no courage to challenge. It is ready to offer edification; it has no courage to break the idols, to shatter the callousness."[11] Religion was distinguished institutions, dogmas, and securities; it is degenerated, petrified, frozen. Heschel felt that religion had ceased to be a living entity, an event. And he did not blame the agnostics for that.

It is customary to blame secular science and anti-religion philosophy for the eclipse of religion in modern society. It would be more honest to blame religion for its defeats. Religion declined not because it was refuted, but because it became irrelevant, dull, oppressive, insipid When religion speaks only in the name of authority rather than with the voice of compassion, its message becomes meaningless.[12]

Further, Heschel criticizes the materialism of modern society and declares how fake and artificial our needs are. His words could have been written today:

Many of the interests and needs we cherish are imposed on us by the conventions of society; they are not indigenous to our essence. While some of them are necessities, others, as I said before, are fictitious, and adopted as a result of convention, advertisement, or sheer envy.[13]

Heschel's analysis is very agreeable to a secular mind like mine. He says that the diseases of our society and culture are not the result of an absence of belief or of a closed heart towards the divine, but of the fact that humanity has lost its compassion and its social solidarity. Seen in this light, Heschel's ideal figure of the prophet can be an ideal figure for me as well:

The mind of the prophets was not religion centered. They dwelt more on the affairs of the royal palace, on the ways and views of the courts of justice, than on the problems of the priestly rituals at the temple of Jerusalem.[14]

---

11. Heschel, *Search*, 244.
12. Heschel, *Search*, 245.
13. Heschel, *Search*, 248–49.
14. Heschel, *Search*, 253.

SOCIAL JUSTICE AND THE PROPHET'S WAY OF THINKING

As we've seen, a crucial aspect of Heschel's thinking was a concern for social justice, human rights, and the misery of human beings. Considering his attitude toward the inseparability of life and thought, I would argue that, for Heschel, we cannot separate the thinker's biography from his philosophy. Heschel expressed this idea as follows: "In the face of the tragic failure of the modern mind, incapable of preventing its own destruction, it became clear to me that the most important philosophical problem of the twentieth century was to find a new set of presuppositions or premises, a different way of thinking."[15]

Heschel indeed found a new way of thinking, an outcome of his own life experience. Heschel managed to escape Europe on the eve of the Second World War. Most of his family, however, perished in the Holocaust, and more than that, all his world, the world of Eastern European Jews before the war, which he portrayed with such great love and nostalgia in his book *The Earth is the Lord's*, was totally annihilated. I would like to suggest that Heschel could not erase the memory of the Holocaust from his theology. It was too colossal an event to be ignored by theologians; the question is too painful to avoid while trying to find a clue or a beginning of an answer.[16]

The more I read Heschel the more I am convinced that his hidden aim was to save the world from another catastrophe. In all the Heschel I've read he rarely mentions the word *Shoah*. But the Holocaust is constantly hovering under the surface of his writings, and I would like to quote one explicit reference to it that I did find.

Life in our time has been a nightmare for many of us, tranquility an interlude, happiness a fake. Who could breathe at a time when man was engaged in murdering the holy witness to God six million times?[17]

---

15. Heschel, *Prophets*, xxviii.

16. Indeed, Jewish theologians are very much preoccupied with this serious problem, which the Holocaust compels believers to face. The attitudes and the "answers" are divergent. I will name some of these theologians, although this is not the place to deal with each thinker's philosophical or theological approach in detail. Some of the main Jewish theologians are Eliezer Berkovits (*Faith after the Holocaust*); Emil Fackenheim, who wrote quite a lot about theology after the Holocaust (*To Mend the World*); Irving Greenberg (*The Jewish Way: Living the Holidays*) and *The Third Era of Jewish History: Power and Politics (Perspective), A Clal Thesis*; Richard Rubenstein (*After Auschwitz: Radical Theology and Contemporary Judaism*. An interesting representation of those thinkers and others can be found in Berger, *Children*, 13–33; Gorny, *Between*, 70–101 (Hebrew); and Morgan, *Beyond* Auschwitz.

17. Heschel, *Truth*, 300–301.

It seems to me that facing the total collapse of the Judeo-Christian civilization, with its rational-modern face, brought him to look for an alternative. He was disappointed with humanity, and he felt that people need guidance, something that will hold them on a short leash. The Aristotelian God, the unmoved mover—a detached perfection, bereft of all involvement and passions, a model of absolute self-sufficiency—was not enough to prevent the destruction of humanity. So Heschel decided to bring God back into history, to restore the intimacy and the immediate relations of God and man. He stressed that as much as man needs God, God needs man, and is looking for him.

The first book by Heschel I read was *The Prophets*, in the English version of the revised and full edition, which he finished editing in 1962. When it comes to the idea of justice, this is his major work. Let me quote some paragraphs from that book that illuminate clearly the mutual dependence of God and man, a dependence which was crucial for Heschel to preserve an amount of justice in the human world. This dependence is vital in minimizing what he calls "the evil of indifference."

>]God's presence in the world is, in essence, His concern for the world . . . The fundamental thought in the Bible is not creation, but God's care for His creation . . . God can be understood by man only in conjunction with the human situation. For of God we know only what he means and does in relation to man. The prophet reflects, not on heavenly or hallowed mysteries, but on the perplexities and ambiguities of history. The prophet refers to God, not as absolute, but always as related to the people. It is an interpretation, not of divine Being, but of the divine interaction with humanity.[18]

God needs humanity, but not at any cost. God puts in front of humanity a demand. This demand includes love and compassion but is primarily a demand for a way of life guided by strict social justice in the human sphere, in person-to-person relations. In such a "prophetic world," a second Shoah cannot happen. Following the dehumanization of human beings in the Shoah, Heschel tries to rehumanize humanity by stressing the idea that God is interested in people, is deeply involved in the affairs of humanity. Moreover, as a religious man who wanted to preserve God as a relevant entity for humanity (and rescue humanity from itself) he had to lessen the idea of the omnipotence of God, since an omnipotent God would not permit the horrors that happen in the world.

---

18. Heschel, *Prophets*, 264–65.

Only a God who is dependent on human activity, only one who is in a mutual relationship with humanity, can secure a society built upon justice: "At times we must believe in Him in spite of Him, to continue being a witness despite His hiding Himself."[19]

In this construct, human beings' responsibility is enormous, for without human deeds, salvation is not possible.

> Messianic redemption is a marvelous promise. The present chaos will not last forever. But fulfillment did not come All we have today is a promise and the expectation. The waiting goes on. However, mere waiting may be a moratorium, a way of marking time, postponing our response to the challenge. The task is never to forget that by each sacred deed we commit, by each word we hallow, by each thought we chant, we render our modest part in reducing distress and advancing redemption.[20]

Heschel wanted to believe in humanity against all the evidence, against history, after the Shoah, so he sanctified humanity by relating it to God, by saying that humanity is "holy of holiness" because God is interested in it. In the image of God, human beings were created. Humanity is the disclosure of the divine. Heschel did not want to eliminate or minimize the "human all too human" features of humanity in order to make humanity holy. On the contrary, what he says is that this creature of flesh and blood, this weird unity of body and soul, is evidence for the presence of the divine on earth.

Heschel wanted so much to believe in women and men, in those very physical creatures, that he tried to sanctify them. But people cannot be saints or angels, since they are a unity of body and soul. If one believes in humanity or sees in it evidence for the presence of God, then one must sanctify physicality, the senses, and the flesh and blood. What a great passion he must have had for that task, one might even say a mission. Therefore, the idea of "God in search of man," of God's need of man, is not a desecration of the divine, but a consecration of humanity. Sensuality has sense and beauty only when it is sanctified, and that was what Heschel was trying to do.

MERCY AND OMNIPOTENCE

I would like now to return to the idea of the omnipotence of God. If God is omnipotent how could we justify his lack of involvement in times of extreme atrocities? How could Heschel explain God's silence during the Holocaust?

19. Heschel, *Truth*, 302.
20. Heschel, *Truth*, 299.

In his Hebrew book *Heavenly Torah*, he has a very interesting discussion of that question in chapters six and eleven. One of the sub-chapters which deals with that issue is titled "decrees or mercy," but I would call it "omnipotence or mercy," and it is about the attributes, or the essence, of the Almighty. The problem is whether God is merciful or almighty, because God cannot be both. They are exclusive terms. It is connected to the unsolved problem of the misfortune of the righteous and the prosperity of the wicked, or, the issue that was most crucial for Heschel: God's participation in human suffering. Heschel witnessed the people of Israel's most painful moment of suffering. How could God watch it and not interfere? Either God is indifferent to the suffering of the innocents, or his power to act in the human sphere is limited. The consequence is that either God is omnipotent but cruel or merciful but limited in power. It is for human beings to decide which image of God they prefer.

For illustrating and introducing the diversity of the Jewish tradition and thinking concerning those questions, Heschel looks to two main figures in the Jewish halakhic world: Rabbi Ishmael and Rabbi Akiva.[21] Both are significant figures when it comes to the way Jewish law and Jewish thought is presented in the Talmud.

Akiva (c. 50–135 C.E.) was one of the outstanding sages, probably the leading scholar of his age. He exercised a decisive influence in the development of Halakha, i.e., the legal side of Judaism, which embraces personal, social, national, and international relationships, and all the other practices and observances of Judaism. Akiva was also one of the most outstanding teachers of his time. He was known for his independence of spirit and his strong mystical orientation. To Akiva the study of Torah was the *raison d'etre* of the Jew. Akiva manifested a broad spirit of universalism in his teachings: "Beloved is a man in that he was created in the image [of God]." His famous statement that "Thou shalt love thy neighbour as thyself" is the fundamental principle of the Torah.

Ishmael Ben Elisha (first half of the second century C.E.) was one of the sages whose personality and teachings had a permanent effect on Talmudic literature and on Judaism as a whole. Akiva was his most intimate colleague, and he disputed with him on Halakha, and in halakhic expositions of the Bible. Both created and developed different approaches to understanding the Torah, and each had a school named after him. The chief difference between the two schools is that Akiva believed that the Torah, as a work of God, contained no redundancies, that even a particular spelling

---

21. Heschel addresses many other theological questions as well in the three-volume *Heavenly Torah*, which is more than 900 pages in the Hebrew original.

has its definite purpose, while Ishmael maintained that the language of the Torah follows normal human usage: "the Torah used human language."[22]

Heschel presented the dilemma of mercy versus omnipotence through the teaching of those two ancient scholars, showing that Akiva is on the side of mercy and Ishmael on the side of almightiness. Therefore, for Akiva it is better to reduce the power of God than to conceive of him as indifferent. Heschel presents Akiva's thinking as follows:

> Compassion is the key. Better to limit the belief in God's power than to dampen the faith in God's mercy. Rabbi Akiva viewed all history through the lens of trust in God's mercy. God participates in His creatures' suffering; it is as if God were wounded by the afflictions of Israel, God's people. If Israel is in exile, the Shekhinah is with them. When Israel is redeemed, God is redeemed.[23]

God can empathize with his suffering people but cannot redeem them, for when they are saved, he is saved with them. But if this is the case, I cannot resist raising the following question: who redeems the suffering people together with God? The implication is serious: is there another alternative power greater than God, one who is responsible for salvation? Or does it mean that the people of Israel, or human beings in general, should redeem themselves? If so, then it is against the passive Jewish attitude of waiting for the Messiah and against the tradition of "not to hasten the end."[24]

Ishmael is on the side of omnipotence, and Heschel interprets his view as follows: "The whole Akivan notion of God's participation in human suffering ... was foreign to Rabbi Ishmael's teaching. In his view, this notion did not befit God's dignity and could lead to a denial of God's power. For him, God's justice and power are key, not God's compassion."[25]

This image of God, angry and harsh, but not compassionate, is very much compatible with the biblical tradition: "For I the Lord thy God am a jealous God, visiting the iniquity of the fathers upon the children unto the third and the fourth generation of them that hate me" (Exodus 20:5).

Those two approaches to the relation between God and humanity, or God and the people of Israel, can be summarized by two different images of the two ancient sages. For Ishmael, "human beings are in the hands of heaven as a servant in the hands of the master," while in Akiva's eyes, in his

---

22. Kahana, "Midreshi Halakhah," (2) (A).
23. Heschel, *Heavenly Torah*, 210.
24. Heschel, *Heavenly Torah*, 220.
25. Heschel, *Heavenly Torah*, 211.

interpretation of the Song of Songs, "the congregation of Israel is compared to a bride, and the holy and Blessed One to her lover."[26]

On which side is Heschel? For me, after reading *God in Search of Man* and knowing his ideas about God, there is no doubt that he is on the side of Akiva. Omnipotent God has no need whatsoever for anything, let alone finite creatures like human beings.

> This is the mysterious paradox of Biblical faith: *God is pursuing man*. It is as if God were unwilling to be alone, and He had chosen man to serve Him. Our seeking Him is not only man's but also His concern and must not be considered an exclusively human affair All the human history as described in the Bible may be summarized in one phrase: *God is in search of man*. When Adam and Eve hid from His presence, the Lord called: *Where art thou*? (Genesis 3:9). It is a call that goes out again and again.[27]

Heschel's notion of the pathos of God is essential to understanding the relationship between God and human beings. The idea of pathos illuminates very clearly Heschel's insistence on God's need of humanity and God's dependence on it. Let me quote what he says about the God of pathos in *The Prophets*:

> God does not reveal himself in an abstract absoluteness, but in a personal and intimate relation to the world. He does not simply command and expect obedience; He is also moved and affected by what happens in the world and reacts accordingly. Events and human actions arouse in Him joy or sorrow, pleasure or wrath. He is not conceived as judging the world in detachment. He acts in an intimate and subjective manner, and thus determines the value of events. . . . This notion that God can be intimately affected, that He possesses not merely intelligence and will, but also pathos, basically defines the prophetic consciousness of God.[28]

Heschel depicts the dilemma of mercy vs. omnipotence very clearly. Does the image of God's suffering with his people "diminish our image of the divine and limit our belief in the creator's omnipotence?" he asks, apparently talking about the Second Temple era but actually referring to his own time, and to the unavoidable doubts in the Almighty: "And a nation that has been belittled by the nations of the world is likely to verge on belittling the great presumptions: that God is merciful and compassionate, and that God

---

26. Heschel, *Heavenly Torah*, 216, 197.
27. Heschel, *Search*, 136–47.
28. Heschel, *Prophets*, 288–89.

is the great and the powerful. If there is mercy, there surely is no power; and if there is power, there surely is no mercy."[29]

What Akiva emphasizes, and I suggest that it is Heschel's point of view as well, is that the pathos of God, i.e., the mutuality in the relationship of God and human beings, the linkage of God to his people, is a participation of the soul. God is related to humanity with love, participates in its sorrow, and suffers with it in the diaspora, and—most important—God is saved with humanity. As much as human beings need God to be saved, so God needs humanity for his salvation. God needs human beings' acceptance, and the human sorrow is his sorrow.

Consequently, this problem is a great dilemma and a challenge to the believer. Heschel expresses this very clearly: at a time of a catastrophe of a nation either God is merciful or he is great and powerful, but in time of crisis it is better to reduce his greatness than to lose confidence in his compassion.

SAVING FAITH IN GOD

I believe that Heschel was trying to save faith in God in an epoch when God's people faced the most horrible catastrophe. Where was this great power when his children were murdered? Why he did not save his people? Where were his mercy and justice? If we need to believe, if we need faith, if we have this inclination to be believers, we cannot ignore those extremely crucial questions. In that case, it is better to believe that God suffers with human beings than to say that although he is omnipotent, he did not make the effort to save his people. This is a way to save the image of God in a time when that notion lost its credibility. Heschel, living in a time of a total collapse of humanity, a time of *hester panim* (God hiding his face from humanity), had to save faith by saying that God needs to get courage from his people. God is not omnipotent, but merciful. There is a mutual dependence of God and man, mutual suffering, and I would say also a mutual responsibility. Hence, God is a part of the destiny of his people, hurt by their misery, saved in their salvation. God participates in human beings' agony, and humanity must take part in God's agony.

But still, how can we abandon the idea of the omnipotence of God? It sounds like a contradiction of the notion of Almighty. Once more, the problem is, how can infinite omnipotent power need salvation? Here Heschel uses the Kabalistic term *tzimtzum*, which refers to the idea of God reducing himself and his presence in the world, in order to make the creation possible.

29. Heschel, *Heavenly Torah*, 118.

Therefore, God reduced himself, reduced his omnipotence, in order to go with his people into exile. Power or mercy? Mercy is priority, says Heschel, and God's mercy is infinite.

> There is an obvious contradiction between the belief in God's omnipotence and the belief that He, too, needs salvation. Perhaps the resolution is this: just as the Creator, whose glory fills the universe, contracted His Shekhinah between the two staves of the Ark in order to reveal His words to Moses, so did God compress His Shekhinah into the history of Israel so that he might be revealed to His chosen nation as they went into exile together. Between mercy and power, mercy takes precedence—and to the mercy of Heaven there is no limit![30]

(The Christian view is similar. In a time of distress and agony on earth, the Divinity compressed himself into a definite object that humans could comprehend—a human figure—and sent Jesus Christ to suffer with humanity and be redeemed with humanity.)

Once I was asked, how can a non-religious person like myself be so fascinated with Heschel? How is it possible that the paradox of God's mercy and omnipotence is such a living question for an unbeliever like me? The answer is on the one hand hard to explain, but on the other hand quite obvious. I do not consider belief a product of the will or the result of rational contemplation. To my surprise and satisfaction, I can say that I share Heschel's view on that matter.

> Faith is not a product of the will. It occurs without intention, without will. . . It is neither an inference from logical premises nor the outcome of a feeling that leads us to believe in His existence; it is not an idea gained by sitting back and observing or by going into the soul and listening to one's inner voice. We do not believe because we have come to a conclusion. It is a turning within the mind by a power from beyond the mind, a shock and collision with the unbelievable by which we are coerced into believing.[31]

I think that being a believer is a matter of inclination. Either one has it or one does not, and neither rational reflection nor a spontaneous decision can lead a person to faith. The ability to believe is like the capacity to distinguish colors or sounds; either we were born with it or we weren't. I must add that, like Heschel, I believe that once a person has that ability, hard and

---

30. Heschel, *Heavenly Torah*, 121.
31. Heschel, *Alone*, 73.

constant work is needed to preserve one's faith. Belief is not for lazy minds. As Heschel wrote: "Faith is the fruit of hard, constant care and vigilance, of insisting upon remaining true to a vision."[32]

I, as an agnostic, did not experience that vision, but I am fascinated by the vision of Heschel. His need to preserve God, to recover God's place in Western philosophy, to make God relevant to humanity, is very moving and profound. I can see in his philosophy an authentic and original answer to the problems discussed above, and I can only admire his honesty and consistency and his commitment to his ideas in his daily life. I also identify with his doubts of whether humanity can get along by itself; after all, we are aware of the failures of humanity. I also think that his concern for the human future, his fear of the human nature, and of what people are capable to do, might be one of his motives for dialogue, but that question I would like to leave for another time.

HESCHEL AS A PROPHET

Finally, I would like to return to *The Prophets*. Heschel portrays the prophets as iconoclasts, challenging the apparently holy. Without fear, they exposed the scandalous pretensions of institutions. They were therefore isolated, sometimes hated, at times stigmatized as odd. I believe that Heschel was that kind of a modern prophet, not hesitating to call things by their true name, courageous enough to face the critics and the timidity of the Jewish establishment of his time. Religion, he says, can become anti-religious; it can distort the genuine call. "Priests themselves had committed perjury . . . condoning violence, tolerating hatred, calling for ceremonies instead of bursting forth with wrath and indignation at cruelty, deceit, idolatry, and violence."[33] Religion, he adds, is not the Temple. The Temple can be a façade that hides evil. Religion is not organizations, hierarchy, priests or institutions. What really counts is not the religious rituals but the deeds of the individual. "Worship preceded or followed by evil acts becomes an absurdity. The holy place is doomed when people indulge in unholy deeds."[34] This is what is so appealing to me in Heschel's thinking: the courage to tell his truth even if the religious establishment was not happy to hear it. The most important thing for a person is not his membership in a certain organization or community, but his deeds. In that respect, we are what we do. Regarding Heschel's deeds I believe that he was a great man, and a beautiful soul.

32. Heschel, *Alone*, 88.
33. Heschel, *Prophets*, 13.
34. Heschel, *Prophets*, 13.

Stanislaw Obirek

A CHRISTIAN PERSPECTIVE

I am a Catholic, but for some years I have been deeply interested in Jewish theology, particularly in the teaching of Abraham Joshua Heschel. To read his writings is to return to the common heritage of Christianity and Judaism. What is at the center of both religions is a human being. This also was the attitude which characterized his way of thinking: "First and foremost, we meet as human beings who have much in common: a heart, a face, a voice, the presence of a soul, fears, hope, the ability to trust, a capacity for compassion and understanding, the kinship of being human." Therefore, it is not surprising that for Heschel, the right way of living is more important than the correct formulation of creed or dogmas: "The mitzvoth are forms of expressing in deeds the appreciation of the ineffable."

To read Heschel is to allow his thoughts to penetrate the deepest part of your heart. My own involvement in the field is an emotional one. It is similar to the journey of Israeli writers coming to Poland, as Shoshana Ronen explains:

> A journey to Poland, in Israeli literature, is not a typical one. A person who decides to travel to Poland is not simply a tourist who wants to explore unknown places, climates, habits, works of art, etc. A journey to Poland in Israeli literature is a very loaded one. The narrator is not an ignorant traveler who is going to a place he does not know anything about, or to a place he has not seen before. The narrator who travels to Poland was there before, even if not physically, he was there psychologically. Even if he was born in Israel and has never been to Poland before, he comes to Poland full of knowledge, stories, stereotypes, prejudice, beliefs, pictures, smells, memories, nostalgia, pain and horror. In this respect, even for those who were not born in Poland, the journey to Poland is a return.[35]

For myself, my encounter with Jewish theology forced a reassessment of my previous theological studies. Until then the central figure was Jesus Christ—the promised Messiah—as the definitive fulfillment of the promises of the Hebrew Bible. However, Jewish theology almost completely ignored him. My question is: is it possible to reconcile both perspectives?

---

35. Ronen, *Pursuit*, 45–46.

Generally speaking, is this not the situation of all Christian theologians who try to read Jewish thinkers? James Carroll, describing his meeting with Abraham Joshua Heschel's thought, uses different concepts than Shoshana Ronen, but the idea behind them is similar: this meeting was a transforming one.

> To read Heschel was to step aboard the endangered but still seaworthy idea that the most transforming adventure of all can be intellectual. Heschel changed my notions not only of Judaism but of religion itself, and of God. As is obvious by now, I had been raised with an anachronistic idea of Judaism: the Scribes and the Pharisees worship at the Temple, the stereotype of the vengeful Old Testament God. Catholics like me knew nothing of the living tradition of Jewish thought and observance; ignorance that reflected the Christian assertion that after Jesus, Israel had been superseded by the 'new Israel,' the Church. Heschel's vital theology rooted in a biblical vision but informed by two millennia of rabbinical wisdom was a stark rebuttal of this. "The central thought of Judaism is a *living God*," he wrote." The craving for God has never subsided in the Jewish soul." Heschel put words on that craving as I experienced it, requiring me to revise entirely what I thought of Judaism. He did something similar for many Catholics.[36]

I'm quoting James Carroll not only as the author of an important book on the relationship between Jews and Catholic Church but also as a critical observer and commentator on the present life of the institution which he served for many years as a priest.

WHAT DO WE HAVE IN COMMON?

Since Heschel's inaugural lecture "No Religion Is an Island" at the Union Theological Seminary in 1965 more than 40 years have passed, but still it is worthwhile to recall the opinion of John C. Bennett, the president of the Union at the time:

> In that lecture he gave two essential messages, one to Christians and one to Jews. He asked Christians not to seek to convert Jews to Christianity. His message to Jews, somewhat less expected by the audience, was: "It is our duty as Jews to remember that it was the Church that brought the knowledge of the God of Abraham to the Gentiles. It was the Church that made the Hebrew

36. Carroll, *Constantine's Sword*, 47.

> Scripture available to all mankind. This we Jews acknowledge with grateful hearts."[37]

These four decades have changed a lot in our mutual relationship, but some of Heschel's remarks have not lost their relevance.

I would like to start with a Jesuitical accent. The questions directed by Heschel to Gustav Weigel I hear, in a way, as questions directed to myself:

> Gustav Weigel spent the last evening of his life in my study at the Jewish Theological Seminary. We opened our hearts to one another in prayer and contrition and spoke of our own deficiencies, failures, hopes. At one moment I posed the question: Is it really the will of God that there be no more Judaism in the world? Would it really be the triumph of God if the scrolls of the Torah were no longer taken out of the Ark and the Torah no longer read in the synagogue, our ancient Hebrew prayers in which Jesus himself worshipped no more recited, the Passover Seder no longer celebrated in our lives, the Law of Moses no longer observed in our homes? Would it really be *ad maiorem Dei gloriam* to have a world without Jews?[38]

Of course, we can say that these are only rhetorical questions; it is obvious that God's will is to preserve Judaism with all its beauty and theological richness. But it is not so obvious when we read some Church documents. Several times I heard this question from my Jewish friends, both religious and agnostic: how can you believe in what the Church and the priests are preaching, particularly in my Catholic Poland? Those questions are louder today than at any time before. It is important to listen carefully to these questions, perhaps more important than to quote the Church's documents. I concur with Heschel: "Humility and contrition seem to be absent where most required—in theology. But humility is the beginning and end of religious thinking, the sacred of faith. There is no truth without humility, no certainty without contrition."[39]

Heschel speaks in his opening lecture of the common elements in Judaism and Christianity. First, we are all human. Second, he underlines the obvious reality that *no religion is an island*. And third, speaking about Jewish-Christian relations, Heschel mentions *pathos*. "First and foremost, we meet as human beings who have much in common: a heart, a face, a voice, the presence of a soul, fears, hope, the ability to trust, a capacity for

---

37. Bennett, "Heschel's Significance for Protestants," 124–25.
38. Heschel, *Moral Grandeur*, 246.
39. Heschel, *Moral Grandeur*, 245.

compassion and understanding, the kinship of being human. My first task in every encounter is to comprehend the personhood of the human being I face, to sense the kinship of being human, solidarity of being."[40] Levinas' passionate defense of otherness comes to mind.

Heschel was deeply aware of the pluralistic reality of world religions:

> The religions of the world are no more isolated than individuals or nations. Energies, experiences, and ideas that come to life outside the boundaries of a particular religion or all religions continue to challenge and to affect every religion.
> Horizons are wider, dangers are greater, *no religion is an island*. We are all involved with one another. Spiritual betrayal on the part of one of us affects the faith of all of us. Views adopted in one community have an impact on other communities. Today religious isolationism is a myth. For all the profound differences in perspective and substance, Judaism is sooner or later affected by the intellectual, moral, and spiritual events within the Christian society, and vice versa.[41]

And he speaks of the third important element for both religions—the divine pathos—which involves the core of each religion:

> The supreme issue is today not the *halacha* for the Jew or the Church for the Christian—but the promise underlying both religions, namely, whether there is a *pathos*, a divine reality concerned with the destiny of man which mysteriously impinges upon history: the supreme issue is whether we are alive or dead to the challenge and the expectation of the living God. The crisis engulfs all of us. The misery and fear of alienation from God make Jew and Christian cry together.[42]

Is this *pathos* still alive in both our religions? And what exactly does it mean? It is not easy to answer, but I think that we can call it the seriousness of life—seen from both the human and divine perspective.[43] It could also be faithfulness to our deepest convictions and, when necessary, courage to change our life project or the direction of our life. Sometimes being faithful means to change!

---

40. Heschel, *Moral Grandeur*, 238.
41. Heschel, *Moral Grandeur*, 237.
42. Heschel, *Moral Grandeur*, 236.
43. Merkle, *Heschel*.

Those three elements—awareness that we all are human, awareness that we are connected and awareness that we have to take our life seriously—are the foundation for a real and honest dialogue:

> Dialogue must not degenerate into a dispute, into an effort on the part of each to get the upper hand. There is an unfortunate history of Christian-Jewish disputations, motivated by the desire to prove how blind the Jews are and carried on in a spirit of opposition, which eventually degenerated into enmity. Thus, any conversation between Christian and Jew in which abandonment of the other's partner faith is a silent hope must be regarded as offensive of one's religious and human dignity.[44]

And the wish of Heschel, which, by the way, is fulfilled by so many Jewish-Christian initiatives, is: "Let there be an end to disputation and polemic, an end to disparagement. We honestly and profoundly disagree in matters of creed and dogma. Indeed, there is a deep chasm between Christian and Jew concerning, e.g., the divinity and messiahship of Jesus. But across the chasm we can extend our hand to one another."[45] And allow me one last quotation from "No Religion is an Island," which suggests the key to the complex problem of all religions claiming a monopoly on the truth:

> Religion is a means, not an end. It becomes idolatrous when regarded as an end in itself. Over and above all beings stands the Creator and the Lord of history, he who transcends all. To equate religion and God is idolatry. Does not the all-inclusiveness of God contradict the exclusiveness of any particular religion? The prospect of all men embracing one form of religion remains an eschatological hope. What about here and now? Is it not blasphemous to say: I alone have all the truth and the grace, and all those who differ live in darkness and are abandoned by the grace of God?[46]

This question is still an important question, for Jews and particularly for Christians. As a Catholic I have to confess that I have a special difficulty accepting the declaration published by Cardinal Joseph Ratzinger, the present Pope Benedict XVI, in 2000, *Dominus Iesus*, in which he claims that the Catholic Church is the only religion with full access to the means of salvation.

---

44. Heschel, *Moral Grandeur*, 243.
45. Heschel, *Moral Grandeur*, 243.
46. Heschel, *Moral Grandeur*, 243.

DIFFERENCES AS A BLESSING

Two years after his opening lecture at the Union Theological Seminary in New York, Heschel was invited to take part in the Congress on the Theology of the Renewal of the Church Centenary of Canada, 1867–1967, where he spoke on "The God of Israel and Christian Renewal." Just being invited by Catholic theologians was for Heschel a blessing: "Is it not a moment of blessing that this congress of illustrious Catholic theologians is willing to submit the great movement of Christian renewal to a confrontation with Jewish understanding of the meaning of the God of Israel?"[47] Heschel is very honest and open in presenting his understanding of a possible and a real dialogue with Christianity. The condition *sine qua non* is mutual respect, or as he calls it "mutual reverence."

> I believe that one of the achievements of this age will be the realization that in our age religious pluralism is the will of God, that the relationship between Judaism and Christianity will be one of mutual reverence, that without denying profound divergences, Jews and Christians will seek to help each other in understanding each one's own commitment and in deepening appreciation of what God means.[48]

In the spirit of understanding, Heschel expresses the difficulty he has with the fundamental Christian view of God and the role of Jesus Christ: "With your permission, I should like to say that it is difficult for a Jew to understand when Christians worship Jesus as the Lord, and this Lordship takes the place of the Lordship of God the Creator. It is difficult for a Jew to understand when theology becomes reduced to Christology."[49] I have to say that the most recent Christological discussions between Christian theologians do not help solve Heschel's problem. Heschel's problem lies at the core of interreligious dialogue and of its relationship to Catholic theology.

The next important difference between Judaism and Christianity is how each religion understands redemption. For Christians the only and universal Redeemer is Jesus Christ, but for Jews the problem is formulated differently:

> The world is unredeemed and deficient, and God is in need of man to be a partner in completing, in aiding, in redeeming. Of all the forms of living, doing is the most patent way of aiding. Action is truth. The deed is elucidation of existence, expressing

47. Heschel, *Moral Grandeur*, 268–85.
48. Heschel, *Moral Grandeur*, 272.
49. Heschel, *Moral Grandeur*, 274–75.

thirst for God with body and soul. The Jewish *mitzvah* is a prayer in the form of a deed. The *mitzvoth* are the Jewish sacraments, sacraments that may be performed in common deeds of kindness. The nature is intelligible if seen in the light of God's care for man. The good act, ritual as well as moral, is a *mitzvah*, a divine offer, and a divine representative. Ultimate issues confront us in immediate situations. What is urgent for the Jew is not the acceptance of salvation but the preparing of redemption, the preparing *for* redemption.[50]

And Heschel concludes this passionate deliberation on the essence of redemption in Judaism with a call to "reveal God's love in His name: The urgent issue is not personal salvation, but the prevention of mankind's surrender to the demoniac. The sanctuary has not walls; the opportunity to praise or to aid has not limits. When God is silent, man must speak in His place. When God is hiding His compassion, man must reveal His love in this name."[51] Heschel understands human activity as an effective collaboration with God in the redemption of the present world. This approach is also very appealing to many agnostics.

LEAP OF ACTION

There are many ways to approach the work of Abraham Joshua Heschel. The growing scholarship on Heschel is testament to how different those approaches can be. But it still seems to me that one of the most important books on Heschel was written and published in 1979 under the title *Divine-Human Encounter: A Study of Abraham Joshua Heschel*, by his disciple Harold Kasimow, who found the hermeneutic key to his master's thought in Heschel's book *God in Search of Man*: "There are three starting points in contemplation about God; three trails that lead to him. The first is the way of sensing the presence of God in the world, in things; the second in the way of sensing His presence in the Bible; the third is the way of sensing His presence in sacred deeds."[52]

Kasimow dedicated the fourth chapter of his book to "Man's Path to God through Holy Deeds," in which we find many references to Heschel's books. To better understand the idea of "sacred deeds" we can look to a paper delivered by Heschel in 1969 in Florence, Italy that was dedicated to the problem of death: "A man's kind deeds are used by Lord as seeds for the

50. Heschel, *Moral Grandeur*, 278.
51. Heschel, *Moral Grandeur*, 278.
52. Heschel, *Search*, 31.

planting of trees in the Garden of Eden. Each man brings about his own trees; each man creates his own Garden of Eden. In Judaism the primary dimension of existence in which meaning is both sensed and created is the dimension of deeds. Sacred acts, deeds of kindness not only imitate the divine, they represent the divine."[53]

As a Christian I'm tempted to look for a connection with the New Testament where we can read a very similar statement made by the King in the Final Judgment: "Whenever you did this for one of the least important of these members of my family, you did it for me!" (Matthew 25:40). And again, in the same chapter of Matthew's Gospel: "Whenever you refused to help one of these least important ones, you refused to help me." (Matthew 25:45)

It is not surprising, then, that for Heschel, the right way of living is more important than the correct formulation of creed or dogmas: "To Jewish tradition, however, right living is what counts most. Follow the pattern of the right living, even though you do not know how to formulate adequately its basic theory."[54] Even more, according to Heschel, human deeds are the only way to reach God: "Sacred deeds are designed to make living *compatible with our sense of the ineffable*. The mitzvoth are forms of expressing in deeds the appreciation of the ineffable."[55]

Shoshana Ronen rightly observed in her paper that the study of biblical prophets brought Heschel to social engagement in defense of human rights and in protest of the war in Vietnam. It is worth remembering that his social engagement brought him isolation and misunderstanding. I would like to recall here the comment made after Heschel's death by the leading Jewish scholar Jacob Neusner: "The Christian world knew Abraham Joshua Heschel chiefly in his roles of holy man and politician. He was a hero to the religious sector of the left, which knew nothing of the man or the intellect." And Neusner added: "Yet I claim this side of Heschel is superficial and unimportant and will be forgotten very soon. The story of his life is not what matters. Theologians and scholars should have not biographies: their work is all that matters."[56] I would say the opposite is true: we remember Heschel exactly because he showed in his life how authentic his ideas were! And that was exactly why he is considered an important part of broader American life, not just religious life. Let me quote once again his friend John C. Bennett from the Union Theological Seminary:

---

53. Heschel, "Death as Homecoming," 375.
54. Heschel, *Search*, 330.
55. Heschel, *Search*, 350.
56. Neusner, "Faith," 209.

Abraham Heschel belonged to the whole American religious community. I know of no other person of whom this was so true. He was profoundly Jewish in his spiritual and cultural roots, in his closeness to Jewish suffering, in his religious commitment, in his love for the nation and land of Israel, and in the quality of his prophetic presence. And yet he was a religious inspiration to Christian and to many searching people beyond the familiar religious boundaries. Christians are nourished in their own faith by his vision and his words.[57]

Let us come back to his books. Already in the 1950s, in *God in Search of Man,* the essence of Heschel's understanding of Judaism was the "leap of action" more than the "leap of thought": "A Jew is asked to take a *leap of action* rather than a *leap of thought*. He is asked to surpass his needs, to do more than he understands in order to understand more than he does. In carrying out the word of the Torah he is ushered into the presence of spiritual meaning. Through the ecstasy of deeds, he learns to be certain of the hereness of God. Right living is a way to right thinking."[58]

The connection between understanding and doing can also be seen between faith and fulfilling the mitzvot, or between believing and acting:

> There is a way that leads *from piety to faith*. Piety and faith are not necessarily concurrent. There can be acts of piety without faith. Faith is a vision, sensitivity and attachment to God; piety is an attempt to attain such sensitivity and attachment. The gates of faith are not ajar, but the mitzvah is a key. But living as a Jew we may attain our faith as Jews. We do not have faith because of deeds; we may attain faith through sacred deeds.[59]

It is interesting that in his chapter on human deeds Harold Kasimow concludes with a quotation where Heschel is dealing with prayer and worship. It is important that Heschel remain a religious thinker; Judaism was for him mainly a religion and not, as for Mordechai Kaplan, a civilization. For Heschel it was very important to underline the real partnership between man and God, that God needs man and his prayer: "We must not overlook one of the profound principles of Judaism. There is something which is far greater than my desire to pray, namely God's desire that I pray How insignificant is the outpouring of my soul in the midst of this great universe!

---

57. Bennett, "Agent," 205.
58. Heschel, *Search*, 283.
59. Heschel, *Search*, 282.

Unless it is the will of God that I pray, unless God desires our prayers, how ludicrous is all my praying."[60]

And Kasimow focuses our attention on a really astonishing statement Heschel made in the same book a few pages later: "Great is the power of prayer. For to worship is to expand the presence of God in the world. God is transcendent, but our worship makes Him immanent. This is implied in the idea that God is in need of man: His being immanent depends upon us."[61]

CONCLUSION

It is hard to stop reading (and quoting!) Heschel; it is not easy to comment on him. But the final effect of this reading is a more open and more optimistic view of the world and particularly of the world of religions. I would like to end with a quotation from his impressive essay "No Religion is an Island": "Perhaps it is the will of God that in this eaon there should be diversity in our forms of devotion and commitment to Him. In this eaon diversity of religion is the will of God."[62]

Harold Kasimow concentrated the last chapter of his book on the implications of this sentence. I can only say that it is exactly this topic that is a source of the most dramatic developments in interreligious dialogue today.

---

60. Heschel, *Quest*, 58.
61. Heschel, *Quest*, 62.
62. Heschel, "No Religion," 14.

6

Abraham Joshua Heschel and the Declaration *Dabru Emet*

Stanislaw Krajewski

Heschel's ground-breaking lecture "No Religion Is an Island" of 1965 contains almost all the ideas that are offered in the unprecedented Jewish declaration on Christianity *Dabru Emet* published in 2000, written by four authors and signed first by over 160, and ultimately by well over 200 (including the present author). This fact seems to have been unnoticed. It means that Heschel's lecture, or more generally his attitude, can be seen as a major source of the declaration, in which Christianity is treated as an equal and valuable partner despite the theological differences and difficult historical heritage.

Unbelievable progress has been achieved in interreligious dialogue and in Christian-Jewish dialogue in particular. The dialogue can include—however rarely and momentarily—a dimension that goes beyond diplomatic acknowledgment of the other religion, beyond the readiness to learn about it, beyond the will to tolerate the fact of religious pluralism. When this dimension is entered, a genuine, absolute respect for the other prevails. In those moments, the other religion is no longer seen as enemy, opponent, competitor, object of study, or even partner, but is treated as Thou, as the other who deserves complete approval, unqualified acceptance, and, to use Abraham Joshua Heschel's term, "reverence."[1] Of course this approach is an idealization; it cannot be the only element in real-life encounters. It is also fleeting, since the other elements in the dialogue inevitably appear, from the memory of the burdens of history, so heavy in the case of the Christian-Jewish relations, to theological disparities, to the dissimilarity of social situations of the dialogue partners. And no genuine proponent of the new dialogue wants to disregard the differences. What is new is the friendly approach, the attitude of reverence, which is an expression of a new vision of interfaith relations. Heschel is a principal representative of the new vision, indeed its prophet, maybe even *the* prophet of it.

How could the thesis about Abraham Joshua Heschel's role in the shaping of the new dialogue be proven? Of course, his life and his writings are primary proofs. It is well known and well documented that he worked closely with some Christian theologians, Protestant and Catholic, and that he was friendly with some Muslims and thinkers belonging to Asian traditions.[2] In his writings the new attitude is clearly present, and indeed the acknowledgment of the utmost importance of other religions is well summarized for instance by the following remark: "We are all involved with one another. Spiritual betrayal of one of us affects the faith of all of us."[3] While it is apparent that Heschel was a trail blazer, it is less clear how strong his impact has been on other thinkers. I believe that his influence has been very strong, and as a telling illustration I propose to consider the formulations contained in the Declaration *Dabru Emet* and compare them with Heschel's own words.

The unprecedented Jewish declaration on Christianity was written by four authors, Tikva Frymer-Kensky, David Novak, Peter Ochs, and Michael Signer, and signed first by over 160 Jewish theologians (in the broadest sense of the term), and ultimately by well over 200 (including the present author). Originally published in the *New York Times* on September 10, 2000, *Dabru Emet* was translated into many languages, the first of which was Polish (It appeared in the daily *Gazeta Wyborcza* on September 30, 2000).[4] The declaration (appended below) articulates better than any other document the acceptance of the new approach to interreligious dialogue by a sizable

---

1. Heschel "No Religion," 11. Hereafter cited in text as either "No Religion" or NR.
2. Kasimow and Sherwin, *Island* is a good source in this respect.
3. Heschel, "No Religion," 6.
4. The English text of *Dabru Emet* can be found in Frymer-Kensky et al, *Christianity*, xvii–xx.

number of publicly active Jews. The signatories, as well as many other Jews who can be thought of as being represented by them, express their recognition of Christianity as an essentially positive phenomenon from the Jewish perspective, despite all the theological differences and the difficult historical heritage.

The aim of my essay is to demonstrate that Heschel's ground-breaking lecture "No Religion Is an Island" of 1965 contains almost all the ideas that are put forward in the declaration *Dabru Emet*. In a few places, other writings by Heschel will be quoted, but the wealth of ideas contained in that lecture is astonishing. They can be seen as the germs of almost all the points of *Dabru Emet*. Heschel is its precursor. Because it seems that no earlier Jewish text contains even a half, or for that matter a quarter, of those statements, Heschel emerges as the forerunner of *Dabru Emet*. Above all, it is Heschel's attitude that is so revolutionary when considered against the background of the traditional attitudes. While there are some divergences between his approach and that of the authors, and presumably of the signers of the declaration (see below the comments to its Points six and seven), his contribution and his attitude can be seen as a major source of the declaration. I would guess it was decisive, even though it is hard to prove it, as the counterfactual history (what would have happened in the interreligious dialogue if Heschel had not been active) would be exceedingly difficult to write. Interestingly, Heschel's pioneering role with regard to *Dabru Emet* seems to have been largely unnoticed.[5]

The introduction to *Dabru Emet* stresses the importance of the changes in the dominant Christian teachings about Jews and Judaism. This motif was not taken as an important point of reference in "No religion," and the reason is clear: the change had not taken place yet. It is worthwhile to note, however, that the moment when Heschel delivered his lecture was a significant point in time in the development of the new teaching. The lecture took place on November 10, 1965.[6] And on October 28, 1965, the Second Vatican Council officially adopted, by an overwhelming majority, the declaration *Nostra Aetate*, and more specifically its chapter four on relations with Jews.[7] This epoch-making document emerged as the result of a rather

---

5. The thesis that Heschel is the forerunner and guiding spirit of *Dabru Emet* was presented in my appendix to the Polish edition of Kasimow and Sherwin, *Island*. Entitled "Polish Rabbi, American Activist and Thinker, World-wide Prophet of Dialogue," this Polish text is the source of the present paper, but it has been modified by omitting some points and expanding other ones. Another Polish article of mine, "Christian-Jewish Dialogue," heavily overlaps with this appendix.

6. Cf. Heschel, *Moral Grandeur*, 236.

7. The subsequent versions and votes are described on the basis of the official

long process. Heschel himself actively participated in the process and contributed to its final result through memoranda and his meetings with Cardinal Augustin Bea as well as with Pope Paul VI.[8] It is, therefore, especially interesting that no mention of that development is made in Heschel's lecture "No religion." Why? The first reason is, it seems, that Heschel was not yet aware of the fact that the declaration had been adopted twelve days before, and certainly he did not know about it when he was preparing the lecture. Yet this explanation is not quite satisfactory. He could have mentioned the process of preparing the document, itself a testimony to the development of the new Christian thinking about Jews; and, indeed, he could have said something about his own involvement. I think that the reason he refrained from that is that the occasion was significantly Protestant in nature. His address was the inaugural lecture for the Harry Emerson Fosdick Visiting Professorship at Union Theological Seminary. The seminary is a Protestant institution, and while in the audience there were certainly Jews and Catholics it was predominantly Protestant. That is why, I assume, Heschel quoted Protestant theologians Reinhold Niebuhr and Paul Tillich, and even a statement of the World Council of Churches (bringing together Protestant and Orthodox Churches), each about the need to abandon proselytism, especially the missions aimed at Jews.[9] This theme understandably constituted a major concern for Heschel. One Catholic theologian is mentioned, Gustave Weigel. He is evoked in a very warm way, and the theme of the conversation, held on "the last evening of his life," was again the erroneous nature of missions to Jews: "Is it really the will of God that there be no more Judaism in the world?"[10] The question is directed at Heschel's audience, and Weigel is not presented as approving of the expected answer. It could seem from the lecture that Catholics did not reach the stage of abandoning the missions to convert Jews. But as a matter of fact the Catholic Church had just adopted an unprecedented official document that reflected just that stage, that is to say, in the words of *Dabru Emet*, it expressed the acknowledgment of God's enduring covenant with the Jewish people. Heschel was among the first Jews who appreciated the move. A short time later, he said that the final version of *Nostra Aetate* "is the first statement of the Church in history—the first Christian discourse dealing with Judaism—which is devoid of any

---

Catholic documentation in, among other places, Ignatowski, *Koscioly* (Polish).

8. Heschel cooperated with the American Jewish Committee. The story is briefly described in Fisher, "Heschel's Impact," 112–15. He quotes the papers by Judith H. Banki and Marc Tannenbaum of the AJC.

9. Heschel, "No Religion," 17, 18.

10. Heschel, "No Religion," 17.

expression of hope for conversion."[11] Heschel admired Pope John XXIII, of whom he said on another occasion, "with John and the Council hearts were opened."[12] It is clear that Heschel was well aware of those developments when he spoke at Union Theological Seminary, but he chose to quote Protestants only.

The fact is that before *Nostra Aetate* no authorized Catholic or Protestant, let alone Christian Orthodox, document proclaimed the new attitude to Jews or any approach free of accusations and disrespect. The change was slowly taking place but had found no official expression yet. And the fact is that the change was due to the shock caused by the Shoah. Christians in the West felt embarrassed when they realized the nature and the scope of the mass murder of Jews in the middle of Christian Europe. All post-war Christian statements on Jews referred to that reality. The first were the Ten Points of Seelisberg of 1947, the product of a group of Protestant and Catholic theologians working together with Jews, but without official backing of the leadership of churches. They appealed to churches, expressing "the firm hope that they will be concerned to show their members how to prevent any animosity towards the Jews which might arise from false, inadequate or mistaken presentations or conceptions of the teaching and preaching of the Christian doctrine, and how on the other hand to promote brotherly love towards the sorely-tried people of the old covenant."[13] The problem of missions to Jews is not directly addressed there. At roughly the same time, in 1948, the World Council of Churches issued an official statement which included a remarkable phrase that "anti-Semitism is sin against God and man."[14] However the new thinking was not present there; it stated that "our churches must consider the responsibility for missions to the Jews as a normal part of parish work," which to Jews is an expression of disrespect.

While the Shoah was a stimulus for the abandonment of the teaching of contempt and of missions to Jews, the issue is more fundamental. Heschel himself began by invoking "the fire of an altar of Satan on which millions of human lives were exterminated to evil's greater glory,"[15] but this statement should not paralyze us. The Shoah may have shown to what anti-Semitism can lead, but the acceptance of the legitimacy of Judaism is a separate matter, as is the Jewish acknowledgment of the legitimacy of Christianity and, more

11. Heschel, "Mission," 2.

12. Heschel, "Choose Life," 255.

13. This text and most other documents can be most easily found at http://www.jcrelations.net. See International Council of Christians and Jews, "Ten Points."

14. See World Council of Churches, *Christian Approach*, or, for example, Croner, *Stepping Stones*, 70.

15. Heschel, "No Religion," 3.

generally, the partnership of religions. Whatever the stimulus, the change of the teaching about Jews and Jewish religion created a fundamentally new situation. Heschel was fully aware of it and would have approved the appeal of *Dabru Emet*: "We believe it is time for Jews to reflect on what Judaism may now say about Christianity." Heschel expressed something similar, but with a characteristic reservation: "The theme of these reflections is not a doctrine or an institution called Christianity, but human beings all over the world, both present and past, who worship God as followers of Jesus, and my problem is how I should relate myself to them spiritually."[16] The first impression is that he does approve of Christians *as* Christians, but at the same time is not sure how to assess the "doctrine or institution." But, on second thought, perhaps Heschel wanted to avoid the necessarily controversial discussion of dogmas (doctrine) and the inevitably critical account of the past actions of the Church (institution), but at the same time did want to develop a respectful "Jewish theology of Christianity."[17] This guess is confirmed by the statement containing the already mentioned term "reverence": "The problem to be faced is: how to combine loyalty to one's own tradition with reverence for different traditions?"[18] This is an expression of the deepest dialogical approach, even stronger than that directly stated in *Dabru Emet*, and certainly more encompassing. It refers to various other traditions, not only Christianity, although primarily to Christianity.

The first point of *Dabru Emet* states that Jews and Christians worship the same God. Obvious to many and criticized by many others, this conviction was clearly stated by Heschel: "Above all, while dogmas and forms of worship are divergent, God is the same."[19] An extension of this thesis is now standard among dialogue practitioners. In the words of *Dabru Emet*: "as Jewish theologians we rejoice that, through Christianity, hundreds of millions of people have entered into relationship with the God of Israel." Possibly this was taken from Heschel as he had stated explicitly: "It is our duty to remember that it was the Church that brought the knowledge of the God of Abraham to the Gentiles. It was the Church that made Hebrew Scripture available to mankind. This we Jews must acknowledge with a grateful heart."[20] The second point of *Dabru Emet*, that Jews and Christians seek authority from the same book, the Bible, is as obvious to some as the

---

16. Heschel, "No Religion," 10.
17. Heschel opposed "spontaneity" present also in the Catholic Church to "the sheer weight of doctrine and institution." See *Moral Grandeur*, 255.
18. Heschel, "No Religion," 11.
19. Heschel, "No Religion," 9.
20. Heschel, "No Religion," 13.

previous point, and criticized by others who remind that the term "Bible" does not mean the same in the two traditions. This was of course obvious to the authors of *Dabru Emet*, who wrote that despite many similarities we "interpret the Bible differently on many points. Such differences must always be respected." Heschel said the same and more:

What unites us? A commitment to the Hebrew Bible as Holy Scripture. Faith in the Creator, the God of Abraham, commitment to many of His commandments, to justice and mercy, a sense of contrition, sensitivity to the sanctity of life and to the involvement of God in history, the conviction that without the holy the good will be defeated, prayer that history may not end before the end of days, and so much more.[21]

Heschel's treatment of the dogmatic differences is noteworthy: "Granted that Judaism and Christianity are committed to contradictory claims, is it impossible to carry on a controversy without acrimony, criticism without loss of respect, disagreement without disrespect?"[22] He states clearly that the problem is caused not by the differences but by the disrespectful approaches. And indeed, deep interreligious dialogue depends on proper attitude, on good will, possible despite the differences and contradictions.

In the third point *Dabru Emet* states that "Christians can respect the claim of the Jewish people upon the land of Israel." In "No Religion" nothing is said about *Eretz Israel*, which seems to fit the basic orientation of Heschel's philosophy of religion stressing the dimension of time in religious existence at the expense of space. Yet somewhat later, in the wake of the 1967 Six-Day War, Heschel wrote a book, *Israel: An Echo of Eternity*, in which the Christian awareness of Jewish ties with that land is mentioned. He quotes Edward H. Flannery, the first spokesman of the Catholic bishops of the United States on Catholic-Jewish relations, who rejected the traditional Christian interpretation of the diaspora as divine punishment of Jews for stubbornness. Flannery said, "Hence, the existence of a Jewish state, be it the state of Israel or another, does not contradict sacred Scripture."[23] While this sounds very modest now, it showed a new awareness, much more widespread now but not uncontested. Heschel was not yet aware of the phenomenon of "Christian Zionism," or pro-Zionism, an important development in Evangelical Churches, which is a source of ambivalent feelings among Jews, as the pro-Israeli attitudes are combined with the expectation of the conversion of Jews. The ambivalence becomes weaker when we realize that the expectation seems to refer to the end of the present era, to Parousia or

21. Heschel, "No Religion," 9.
22. Heschel, "No Religion," 11.
23. After Heschel, *Israel*, 163.

Messianic times, and nobody can really be sure how to imagine that future. Be that as it may, we are surrounded by either the passionate pro-Zionism or a mild acknowledgment of Jewish ties to the Holy Land, as for example, in the statement of the National Conference of Catholic Bishops of 1975: "Whatever difficulties Christians may experience in sharing this view they should strive to understand this link between land and people which Jews have expressed in their writings and worship throughout two millennia."[24] It is to this reality that the authors of *Dabru Emet* were referring. Heschel did not witness this reality yet, but he was penetrating enough to mention a beginning of such views: some commentators interpreted the words of Luke (Luke 21:24) as a prediction of "the re-establishment of Jerusalem as a capital of the Jewish nation."

In the fourth point of *Dabru Emet* it is maintained that "Jews and Christians accept the moral principles of Torah." This formulation is not standard and can be criticized on the basis that Torah is hardly the traditional term for the church. In addition, the oral Torah is part and parcel of the entity called Torah in the Jewish tradition, and it is precisely what the Church has rejected. Nevertheless, the thought expressed in this point was also stated by Heschel. He said that Jews and Christians "claim brotherhood by being subject to His commandments."[25] In Judaism the expressions "commandments" and "principles of Torah" have very similar meanings. In the same paragraph *Dabru Emet* contains a rather standard indication of the metaphysical common ground: "Central to the moral principles of Torah is the inalienable sanctity and dignity of every human being. All of us were created in the image of God." Heschel says the same in much more dramatic way: "To meet a human being is an opportunity to sense the image of God, *the presence* of God."[26]

The fifth point was criticized by some Jews as too soft on the Church's role in the Holocaust. According to *Dabru Emet*, "Nazism was not a Christian phenomenon." Heschel stated a related thesis: "Nazism resolved that it must both exterminate the Jews and eliminate Christianity and bring about instead a revival of Teutonic paganism."[27] From this it can be understood that for Heschel Nazism was essentially an anti-Christian rather than Christian phenomenon. Of course, this is compatible with the truth that Christian anti-Semitism prepared the ground for the Shoah. This was as clear to Heschel, who directly experienced Nazism and the policies of German

---

24. National Conference of Catholic Bishops USA, *Statement*.
25. Heschel, "No Religion," 10.
26. Heschel, "No Religion," 8.
27. Heschel, "No Religion," 4.

churches, as it was to the authors of *Dabru Emet*, who stated: "Without the long history of Christian anti-Judaism and Christian violence against Jews, Nazi ideology could not have taken hold nor could it have been carried out." Heschel's remark about Nazis' aim to eliminate Christianity is echoed by the formulation occurring in the fifth point: "If the Nazi extermination of the Jews had been fully successful, it would have turned its murderous rage more directly to Christians. "

Point six of *Dabru Emet* contains some of the most profound dialogical insights expressed in the declaration. It begins by saying that "the humanly irreconcilable difference between Jews and Christians will not be settled until God redeems the entire world as promised in Scripture." Or as Heschel says, we should not try to overcome the differences: "The prospect of all men embracing one form of religion remains an eschatological hope. What about here and now? Is it not blasphemous to say: I alone have all the truth and the grace . . . ?"[28] Heschel states explicitly the view which is relatively easy for a Jew to adopt. Namely, "in this aeon diversity of religions is the will of God."[29] The authors of *Dabru Emet* go further. They include a modest-looking statement: "Christians know and serve God through Jesus Christ and the Christian tradition. Jews know and serve God through Torah and the Jewish tradition." To me it is a spectacular formulation. It is more than an expression of theological legitimacy and religious respect. Of course, it is also this and Heschel's lecture contains similar appreciation of Christianity from the Jewish perspective. Thus, "a Jew . . . ought to acknowledge the eminent role and part of Christianity in God's design for the redemption of all men."[30] Also, the same meaning is carried by the already mentioned remark about those "who worship God as followers of Jesus."[31] However, two additional aspects of the statement on how Christians and Jews know and serve God seem absent, or at least not present explicitly, in Heschel's lecture and his other writings. The first is the consequence of the very form of the statement, the two parallel sentences. This form suggests that the parallel ways, one Christian, one Jewish, have the same value. This equivalence is not directly stated, but the form and the context (in particular point one of the Declaration) constitute a very strong suggestion. Heschel indicates something similar, but indirectly: "Or should we pray for each other's health, and help one another in preserving one's respective legacy, in preserving a common legacy?"[32] The

28. Heschel, "No Religion," 14.
29. Heschel, "No Religion," 14.
30. Heschel, "No Religion," 12.
31. Heschel, "No Religion," 10.
32. Heschel, "No Religion," 6.

acknowledgment of a fundamental equality of Judaism and Christianity, and other traditions as well, is present in Heschel's thought on a deeper level. It occurs in the realm described by his "depth theology"; therein religiosity is rooted before it takes a specific form associated with some revelation. "The language, the imagination, the concretization of our hopes are different, but the embarrassment is the same . . . "[33] Heschel makes a general philosophical point: "One truth comes to expression in many ways of understanding . . . because we can only speak in the tentative language of man."[34] More importantly, "the misery and fear of alienation from God make Jew and Christian cry together."[35]

The second aspect that singles out *Dabru Emet* from all other Jewish documents, including Heschel's writings, is the use of the term "Jesus Christ." I was surprised, even shocked, when I first saw it. *That* name in a *Jewish* document? I had avoided it because, after all, it means "Jesus the Messiah," which contradicts the Jewish tradition. True, there have been efforts to overcome the contradiction by theological refinements of the concept of Messiah, but the attempts—may they continue—have been neither mature enough nor sufficiently known to serve as the implicit point of reference. I had avoided the term "Christ," unless quoting someone else, to avoid the impression that I share the Christian understanding of Messianism. When I saw the term in *Dabru Emet* I knew that its authors must have felt the same. The fact that they decided to write "Jesus Christ" taught me an important lesson. I immediately realized that they did something right. Namely, they drew consequences from a principle that is preached but rarely followed: always present the dialogue partner in the way he would like to be presented. Let me add another illustration of this issue since the above example may be hard for a Christian reader to appreciate.

However sympathetic and faithful should be the representation of Christianity by Jews, any attempt to convert, any hint of missionary activities is wrong and threatening. This is stated in the same point: "Neither Jew nor Christian should be pressed into affirming the teaching of the other community." While expressed as a principle for both religions, it applies basically only to Christians. Nowadays this imperative to abstain from missions is understood much more widely than in 1965. Still, even then Heschel could say: "Fortunately there are some important Christian voices [like Niebuhr and Tillich] who expressed themselves to the effect that the

---

33. Heschel, "No Religion," 9.
34. Heschel, "No Religion," 15–16.
35. Heschel, "No Religion," 5.

missionary activities to the Jews be given up."[36] Since the Second Vatican Council, the Catholic Church has not missionized Jews. This is not the case, however, for many Protestant churches.

The seventh point of *Dabru Emet* rejects in advance the criticism that has indeed been made since the declaration was released: according to the critics, it is just a capitulation, an acceptance of assimilation. The authors predicted that attack: "A new relationship between Jews and Christians will not weaken Jewish practice." I am convinced this belief is right, but one can ask whether this conviction is a wishful thinking or is based on some premises. For me, and I would guess for many signatories of the declaration, the main reason for the conviction that deep dialogue is not threatening is provided by the actual experience of dialogue. The actual experience of Heschel was the same. He was among the first Jews, if not the first, raised in an absolutely traditionalist milieu who engaged in a serious sustained dialogue with Christians, based on respect and affirmation of the other faith. At the same time, he continued living a traditional Jewish religious life. Of course, he was also familiar with secular life and Reform and Conservative Judaism, and he did not avoid criticism by traditionalists. Still, only ill-will can lead one to doubt his devotion to traditionally conceived Judaism.

Both *Dabru Emet* and "No Religion" are clear that there is one condition that must be fulfilled to make sure that Jewish practice will not be weakened: "Only if we cherish our own traditions can we pursue this relationship with integrity." Similarly, for Heschel, "Interfaith must come out of depth, not out of a void absence of faith. It is not an enterprise for those who are half-learned or spiritually immature."[37] This reservation makes a lot of sense, but it is treated so seriously by Heschel that he adds a stronger postulate for interreligious dialogue: "If it is not to lead to the confusion of the many, it must remain a prerogative of the few."[38] This postulate, completely absent from *Dabru Emet*, is probably caused by personal experiences and very high demands on the knowledge and maturity of participants, but it strikes me and many among us now as being too severe. Probably it reflects the initial stage of Christian-Jewish dialogue. Nowadays many more people participate. The group of signers of *Dabru Emet* is considerable, and it constitutes just the tip of the iceberg. Besides, it includes almost nobody from outside the English-speaking circles, and among American Jewish theologians many did not sign only because they unsuccessfully proposed changing one formulation or another, but their general attitude is very similar to

---

36. Heschel, "No Religion," 17.
37. Heschel, "No Religion," 11.
38. Heschel, "No Religion," 11.

that of the signatories. Dialogue, also the deep dialogue of equal partners, is not so uncommon today. We have moved beyond the level known to Heschel. This is not to say that his worries do not apply anymore. If we enter the dialogue without proper preparation and competence, we still face the risk of confusion regarding religious truth, the danger of shallowness of one's religious identification, the threat of religious syncretism, and the menace of putting politics, or allegedly dialogical drive to compromise on every issue, above the participating religions. Still, I believe that Heschel would be glad to witness the selectiveness of dialogue reduced. Elitism in some sense is still there, because the genuine interest in a deep interreligious dialogue occurs relatively rarely. To me this is a weakness rather than a virtue.

The final point of *Dabru Emet* contains an appeal for cooperation: "Jews and Christians must work together for justice and peace." It is well known that Heschel not only thought the same but was deeply involved in social issues. The need to cooperate was so obvious to him that he made no appeal in his lecture. Instead, he mentioned the reasons for interreligious cooperation. First, it is "to help one another; . . . and what is even more important to search in the wilderness for well-springs of devotion, for treasures of stillness, for the power of love and care for man."[39] Second, it is to help survive genuine, living religiosity: "It is on the issue of saving the radiance of the Hebrew Bible in the minds of man that Jews and Christians are called upon to work together. *None of us can do it alone*. Both of us must realize that in our age anti-Semitism is anti-Christianity and that anti-Christianity is anti-Semitism."[40] It is a striking statement, a confirmation that Heschel is as sensitive to the Christian tradition as to his own. Heschel's phrase equating antisemitism as anti-Christianity and anti-Christianity as antisemitism was used by John Paul II when he was in Israel in 2000.

Dabru Emet ends with a citation from Isaiah, and, to state the obvious, nothing is closer to Heschel, the author of works on the prophets, than the prophetic appeals. In "No Religion" he wrote, "Is it not our duty to help one another . . . in seeking to respond to the voice of prophets?"[41]

The above quotes demonstrate that Heschel did express almost all the ideas that are proposed in *Dabru Emet*. The main points of divergence are the complete and explicit parallelism of Christian and Jewish ways and the use of the name "Christ," both present only in the declaration, and the plea for an elitist character of the dialogue, present only in Heschel's address. I believe, however, that forty years later he would have been much closer

39. Heschel, "No Religion," 22.
40. Heschel, "No Religion," 4.
41. Heschel, "No Religion," 12.

to the authors and signatories of *Dabru Emet* on all those issues. In a very strong way, he is the precursor and spiritual father of the declaration.

It is also apparent that compared to the declaration, Heschel's words sound more daring, more powerful, more poetic, and certainly more prophetic. This remark is not made to cast doubts on the value of *Dabru Emet*. It is a milestone in Christian-Jewish dialogue and most probably will remain such for a long time. Only its character is different from Heschel's visionary personal appeal. While he was addressing his mostly Protestant Christian audience, the authors of *Dabru Emet* were talking primarily to Jews and did a lot to balance their formulations, which unfortunately did not prevent vicious criticisms. The affinity of the two statements means that in principle Heschel should be equally exposed to those criticisms. I think that at least some of the critics would have hesitated if they had realized that their reproach is as much aimed at Heschel.

Heschel is a—if not *the*—prophet of the deep interreligious dialogue and the forerunner of *Dabru Emet*. Curiously enough, its authors seem not to be fully aware of it. When they say, "it is time for Jews to reflect on what Judaism may now say about Christianity. As a first step, we offer eight brief statements . . ." it sounds as if there were no precursors who had taken the first step. I think that this difficulty with acknowledging Heschel's role is a tribute to him. It is because Heschel's insights and proposals have been absorbed by most Jews who are active in interreligious dialogue, and they are no longer aware of the origins of those ideas. I must avow that when I reread "No Religion" after many years I was struck by the extent to which I had been speaking using Heschel's phrases without being aware of it. There can be no higher praise for a thinker. When one's ideas become everyone's property and nobody remembers how they were introduced, they can be called "classic." This has happened to some of Heschel's ideas, and I believe this process will continue. He, as their author, can therefore be called a classic.

APPENDIX: *DABRU EMET*

A Jewish Statement on Christians and Christianity (Released September 10, 2000)

In recent years, there has been a dramatic and unprecedented shift in Jewish and Christian relations. Throughout the nearly two millennia of Jewish exile, Christians have tended to characterize Judaism as a failed religion or, at best, a religion that prepared the way for, and is completed in, Christianity. In the decades since the Holocaust, however, Christianity has changed dramatically. An increasing number of official Church bodies, both Roman Catholic and Protestant, have made public statements of their remorse about Christian mistreatment of Jews and Judaism. These statements have declared, furthermore, that Christian teaching and preaching can and must be reformed so that they acknowledge God's enduring covenant with the Jewish people and celebrate the contribution of Judaism to world civilization and to Christian faith itself.

We believe these changes merit a thoughtful Jewish response. Speaking only for ourselves—an interdenominational group of Jewish scholars—we believe it is time for Jews to learn about the efforts of Christians to honor Judaism. We believe it is time for Jews to reflect on what Judaism may now say about Christianity. As a first step, we offer eight brief statements about how Jews and Christians may relate to one another.

Jews and Christians worship the same God. Before the rise of Christianity, Jews were the only worshippers of the God of Israel. But Christians also worship the God of Abraham, Isaac, and Jacob, creator of heaven and earth. While Christian worship is not a viable religious choice for Jews, as Jewish theologians we rejoice that, through Christianity, hundreds of millions of people have entered relationship with the God of Israel.

Jews and Christians seek authority from the same book—the Bible (what Jews call "Tanakh" and Christians call the "Old Testament"). Turning to it for religious orientation, spiritual enrichment, and communal education, we each take away similar lessons: God created and sustains the universe; God established a covenant with the people Israel; God's revealed word guides Israel to a life of righteousness; and God will ultimately redeem Israel and the whole world. Yet, Jews and Christians interpret the Bible differently on many points. Such differences must always be respected.

Christians can respect the claim of the Jewish people upon the land of Israel. The most important event for Jews since the Holocaust has been the reestablishment of a Jewish state in the Promised Land. As members of a biblically based religion, Christians appreciate that Israel was promised—and given—to Jews as the physical center of the covenant between them and God. Many Christians support the State of Israel for reasons far more profound than mere politics. As Jews, we applaud this support. We also recognize that Jewish tradition mandates justice for all non-Jews who reside in a Jewish state.

Jews and Christians accept the moral principles of Torah. Central to the moral principles of Torah is the inalienable sanctity and dignity of every human being. All of us were created in the image of God. This shared moral emphasis can be the basis of an improved relationship between our two communities. It can also be the basis of a powerful witness to all humanity for improving the lives of our fellow human beings and for standing against the immoralities and idolatries that harm and degrade us. Such witness is especially needed after the unprecedented horrors of the past century.

Nazism was not a Christian phenomenon. Without the long history of Christian anti-Judaism and Christian violence against Jews, Nazi ideology could not have taken hold nor could it have been carried out. Too many Christians participated in, or were sympathetic to, Nazi atrocities against Jews. Other Christians did not protest sufficiently against these atrocities. But Nazism itself was not an inevitable outcome of Christianity. If the Nazi extermination of the Jews had been fully successful, it would have turned its murderous rage more directly to Christians. We recognize with gratitude those Christians who risked or sacrificed their lives to save Jews during the Nazi regime. With that in mind, we encourage the continuation of recent efforts in Christian theology to repudiate unequivocally contempt of Judaism and the Jewish people. We applaud those Christians who reject this teaching of contempt, and we do not blame them for the sins committed by their ancestors.

The humanly irreconcilable difference between Jews and Christians will not be settled until God redeems the entire world as promised in Scripture. Christians know and serve God through Jesus Christ and the Christian tradition. Jews know and serve God through Torah and the Jewish tradition. That difference will not be settled by one community insisting that it has interpreted Scripture more accurately than the other: nor by exercising political power over the other. Jews can respect Christians' faithfulness to their revelation just as we expect Christians to respect our faithfulness to our revelation. Neither Jew nor Christian should be pressed into affirming the teaching of the other community.

A new relationship between Jews and Christians will not weaken Jewish practice. An improved relationship will not accelerate the cultural and religious assimilation that Jews rightly fear. It will not change traditional Jewish forms of worship, nor increase intermarriage between Jews and non-Jews, nor persuade more Jews to convert to Christianity, nor create a false blending of Judaism and Christianity. We respect Christianity as a faith that originated within Judaism and that still has significant contacts with it. We do not see it as an extension of Judaism. Only if we cherish our own traditions can we pursue this relationship with integrity.

Jews and Christians must work together for justice and peace. Jews and Christians, each in their own way, recognize the unredeemed state of the world as reflected in the persistence of persecution, poverty, and human degradation and misery. Although justice and peace are finally God's, our joint efforts, together with those of other faith communities, will help bring the kingdom of God for which we hope and long. Separately and together, we must work to bring justice and peace to our world. In this enterprise, we are guided by the vision of the prophets of Israel:

It shall come to pass in the end of days that the mountain of the Lord's house shall be established at the top of the mountains and be exalted above the hills, and the nations shall flow unto it . . . and many peoples shall go and say, "Come ye and let us go up to the mountain of the Lord to the house of the God of Jacob and He will teach us of His ways and we will walk in his paths" (Isaiah 2:2–3).

7

Heschel Book Reviews

BYRON L. SHERWIN, SPERTUS INSTITUTE OF JEWISH STUDIES (CHICAGO, ILLINOIS)

REVIEW OF *THE EARTH IS THE LORD'S*, ABRAHAM JOSHUA HESCHEL. NEW YORK: HENRY SCHUMAN, 1950.

Review of *A Passion for Truth*, Abraham Joshua Heschel. New York: Farrar, Straus and Giroux, 1973.

During the late 1960s, when "Holocaust theology" was the rage, Heschel was criticized for not articulating a theological response to the Holocaust. During those years, Heschel was also criticized for being overly involved in social action, and not adequately engaged with the spiritual condition of American Jewry. Both criticisms are unfounded. For example, as the Protestant scholar W. D. Davies observed soon after Heschel's death, Heschel's social action was, in substantial measure, part of his response to the Holocaust.[1] Further, as Morris Faierstein has demonstrated, Heschel—especially in his Yiddish writings—offered a (theological) response to the Holocaust that "was very

---

1. Davies, "Conscience, Scholar, Witness," 213.

much in line with the response of the remnant of East European Jewry which survived the Holocaust."[2] In addition, in his essays and addresses (collected in *The Insecurity of Freedom* [1966] and *Moral Grandeur and Spiritual Audacity* [1996]) as well as in daily conversation with his students, Heschel constantly articulated his views about the spiritual condition of American Jewry.

Toward the end of his life, as individuals such as Richard Rubenstein, Arnold Jacob Wolf, and I and others can attest, Heschel would often use bold imagery to depict the spiritual condition of American Jewry and his prognosis for it. For example, Rubenstein quotes Heschel as saying to him, "When I think of what our people have accumulated over the centuries that nobody will ever know about, it seems like a second holocaust. Hitler destroyed our people. Now we let their spirit die."[3] Similarly, Arnold J. Wolf reports a conversation he had with Heschel weeks before Heschel's death in which he was very pessimistic about the continuity of Jewish learning and spirituality in America, and about the possibility of a renaissance of Jewish values in the diaspora. Wolf quotes Heschel as saying, "[I]n America we have ten more years. (That was not his usual style.) He didn't say thirty or forty or sixty—but he said *ten*. After that some factors will be irreversible."[4] In 1965, in an address to the Council of Jewish Federations and Welfare Funds, Heschel said, "We may claim to be a success, but in the eyes of Jewish history we may be regarded as a failure."[5]

Heschel's response to the Holocaust, the articulation of his concerns about the spiritual condition of American Jewry, and his observation that the spiritual suicide of American Jewry was leading to a "second holocaust" all relate to his apprehension that the spiritual legacy of East European Jewry was being lost, forgotten and dismissed, or distorted by the American Jewish community. In his early work, *The Earth is the Lord's*, and in his last work, *A Passion for Truth*, this apprehension is clearly articulated. Heschel considered the preservation and the conveyance of the spiritual heritage of East European Jewry, especially Hasidism, as the key to the continuity of an authentic form of Judaism in post-Holocaust America. He would have agreed with Chief Rabbi Lau's tongue-in-cheek remark that "the religion closest to Judaism is Hasidism."

In January 1945, as World War II moved toward an end in Europe, and as the catastrophe that had decimated European Jewry was becoming public knowledge, Heschel delivered a lecture in Yiddish at YIVO in New

---

2. Faierstein, "Heschel and the Holocaust," 255–75.
3. Rubenstein, *Power Stuggle*, 128.
4. Wolf, "What We Learned," 39.
5. Heschel, *Moral Grandeur*, 23.

York in which he offered his eulogy for the now lost Atlantis of east European Jewry. This lecture, published in Yiddish as "The East European Jew," metamorphosed into his 1950 English volume, *The Earth is the Lord's: The Inner World of the Jew in East Europe*.[6] When Heschel completed his lecture, the audience of several thousand Yiddish-speaking Jews, containing a large contingent of secular Yiddishists, spontaneously arose, and with tears in their eyes, they recited the Mourner's *Kaddish*.[7]

Throughout his life in America, Heschel continuously spoke and wrote about the spiritual heritage of East European Jewry. Beginning with *The Earth is the Lord's* and concluding with his posthumously published *A Passion for Truth*, Heschel's English writings on this subject were directed to an American Jewish readership that was becoming progressively detached from their East European Jewish roots. In a 1963 interview with a Yiddish newspaper, Heschel said, "Since I came to America I keep speaking about East European Jewry, and not forgetting the source, the crown of Jewry, is the primary task for American Jewry. With certain exceptions, American Jews have made great efforts to forget their roots Modern Jewish leaders have no understanding of their roots. This is the main tragedy of our generation. How can we expect the tree to bloom without roots?"[8]

For Heschel, post-World War II American Jewry held the future of Judaism in its hands: "A world has vanished. We of this generation are still holding the key. Unless we remember, unless we unlock it, the holiness of the ages will remain a secret of God. If we mislay the key, we shall elude ourselves. . . . We are either the last Jews or those who will hand over the entire past to generations yet to come."[9]

Like Eliezer Berkovits and others, for Heschel the Holocaust demonstrated the failure of western culture. Neither modern western philosophy with its insistence on individual moral autonomy, nor western aesthetics with its detachment from ethics, could provide direction for dealing with contemporary moral or spiritual realities. He derides the secular Jewish intellectuals—the "plate-lickers of non-Jewish culture," detached from the wellsprings of Jewish tradition—who "were blinded by the light of western civilization" and who could not therefore "appreciate the value of the small fire of our eternal light."[10] For Jewish continuity to be assured, for the wis-

---

6. On this metamorphosis, see Shandler, "Heschel and Yiddish," 269–84.
7. See e.g. Moore, *East European Jews*, viii.
8. Translated as an appendix in Faierstein, "Heschel and the Holocaust."
9. Heschel, *Earth*, 107.
10. See Faierstein, "Heschel and the Holocaust," appendix, where he also translates Heschel's article, "After Majdanek."

dom of the past to address the perplexities of the present, the day had to come "when the hidden light of the East European era may be revealed."[11]

In *The Earth is the Lord's* Heschel depicts East European Judaism as the quintessence of Judaism, the crystallization of the best of Jewish spirituality as a way of living, thinking and looking at the world. For Heschel, the spiritual wisdom of East European Jewry offers not only an authentic foundation for American Jewish life and thought, but also a wisdom-tradition "that the world is hungry to hear" as it confronts contemporary problems.

For Heschel, a culture is best evaluated not by its artistic or scientific achievements, but by the quality of "inwardness," "holiness," and "spiritual integrity" manifested in the daily life of the people. Heschel claims that in Jewish history, the "highest degree of inwardness" was attained by Ashkenazic Jewry, particularly in Eastern Europe, and especially by the followers of Hasidism. This for Heschel was the now decimated "golden period in Jewish history, in the history of the Jewish soul."[12]

In depicting the experience of East European Jewry as *the* "golden age" of Jewish history, Heschel polemicizes against the prejudices of Western Jewry against East European Jewry. He rejects as a model for modern Jewry the multicultural achievements in literature, science, and philosophy of the so-called "golden age" of medieval Spanish Jewry that were extolled as a model for post-Emancipation Jewish life in western Europe and America by leading European and American scholars. For Heschel, the Jewish authenticity of Sephardic thought had been compromised by its program of forging a synthesis between Judaism and other cultures, its focus on emphasizing what Judaism has in common with other cultures rather than articulating its own unique characteristics, its elitist and aristocratic nature, its use of non-Jewish languages to articulate Jewish ideas.[13] In contrast, Heschel extols the authenticity of Ashkenazic Jewish teachings, developed in its own categories, in its own language, and therefore of untainted Jewish authenticity. He describes the Ashkenazic penchant for the democratization of Jewish education where Jewish learning and Talmudic scholarship "ceased to be the monopoly of the few," where mystical piety became a hegemony of the masses.[14] Throughout his thought, Heschel emphasized the existence of a uniquely Jewish way of thinking,[15] found in ancient times in the Bible, Tal-

---

11. Heschel, *Earth*, 99.
12. Heschel, *Earth*, 10.
13. Heschel, *Earth*, 23–38. See also Heschel, "Two Great Traditions," 416–22.
14. Heschel, *Earth*, 65.
15. See e.g., Heschel, *Moral Grandeur*, 156

mud, and midrashim, and articulated most profoundly in the works of East European Jewry, especially the Hasidim.

In *A Passion for Truth*, Heschel provides the English reader with an introduction to the life and thought of Rabbi Mendel of Kotzk, discussed in greater detail in his two-volume Yiddish work on this nineteenth-century Hasidic master.[16] Here, Heschel continues to explore themes presented in *The Earth is the Lord's*. Written during the beginning of the Watergate scandal and during the times of Lyndon Johnson's "credibility gap," Heschel marshals the Rabbi of Kotzk's war against mendacity to demonstrate the pertinence of the teachings of a neglected Hasidic Jewish thinker for addressing contemporary realities both in Jewish and non-Jewish life. For this reason, Heschel claims that "his legacy must necessarily influence if Judaism is to survive as more than a mere commonplace."[17] Again emphasizing Jewish authenticity over accommodationist approaches, Heschel writes that "[m]any interpreters [of Judaism] have sought to accommodate Judaism to preconceived points of view; for the Kotzker, Judaism was *the* point of view."[18]

Advocating "radical self-inspection," the Rabbi of Kotzk took the East European quest for *penimiut* (inwardness, spirituality) to radical extremes, aimed at inner transformation. "The Kotzker would say that Judaism is truth," writes Heschel. "Truth is inwardness, inwardness is authenticity, and authenticity is attained through intense, passionate inner action. Only integrity can save man and his faith."[19]

Like the Kotzker, Heschel criticized the "spiritual vapidity of his fellow Jews," his fellow rabbis who "canonized religious mediocrity," the "salesmen of their own delusions." Like the Kotzker, he sees a Judaism that "had been weakened from within, its insights had become clichés, its loyalties stale."[20] Like the Kotzker, he denounced "the equation of religion and self-interest whether it is the survival of the people within the Jewish context or the personal salvation that is the center of concern in Christianity."[21] For Heschel, the issue is not "to be or not to be" a Jew, but why and how to be a Jew. The prime directive for Jews, even after the Holocaust, is not sheer survivalism.[22] Rather, "the gravest sin for a Jew is to forget what he represents."[23] For

---

16. Heschel, *Kotzk*.
17. Heschel, *Passion*, 318.
18. Heschel, *Passion*, 127.
19. Heschel, *Passion*, 127.
20. Heschel, *Passion*, 153, 318, 320, 314.
21. Heschel, *Passion*, 316.
22. Heschel, *Moral Grandeur*, 30.
23. Heschel, *Earth*, 109.

Heschel, American Jewry has forgotten what it represents; it has become a messenger who has forgotten the message. And, that message is the spiritual legacy of East European Jewry. Devoid of its wisdom, American Jewry has become a conclusion without a premise, a fallacy; a community characterized by smugness and "intellectual vulgarity," wrapped in its own self-delusions of inauthenticity, and engaged in its own spiritual suicide, a "second holocaust." American Jewry had become the epitome of the Kotzker rebbe's observation that it is bad enough to be in a state of exile and alienation, but it is even worse to be in such a state and not even to know it.

REUVEN KIMELMAN, BRANDEIS UNIVERSITY

Review of *The Sabbath*, Abraham Joshua Heschel. New York: Farrar, Straus and Young, 1951.

The Sabbath is likely Abraham Joshua Heschel's most widely read book. Widely translated, it merited a second translation into a resonant Hebrew. It achieved fame when published jointly with *The Earth is the Lord's* (1950). The books complement each other: the earlier portrays the sanctity of space, the later expounds the sanctity of time. Together they express the Heschelian space-time dialectic.

From its biblical inception to its modern expression, no practice of Judaism has garnered more attention than the Sabbath. Heschel's *The Sabbath* subtitled "Its Meaning for Modern Man," culminates a series of such attempts. In the century prior to Heschel's *The Sabbath*, major explanations of the Sabbath were proffered primarily by German and Hasidic thinkers. In the late nineteenth century, Samson Raphael Hirsch stressed the idea that one rules the world six days a week but ceases on the seventh in order to realize one's creatureliness and appreciate one's Creator. Herman Cohen in his essay on the Sabbath (1869) and in his book *Religion of Reason* (1919) stressed the social significance of the Sabbath as a realization of ideal human existence, the day on which God's love is manifest, and a demonstration to humanity of pure monotheism. Leo Baeck and Franz Rosenzweig, two of Cohen's followers, also made contributions. Baeck underscored the Sabbath as a day of liberation for slaves and the oppressed, and as a balance to the bustle of the week. For Rosenzweig, the Sabbath whets our appetite for eternity by getting us to commemorate creation, sense revelation, and anticipate redemption. In the same year that *The Sabbath* came out, Erich Fromm published *The Forgotten Language* with its essay on the Sabbath, based on his German essay of 1927. For Fromm, the Sabbath is "man's victory over time," for "by stopping interference with nature for one day you eliminate time." "Instead of a Sabbath on which man bows down to the lord of time, the Biblical Sabbath symbolizes man's victory over time."

None of these figure in Heschel's otherwise heavily documented presentation (Cohen is cited once, but on a different subject) though he incorporates many of their insights when he writes, "Man's royal privilege to conquer nature is suspended on the seventh day" or "The seventh day is the armistice in man's cruel struggle for existence, a truce in all conflicts, personal and social, peace between man and man, man and nature, peace within man."[24]

Instead, references to Rabbinic literature, the liturgy, Kabbalah, and Hasidic literature predominate. *The Sabbath*'s immediate precursors, especially on the subject of the sacredness of time, are *Kedushas Shabbat* of R. Zadok ha-Kohen of Lublin (1823–1900) and *Sefas Emes* of R. Yehudah Leib of Gur (1847–1905). Albeit rabbinically based, Heschel's portrayal is drawn with liturgical-mystical hues. His chapters revolve around time, (Divine) Presence, eternity, and holiness. The balance between space and time can be gauged by the ratio of their mention in the table of contents: five for time, two for space, and two more for time extended, eternity. His opening metaphor for the Sabbath, "A Palace in time"—elsewhere called "cathedrals in time"—is a classical Kabbalistic image. Kabbalah loves to mix temporal and spatial metaphors. In fact, its focus on the Sabbath and Jerusalem is a focus on the sacred in time and space. Both the Sabbath and Jerusalem are the centers of their respective categories of the sacred. Jerusalem is the spatialization of the holy as the Sabbath is its temporalization. Therefore, were one to profane the Sabbath by treating it as one of the six days of the week, one could be ejected from the sacred center in space to the periphery of the exile. In the same vein, were one to properly observe the Sabbath in time, one could be restored from the profane periphery to the sacred center in space, namely Jerusalem. Thus, the rebuilding of Jerusalem is dependent upon Sabbath observance.

Still Heschel rarely employs Kabbalistic terminology, though it pervades his analysis. In his discussion of the feminization of the Sabbath, he says: "The idea of the Sabbath as a queen or a bride is not a personification of the Sabbath but an exemplification of a divine attribute, an illustration of God's need for human love; it does not represent a substance but the presence of God, His relationship to man."[25] This is the Kabbalistic understanding of *Shekhinah* or *Malkhut*, the *sefirah* that hovers over humanity.

24. Heschel, *Sabbath*, 29.
25. Heschel, *Sabbath*, 60.

As Heschel further expounds, "The Sabbath is the presence of God in the world, open to the soul of man. It is possible for the soul to respond in affection, to enter into fellowship with the consecrated day." Were one to translate this into Kabbalistic Hebrew, one might think it came straight out of *Sod ha-Shabbat* of Meir ibn Gabbai. Like ibn Gabbai, Heschel succeeds in integrating temporal, human, and divine axes. In general, Kabbalah operates on four levels, frequently simultaneously: the spatial, the temporal, the human, and the *sefirotic*. Its multivalent language embraces the totality of space, time, humanity, and the sefirot under the canopy of the holy in order to bring about a world/age that is wholly Sabbatical.

As Heschel notes, the expression *Kabbalat Shabbat* has two meanings. In early post-Talmudic legal literature, it denotes the assumption of the obligation of Sabbath observance. In haggadic literature, especially Kabbalistic literature, it connotes the welcoming of the Sabbath as a bride. Additionally, in early legal literature the Sabbath is personified primarily as king, whereas in post-Zoharic Kabbalistic literature the personification as bride or queen predominates. The feminization of the Sabbath is a victory of Kabbalistic literature. Its victory is due to the fact that it understood the welcoming of the Sabbath and the acceptance of its authority through a series of integrated metaphors such as the acceptance of kingship, the acceptance of the crown, the acceptance of a supernal soul, the welcoming of the bride, and the entrance into the canopy of marriage. Viewing the coronation metaphor through the prism of a marriage metaphor led to the comparison of a king without a queen or a people to that of a man without a wife.

After Heschel, there appeared two academic Kabbalistic books on the Sabbath which took their cue from *The Sabbath*. The first was *The Sabbath in the Classical Kabbalah* by Eliot Ginsburg. Its opening citation is from *The Sabbath*. The second is my Hebrew, soon to be translated, *The Mystical Meaning of 'Lekhah Dodi' and 'Kabbalat Shabbat.'* In a sense both, but especially the latter, are footnotes to my teacher's book *The Sabbath*.

EDWARD K. KAPLAN, BRANDEIS UNIVERSITY

Review of *Man Is Not Alone: A Philosophy of Religion*, Abraham Joshua Heschel. New York: Farrar, Straus and Young, 1951.

I was earning a Ph.D. in French literature, with a specialty in poetry, when I first read *Man Is Not Alone*. Enthralled by the intensity of Heschel's prose, I was seduced by lyrical sentences such as this: "Words expire when uttered, and faith is like the silence that draws lovers near, like a breath that shares in the wind."[26] Most significantly, it was the first Jewish book that convincingly evoked for me the presence of God. What I did not find in Hindu philosophy, Buddhism, or even in Martin Buber, I found in Heschel, an entrance to Jewishness that aspired to a concrete experience of the divine. I met Heschel and participated with him in the religious opposition to the Vietnam war, deciding to entrust my personal quest to Judaism.

Man Is Not Alone is both poetic and philosophical, expressive, analytic, and mystical. It is Heschel's blueprint for a theological revolution, intended to train readers to receive nothing less than divine revelation. He developed the book from articles he wrote in the 1940s on prayer, faith, and "The Quest for Certainty in Saadia's Philosophy." The book's biographical unity is demonstrated by Heschel's germinal essay, "An Analysis of Piety," first published in 1942 and transported almost verbatim, with only subtitles added, to form the concluding chapter, "The Pious Man." This model of devoutness as a constant awareness of God's presence should inspire readers to lead a holy and righteous life.

The book is divided into two parts. Part I, "The Problem of God" (chapters 1–17), appeals to thoughtful, open-minded, and self-critical seekers, introducing the "cognitive emotions" of awe and wonder leading to a state of "radical amazement." Awareness of "the ineffable" prepares the mind for receptivity to transcendence. These opening chapters deploy a sort of philosophical housecleaning, a rigorous questioning of conventional ways of thinking about ultimate meaning. Heschel compels the person to abandon secular preconceptions and even drives the mind into a state of despair. Plunged into anguish, the person can surrender the ego; radical amazement should lead to radical insight. Heschel's philosophical goal was to train readers to achieve "certainty" in the divine reality.

Heschel recapitulates this itinerary in chapter 9, "In the Presence of God," which can be read as a prose poem with its own internal commentary. The seeker enters a new phase with "dark apathy," a loss of self that allows the living God to enter human consciousness: "But, then, a moment comes like a thunderbolt, in which a flash of the undisclosed rends our dark apathy asunder. It is full of overpowering brilliance, like a point in which all moments of life are focused or a thought which outweighs all thoughts ever conceived of Apathy turns to splendor unawares."[27] Normal, ego-centered thinking is reversed: "We are penetrated by His [God's] insight. We cannot think any more as if He were there and we here. He is both there and here."

---

26. Heschel, *Alone*, 73.
27. Heschel, *Alone*, 78–79.

The mind receives a jolt of God's presence at the initiative of the divine. I call this event mystical illumination; Heschel calls it intuition or insight.

Whatever the label, this paradigm shift comprises Heschel's theological revolution: the recentering of human subjectivity from the self to God. (Kant's "Copernican revolution" in philosophy placed the emphasis on the human subject.) In religious awareness, the mind is illumined by a radical "turning" to God-centered thinking. God is the Subject of whom I am the object. Rather than speaking of a mystical encounter with God, he used philosophical terms, a "categorical imperative" analogous to Kant's rationalism. But mystical it is, for the person receives an unmediated incursion from the living God. Heschel trusted that all readers might eventually welcome this modern form of divine revelation and prophetic inspiration.

Man Is Not Alone assumes that all readers can receive God's presence directly. In this Heschel vied implicitly with Rosenzweig's *Star of Redemption* and Buber's *I and Thou*, both of which were then barely known to the American public, and which emphasize the human side of the religious quest. Heschel's spiritual itinerary is more straightforward and elegant than Rosenzweig's philosophical masterpiece, and more authentically biblical (and rabbinic) than Buber's humanistic "dialogue" with the sacred.

Along with his analysis of religious insight, in chapter 16, "The Hiding God," Heschel confronts the excruciating problem of human evil. In one of the earliest reflections on what became known as the Holocaust, the chapter opens with this inexorable question: "For us, survivors of history's most terrible horrors, it is impossible to meditate about the compassion of God without asking: Where is God?"[28] What I call Heschel's "spiritual radicalism" subordinates theology to ethics, as he rejects both a negative theology of divine indifference or absence and human impotence: "Emblazoned over the gates of the world in which we live is the escutcheon of the demons. The mark of Cain on the face of man has come to overshadow the likeness of God. The major folly of this view seems to lie in its shifting the responsibility from man's plight from man to God, in accusing the Invisible though the iniquity is ours."[29]

In Part II, "The Problem of Living" (chapters 18–26), Heschel applies his paradigm shift to ritual observance and practical ethics. Rather than explain religion as a fulfillment of human needs, he understands the essence of the human as being a need of God. The Bible was not human theology but God's anthropology. In his famous phrase, God is in search of man.

---

28. Heschel, *Alone*, 151.
29. Heschel, *Alone*, 151.

Man Is Not Alone earned national renown for Heschel with a review by Reinhold Niebuhr, America's leading Protestant theologian, in the *New York Herald Tribune*. Niebuhr dramatically predicted that Heschel "will become a commanding and authoritative voice not only in the Jewish community but in the religious life of America." This gratifying declaration was followed by a longer, more detailed review in *Congress Weekly* by Jacob B. Agus, a leading thinker in the Conservative rabbinate and author of *Modern Philosophies of Judaism*, the first major presentation in English of Rosenzweig and Buber. Agus underscored Heschel's immediate relevance: "A profound hunger for faith is now felt in every walk of life."

If Judaic Studies had been an established academic discipline at the time, Agus's review might have initiated a systematic interpretation of Heschel's works. (The Association for Jewish Studies was not founded until 1969.) But in 1951, there were only general forums such as *Commentary* in which new works of Jewish philosophy might be carefully examined. Heschel needed allies to help overcome resistance to his God-centered vision. Only in 1959, with the publication of Fritz Rothschild's carefully constructed anthology, *Between God and Man*, was it possible for readers to grasp the outlines of Heschel's dynamic system.

The key to Heschel's theory of religious knowledge, and to his own multilayered discourse, is poetry. His lush literary style combines incisive philosophical analysis, lyrical passages vivified by comparisons, and images appealing to memory and emotions, with aphorisms that condensed insights. Like musical scores, the author repeats and orchestrates moments of sensitivity to holiness. This manner of thinking and writing calls for an imaginative, participatory reading strategy. No wonder that his books have become devotional reading for Christians as well as for Jews.

Man Is Not Alone is a book to return to, again and again, slowly, with meditative intent. Reading his other works, we understand how this first magnificent sketch of his "philosophy of religion" contains them all in seed. In the end, Heschel's poetry, his mastery of both the Judaic and Western canons, his Hasidism, and his spiritual commitment welcome all of us into the sanctuary.

VIOLETTA REDER, INTERFACULTY INSTITUTE OF ECUMENISM AND DIALOGUE/PONTIFICAL ACADEMY OF THEOLOGY (KRAKOW, POLAND)

Review of *Man's Quest for God: Studies in Prayer and Symbolism*, Abraham Joshua Heschel. New York: Charles Scribner's Sons, 1954.

Rabbi Abraham Joshua Heschel had a universal message important for Christians as well as Jews. Inspired by the example of the biblical prophets, Rabbi Heschel spoke on issues crucial to all humanity. It is prophetic audacity that made him deplore both the "spiritual absenteeism of the synagogue" and the "separation of Church and God."

Man's Quest for God is written in the language of a modern Jewish mystic and scholar who can both appreciate the whole of his tradition and distinguish its universal threads. In response to a world that found itself in a "pit full of snakes," Heschel reminds readers of the mystical lift of *Shekhinah* and *mitzvot*. In essence, *Man's Quest for God* is a guidebook for transcendence.

In this attempt by a rabbi to encourage Jews to renew their Covenant with God after the Shoah, Catholics will find a map to the Church's biblical and liturgical roots. The whole of *Man's Quest* is an explication of *Shema Israel*—the absolute priority of God in human life. To prioritize God means to make room for His presence, *Shekhinah*, and His Word, the *Torah*, and to answer God's will as formulated in the Revelation.

In *Man's Quest for God*, Heschel makes it clear that the essential thing in life—worship of God with the whole of all human powers (as directed by the Commandment of Commandments)—has two inextricable aspects: prayer and deeds. This is explained in his paradoxes: "Prayer is the queen of all commandments," but "a mitzvah is a prayer in the form of a deed." "The philosophy of Jewish living is essentially a philosophy of worship," but, at the same time, "Judaism stands and falls with the idea of the absolute relevance of human deeds." Given this key, we notice that the definitions of prayer throughout the book reflect the role of mitzvot as well: prayer means "feeling God's concern," "coming close to hearing the eternal theme and discerning our place in it," "expressing God," "participation in the mystery," "expanding God's presence in the world," "establishing His kingship," "bringing God back to the world."

And it is no wonder that this should be so. At the source of Jewish religious integrity there is the word *Shema* ("Listen"), which epitomizes worship. Isn't the full meaning of *Shema* "hear and fulfill"? Or sometimes even "fulfill and hear?" Similarly, the religious integrity in Judaism is guarded by the central Jewish idea of *kiddush-ha-Shem*. As Heschel says, "to Judaism religion is . . . an answer to Him who is asking us to live in a certain way"; it is "an order of all man's existence." This notion of an integral religious life—with the centrality of both prayer and human action—can serve as a model for Christians.

Moving with Heschel between the poles of *aggadah* and *halacha, kavanah* and external performance, "spontaneity" and "continuity," we see that the paradox of living with the God of Israel can be also summed as follows: The very heart of God's Law addresses the human heart! "You shall love the Lord your God"—and serve Him (Deut 11:13)—"with all your heart and with all your soul and with all your might" (Deut 6:5). "If the heart could be offered alone [without words], this would be enough to fulfill the commandment." Thus, "prayer is sacrifice." But "we do not sacrifice. We are the sacrifice."

If only people meditated on this central directive/petition of God every day, would this not bring Heschel's dream of spiritual revolution to the world? For many modern humans, this idea is divine *chutzpah*, some peculiar excess. But in biblical terms, this is the reality of responding to God. In the year 1943—the peak of the Shoah, the year that portions of *Man's Quest for God* were first published—Heschel exhorted humanity to return to this biblical mindset. For Heschel, there is no middle ground in loving God. "The world is not a vacuum. Either we make it an altar for God or it is invaded by demons," he says. "There can be no neutrality. Either we are ministers of the sacred or slaves of evil."

One of the chapters offers an analysis of human language as a tool of prayer with the *siddur*, which Heschel ironically calls "one of the least known books in Jewish literature." Both the breviary (more than 50 percent of its content derives from the Hebrew Bible)—once reserved only for religious orders—and the religious rules (*qui regulae vivit Deo vivit!*), with their paragraphs like new *mitzvot*, remind us that Christians do need a *halakhah* based on their Covenant with God. With this reflection we come close to Heschel's spirit: "How grateful I am to God that there is a duty to worship, a law to remind my distraught mind that it is time to think of God, time to disregard my ego for at least a moment! . . . There is something far greater than my desire to pray, namely God's desire that I pray."

A Christian reader will know how to apply this fascination with *mitzvot* and *halacha*: words revealing God's will should be taken to the heart as commandments, as seriously and lovingly as Jews take *mitzvot*. "Take and eat; this is my Body" (Matt 26:26). "Pursue justice. Guide the oppressed. Uphold the rights of the fatherless. Plead with the widow's cause" (Isa 1:17).

The chapter on symbols reiterates the *Adonai Ehad* principle in one more sense: by separating symbolism from true worship. Rabbi Heschel defends man against a man-made god, god made after the image of man. The Holy One did not reveal Himself in symbols, but in events and commands. Therefore, the days commemorating those events are holy days, and fulfilling His will is the source of sanctification.

Having traced the golden thread of Heschel's message, I would be remiss if I did not mention the mystic, transcendent nature of Heschel's style. Here is a writer united with the reality he is trying to speak about: he himself is an "expression of God." This results in accuracy and immediacy filling one with awe. For one who has stood in the presence of God at least once, Heschel's text is evocative of that ineffable mysterious moment when the presence of God is more obvious than that of one's own self. Sometimes, a terse and accurate sentence hits the point with such lingering power that it becomes an instant aphorism. "God is of no importance unless He is of supreme importance." "To pray is to dream in league with God." There is no rattle of redundancy, just condensation of insight. Sometimes, it reads like sheer poetry, the whole world opening its gates to metaphors that could help render what there is between God and man: "God's grace resounds in our lives like a staccato. Only by retaining the seemingly disconnected notes comes the ability to grasp the theme." Insights sparking off insights, this book has the potential to make one open to the presence and will of God with fascination.

JOHN P. KEENAN, ST. MARK'S EPISCOPAL CHURCH (NEWPORT, VERMONT)

Review of *God in Search of Man: A Philosophy of Judaism*, Abraham Joshua Heschel. New York: Farrar, Straus and Giroux, 1955.

Books are alike only in that they contain writings bound in some fashion, usually nowadays in hard or soft cover. Beyond that, they come in every variety—essay or poetry collection, scholarly study, literary or popular fiction. In quality, the writing may be lyrical or persuasive, or it may lack grace and coherence, character development, or verisimilitude. That is why it is so basic to determine first the genre of a book, that it may be judged for what it tries to do and not for what the reviewer wanted the author to do. And, partial as I am to the reading and writing of theology, that was my first task in thinking about Heschel's *God in Search of Man*.

This book is indeed rich in theology, and its themes, enunciated in that striking title *God in Search of Man*, do capture Heschel's theology well: that God loves humans and that for some strange reason he seeks them out, makes covenants with them, bestows blessings upon them, and holds them as the apple of his eye. These themes are so grounded in the scriptures that one can hardly disagree unless one is a deist or something of that ilk. But this is not a theology book; it develops no new argument and presents no theological thesis for discussion or debate.

In genre *God in Search of Man* is a book of meditations. The term "philosophy" in the subtitle means not systematic analysis but love of wisdom, the wisdom of the scriptures and the tradition. I am familiar with books of this kind from my Roman Catholic upbringing and seminary training. Early each morning in the seminary, beginning at 5:40 AM, we would meditate for twenty minutes in silence. As a focus for our meditation, we were directed to use meditation manuals, some better than others. The genre continues, perhaps exemplified by Kathleen Norris's *Amazing Grace*, which contains a series of thought-provoking passages on faith and life, each taking up but a few brief pages. The point was never to read the meditations to memorize their content or learn something not heretofore known. Norris's book and others of this kind are meant to trigger meditative thought and quietude. In seminary we meditated on specific scripture texts or scenes, wherein we were to focus on truths so large they could hardly be contained in ordinary words.

Such I find Heschel's book to be. He writes as himself a prophet, announcing the scriptural word. He weaves texts and observations. He triggers things in the reader's consciousness that have been perhaps forgotten or overlooked. And his words can be read only slowly, passage by passage, with no hurry and no need to do aught but sit quietly and imbibe his sense of the Lord who encompasses us all and the life he seeks to bestow upon us. There is no reviewing Heschel's *God in Search of Man*. Of all the postmodern quips, of this volume it is particularly true to say that the text reads us; it reviews our lives and how we live them, all of us within the Abrahamic covenant. Heschel's language is so rich that one can of a morning stop after reading only a sentence or two and call it enough, for the eloquence of his diction catches one and fixes the mind in focused concentration on a particular text or biblical theme.

And so, I keep the book by my bedside that I might read a portion every morning. No longer do I arise as early as I used to, and sometimes I rise only begrudgingly. But then there is Heschel waiting, usually with some theme that not only comforts but also awakens depths of prayer and meditation in response to God's searching.

I remember the older meditation manuals of my youth—St. Francis de Sales's *Introduction to the Devout Life*, Thomas à Kempis' *Imitation of Christ*, and a host of others whose titles escape me. For now, however, it is Abraham Joshua Heschel's *God in Search of Man* that resides on my bedside table and begins my days.

RICHARD SIMON HANSON, LUTHER COLLEGE (DECORAH, IOWA)

Review of *The Prophets*, Abraham Joshua Heschel. New York and Evanston: Harper and Row; Philadelphia: The Jewish Publication Society of America, 1962.

As I worked my way afresh through *The Prophets* I realized again why this was such a popular textbook in seminary curricula for several decades of the twentieth century. Heschel's thorough treatment of the subject recommends it as a basic interpretation of classical prophecy. His conservative appreciation of the biblical material as it stands is a comfort to cautious minds, and his keen insights stretch readers to understanding beyond familiar points of view. As a textbook it proved to be both safe and exciting for those training to be either pastors or rabbis.

I think of the book as two series of lectures. The first is composed of compact studies of seven prophets from the classical era and is prefaced by a chapter titled "What Manner of Man is the Prophet." The second and larger series seeks to understand the phenomenon of prophecy in general but with emphasis on the Israelite Biblical tradition.

Heschel holds a special reverence for the prophets. In treating their message as the heart of the Bible's witness, he plants himself solidly in Reform Judaism's legacy of considering the prophets to be the core of Judaism's contributions to the world, in contrast to the Orthodox position that puts the Torah at the center. In "What Manner of Man is the Prophet," he says, "The significance of Israel's prophets lies not only in what they said but in what they were" and writes that the prophet "is a person, not a microphone" and also a "poet, preacher, patriot, statesman, social critic, moralist."

The seven prophets Heschel focuses on in his first series are Amos, Hosea, Isaiah, Micah, Jeremiah, Habakkuk, and the Second Isaiah. In each chapter he discusses the life and message of the prophet in the context of his historical and political circumstances. Aiming for nothing less than "an understanding of what it means to think, feel, respond and act as a prophet," Heschel brilliantly recreates the ancient world of these great men.

One of the distinctive features of Heschel's approach to the prophets is the way he sees the prophets as a singular, unified phenomenon. From his analysis of the prophets, he abstracts a composite type whom he calls "the prophet." While his descriptions of "the prophet" tend to elevate the role into a Platonic, universal ideal, Heschel never loses sight of the historical relevance of the classical prophets' work. Heschel sees them as the "first men in history to regard a nation's reliance on force as evil":

> Why were so few voices raised in the ancient world to protest against the ruthlessness of man? Why are human beings so obsequious, ready to kill and ready to die at the call of kings and chieftains? Perhaps it is because they worship might, venerate those who command might, and are convinced that it is by force that man prevails. The splendor and pride of kings blind the people. The Mesopotamian, for example, felt convinced that authorities were always right The prophets repudiated the work as well as the power of man as an object of supreme adoration. They denounced "arrogant boasting" and "haughty pride" (Isa. 10:12), the kings who ruled the nations in anger, the oppressors (Isa. 14:4–6), the destroyers of nations, who went forth to inflict waste, ruin, and death (Jer. 4:7), the "guilty men, whose own might is their god" (Hab. 1:11).[30]
>
> When the prophets appeared, they proclaimed that might is not supreme, that the sword is an abomination, that violence is obscene. The sword, they said, shall be destroyed.
>
> They shall beat their swords into plowshares,
> And their spears into pruning hooks;
> Nation shall not lift up sword against nation,
> Neither shall they learn war any more. Isaiah 2:4

Heschel also gives them credit for having a historically progressive view of social justice: "The threat of punishment is one of the most prominent themes of the prophetic orations. Yet the prophets themselves seem to have questioned the efficacy of punishment. Punishment has three aims: retributive, deterrent and reformatory. The divine intention, according to the prophets . . . is deterrent and reformatory."

This focus on justice is no surprise considering Heschel's very public commitment to social justice in the American civil rights and anti-war movements. In Heschel's view, "the world exists for the sake of justice rather than justice for the sake of the world."[31] Heschel calls justice "the personal

---

30. Heschel, *Prophets*, 167.
31. Heschel, *Prophets*, 215.

will of God"[32] and speaks of history as the arena for justice, with the prophets cast as advocates for victims of injustice. Indeed, Heschel was known to attribute his activism to his intellectual encounter with the prophets.

The eleventh through fourteenth chapters spell out what may be Heschel's most original contribution to biblical theology: his "theology of pathos." Early in the first of this series he writes, "The prophets had no theory or idea of God To the prophets God was overwhelmingly real and shatteringly present. . . . They lived as witnesses [to God] . . . rather than as explorers engaged in an effort to ascertain the nature of God; their utterances were the unloading of a burden."

In Heschel's view, God's pathos is not merely intentional—that God empathizes with humanity. It is also transitive—that the prophets can feel and transmit God's empathy towards humanity:

> The basic feature of pathos and the primary concern of the prophet's consciousness is a *divine attentiveness and concern.* Whatever message he appropriates, it reflects that awareness. It is a divine attentiveness to humanity, an involvement in history, a divine vision of the world in which the prophet shares and which he tries to convey. And it is God's concern for man that is at the root of the prophet's work to save the people.[33]

Heschel sees this notion of an engaged, concerned God as distinct from the conceptions of the self-centered Greek gods and the notions of God offered by philosophers like Plato, Theophrates, and Epicurus and Eastern schools of thought like Hinduism, Taosim, and Buddhism. "At the heart of the prophets' affirmation," he says, "is the certainty that God is concerned about the world."[34]

But Heschel makes clear that pathos is a double-edged sword. If God can empathize with humanity's suffering, then he can also be enraged by humanity's sins:

> Pathos is always disclosed as a particular mode or form. There are, as we have seen, many and variable modes of pathos, such as love and anger, grief and joy, mercy and wrath. What is the basic feature they have in common? What is the ultimate significance of pathos? . . .
>
> The great secret is God's hidden pathos. A divine attachment concealed from the eye, a divine concern unnoticed or forgotten, hovers over the history of mankind. Yet there are

---

32. Heschel, *Prophets*, 199.
33. Heschel, *Prophets*, 483.
34. Heschel, *Prophets*, 259.

moments when attachment turns to detachment, when concern is overshadowed by anger.[35]

With his theology of pathos, Heschel could be accused of humanizing God by attributing humanlike reason to the Almighty. But he is only taking the lead from his prophetic sources, who assumed that God could think or even feel as humans think and feel. In the later chapters, he says "the prophet is a poet," and "what the poets know as poetic inspiration the prophets called divine revelation."[36] In conjunction with that he encourages people to read the Bible as literature.

In the final chapter Heschel returns to "the theology of pathos": Pathos in all its forms reveals the extreme pertinence of man to God, His world directedness, attentiveness, and concern. God "looks at" the world and is affected by what happens in it; man is the object of His care and judgment.

Overwhelmingly, mysteriously different from man, God was not the object of imagination. He could not be captured in a myth or comprehended in a concept or a symbol. Challenging, involved, and concerned, His presence pierced the impregnable walls of His otherness. The dilemma was overcome by abstaining from any claim to comprehend God's *essence*, His inmost being, or even to apprehend His inscrutable thoughts, unrelated to history, and by insisting upon the ability to understand His presence, expression, or manifestation. The prophets experience what He *utters*, not what He *is*.[37]

For Heschel, the prophets were an unrepeatable phenomenon to be studied and emulated for millennia to come. He allowed himself to be so taken into the messages of the prophets as to enter their reality, their perceptions, and their own convictions. As they communicated the message of God to humanity so Heschel can communicate their message to us.

JOHN C. MERKLE, COLLEGE OF ST. BENEDICT/ ST. JOHN'S UNIVERSITY (ST. JOSEPH AND COLLEGEVILLE, MINNESOTA)

Review of *Who Is Man?* Abraham J. Heschel. Stanford, CA: Stanford University Press, 1965.

Like all Heschel's books but in a more concentrated and explicitly philosophical way, *Who Is Man?* is an eloquent defense of the transcendent dignity of

---

35. Heschel, *Prophets*, 483.
36. Heschel, *Prophets*, 367.
37. Heschel, *Prophets*, 483–84.

being human—a transcendent dignity grounded in the human orientation toward and manifestation of meaning that transcends the human.

Heschel has often been acclaimed as one of the most profound and poetic spiritual writers of our age. But he has not gained the recognition he deserves as a philosopher. This is probably due precisely to the poetic—rather than the strictly systematic—quality of his writing. But the fact that his writing is not systematic *in the strict sense* does not mean it is unsystematic. It is an organic system in that there is an order, direction, and inner consistency to it. In my view, Heschel's books are every bit as philosophical as they are poetic, and this is especially true of *Who Is Man?* whose title states the question at the heart of Heschel's philosophical exploration.

"We ask: *What is man?* Yet the true question should be: *Who is man?* As a thing man is explicable; as a person he is both a mystery and a surprise."[38] In responding to the question "Who is man?" Heschel engages in what he elsewhere calls "situational thinking" as contrasted with "conceptual thinking."[39] The latter deals with concepts by way of detached analysis; the former deals with situations by way of concerned involvement. By conceptual thinking Heschel does not simply mean thinking in concepts, which even situational thinking must include, but thinking about concepts rather than the situations underlying them. Situational thinking is the reverse, attending to the situations that give rise to the concepts. Conceptual thinking is an important way of dealing with many intellectual questions, but ultimate questions such as "Who is man?" are not merely intellectual issues but existential problems. Situational thinking is necessary when dealing with such problems: "No genuine problem comes into being out of sheer inquisitiveness. A problem is the outcome of a situation. To understand the meaning of the problem and to appreciate its urgency, we must keep alive in our reflection the situation of stress and strain in which it comes to pass."[40]

It is easier to keep alive the conceptualization of a problem than the situation in which it emerged, and it is easier to spawn a conceptual problem than to grapple with a situational problem. But the conceptualization of a problem is not the problem itself and is often a distortion of it. "The predicament of much of contemporary philosophy is partly due to the fact that ongoing conceptualizations have so far outdistanced the situations which engender philosophizing that their conclusions seem to be unrelated to the original problems."[41] Situational thinking focuses on "the human

---

38. Heschel, *Who Is Man*, 28.
39. Heschel, *Search*, 5.
40. Heschel, *Who Is Man*, 1.
41. Heschel, *Who Is Man*, 2.

situation"[42] and its original problems more than on concepts or speculations about human nature. Therefore, writes Heschel: "Our question is not only: What is the nature of the human species? but also: What is the situation of the human individual? What is human about a human being? Specifically, our theme is not only: What is a *human being*? but also: What is *being human*?"[43]

For Heschel, any description of human existence that does not consider human relatedness to transcendence is inadequate. But classical definitions of human beings as "tool-making animals," "rational animals," "political animals," etc. fail to capture what is distinctive about human beings—"not the undeniable fact of [their] animality" but the enigma of what they do "with and apart from [their] animality."[44] We can attain an adequate understanding of human existence only if we think in distinctively human terms and avoid categories developed in the study of other forms of life.[45] Thus, any doctrine that describes human beings as qualified animals precludes a genuine understanding of human existence. "Man is a peculiar being trying to understand his uniqueness. What he seeks to understand is not his animality but his humanity."[46]

Priority must therefore be given to the category of the human. "The attribute 'human' in the term 'human being' is not an accidental quality, added to the essence of his being. It is the essence."[47] Human beings may at times act like tool-making animals, or rational animals, or even like machines, but defining human existence in such terms by no means does justice to the essential meaning of being human. Instead, such descriptions "contribute to the gradual liquidation of man's self-understanding," says Heschel. "And the liquidation of the self-understanding of man may lead to the self-extinction of man."[48] Heschel claims that there is a "creeping self-disparagement" about humanity in contemporary literature, and that "moral defamation of man may spell the doom of all of us."[49]

Thus, Heschel is concerned with proper self-understanding and with the preservation and promotion of authentic human living. He begins his response to the question "Who is man?" by elucidating what he calls

42. Heschel, *Who Is Man*, 14.
43. Heschel, *Who Is Man*, 28–29.
44. Heschel, *Who Is Man*, 21.
45. Heschel, *Who Is Man*, 3.
46. Heschel, *Who Is Man*, 22.
47. Heschel, *Who Is Man*, 29.
48. Heschel, *Who Is Man*, 25.
49. Heschel, *Who Is Man*, 27.

"necessary components which constitute the essence of being human":[50] a sense of the preciousness and uniqueness of human existence; an appreciation of the boundless opportunity and non-finality of being human; the interplay in human life of physical processes and spiritual events and of solitude and solidarity; the power of reciprocity; sensing and living the sanctity of human life. The remainder of the book is, for the most part, a profound elaboration of this claim: "the essence of being human is concern for transcendent meaning" which means that "openness to transcendence is a constitutive element of being human."[51]

This concern for transcendent meaning or openness to transcendence is also a premise of religious faith, and, at its core, *Who Is Man?* is an argument that the transcendent God of biblical faith is the only viable answer to the question about the ultimate meaning of human being. The thesis is that only a personal God who cares for us can qualify as our ultimate meaning because "the cry for meaning is a cry for ultimate relationship, for ultimate belonging."[52] In view of this, "ultimate meaning as an idea is no answer to our anxiety" because human existence "is more than an intellectual structure; it is a personal reality."[53] Only a personal reality may serve as the ultimate meaning for another personal reality. Therefore, the ultimate question is not "What is the meaning of being human," which reduces the meaning of a person to a thing or an idea, but rather "*Who is man's meaning?*"[54]

The answer obviously cannot be nature because, unlike humanity, nature is not a personal reality. Neither can humanity, nor any human being or group of human beings, be the ultimate meaning for any of us because being human involves responding to transcendent meaning. Spellbound by the splendor of being, by the marvel of our own existence; humbled by the fact that we often fail to realize the meaning within the marvel, we human beings must confess that we are not sovereign in the realm of being, nor have we authored the realm of meaning. Only a reality beyond the world of nature and humanity can be the ultimate source of all being and meaning. And only an ultimate presence—a transcendent, personal reality—can be ultimately meaningful to human beings as personal beings in need of transcendent meaning.

But how do we know transcendent meaning as ultimate presence? Finding ourselves involved in the inescapable context of meaning, we

50. Heschel, *Who Is Man*, 31.
51. Heschel, *Who Is Man*, 66.
52. Heschel, *Who Is Man*, 73.
53. Heschel, *Who Is Man*, 73.
54. Heschel, *Who Is Man*, 72.

come to realize that meaning is something we discover rather than invent. Moreover, we realize that the discovery of meaning is born of "meaning that drives us to think about meaning."⁵⁵ Realizing this, we sense that our anxiety about meaning is "a response to a challenge."⁵⁶ The challenge must issue from a source that transcends humanity because all human beings, individually and collectively, live under the challenge. Thus, the challenge we face issues from "a transcendence called the living God."⁵⁷ Moreover, this challenging transcendence signifies "transcendent concern"⁵⁸ because there would be no challenge to us without a concern for us. This challenging and concerned transcendence is what Heschel means by God. As such, God is the ultimate meaning in whose presence we find meaning by responding to the divine challenge to share in divine concern. Thus, Heschel concludes his book with these words: "Who is man? *A being in travail with God's dreams and designs*, with God's dream of a world redeemed God's dream is not to be alone, to have mankind as a partner in the drama of continuous creation. By whatever we do, by every act we carry out, we either advance or obstruct the drama of redemption; we either reduce or enhance the power of evil."⁵⁹

MONIKA ELLIOTT, WARSAW UNIVERSITY

Review of *The Insecurity of Freedom*, Abraham Joshua Heschel. Philadelphia: The Jewish Publication Society of America, 1966.

> "It is the beginning of wisdom to be amazed at the fact of our being free."⁶⁰

Freedom appears in much of contemporary public discourse as a conceptual placeholder in a larger arrangement of oppositions and dichotomies which are employed to relieve or deprive us of the difficulty associated with independent political reasoning. It would be no exaggeration to say that in many of our societies, "freedom" is left sounding like little more than a hollow slogan for those who wish to avoid the trouble of understanding an infinitely complex world. Particularly for those of us living amongst the "coalition of the willing," there certainly has been no shortage of opportunities to witness

---

55. Heschel, *Who Is Man*, 64.
56. Heschel, *Who Is Man*, 74.
57. Heschel, *Who Is Man*, 69.
58. Heschel, *Who Is Man*, 92.
59. Heschel, *Who Is Man*, 119.
60. Heschel, *Insecurity*, 18.

the deployment of "freedom" as an ideological silencer used to stifle debate and curtail dissent. There are friends of freedom, and there are enemies of freedom. Of course, human circumstances will always fail to conform to such simplistic reductions, and therefore, out of necessity, the concept of freedom must be recaptured in all its difficulty and possibility. The lesson of Abraham Joshua Heschel's theological discourse on freedom is that freedom is fatally misunderstood when conceptualized as "mere emancipation" or thought of as a license "to be or act as I desire."[61] Therefore, freedom is not a category or simple attribute to which one may subscribe and use to determine the coordinates of the world by which one is surrounded. Instead, freedom requires the effort to learn to be responsive to the entirety of creation and the strength to bear the load of responsibility for all of humanity and heaven. "Freedom is a burden that God has thrust upon man."[62]

The Insecurity of Freedom, a volume of collected essays written by Heschel between the late 1950s and mid-1960s, concerns how men may retain their humanity in the face of modern existence or "remain human in the skyscrapers."[63] The method that Heschel advocates for the retention of our humanity is a vigorous defense of freedom intended to recapture the urgency of freedom as a practice in human responsibility for the salvation of the world.[64] That is to say that for Heschel the only way that mankind may retain its humanity is by means of the work of freedom, the very practice by which humanity transcends itself and its limitations.[65] Heschel's work involves the intricate relation between concrete historical realities and the eternal truths of religious thinking. Therefore, Heschel concerns himself with not only with perennial questions of prayer or good and evil, but also with status of Soviet Jews and the American Civil Rights Movement. The interweaving of these two distinctive fields of attention is fundamental to Heschel's argument that universal divine concern always lies within the field of particular human realities, and the work of concrete emancipation of mankind is always the work of realizing divine concern. Therefore, freedom is the difficult task to which mankind must awaken in order to show reverence for the world and for fellow men.

Heschel advocates a variety of means by which man may come to confront the challenge of freedom; chief amongst them is education. For if our freedom is precariously bound to our willingness to be responsive

---

61. Heschel, *Insecurity*, 14.
62. Heschel, *Insecurity*, 13, 21.
63. Heschel, *Insecurity*, 23.
64. Heschel, *Insecurity*, 21.
65. Heschel, *Insecurity*, 14.

to the world, then we must learn how to listen. Accordingly, education is not a process of accumulating a set of facts and knowledge, but instead a process of attunement, of learning how to listen. "Let us remember that it is not enough to impart information. We must strive to awaken appreciation as well."[66] Therefore, Heschel seeks to capture the essence of education, in the broadest sense, and specifically to articulate the features of an active and effectual religious education. The basic function of religious education is to "dedicate, to consecrate . . . the ability to experience the suffering of others, compassion and acts of kindness; sanctification of time, not the mere observance of customs and ceremonies; the joy of discipline, not the pleasures of conceit; sacrifice not casual celebrations; contrition rather than national price."[67] Religious education, which must emerge from dynamic religious thinking and pedagogy, must not function as a mere supplement to secular education; any form of religious education that looks to secular or scientific reasoning for directives or approval is fundamentally lost. "In the face of fabulous progress made in secular civilization, the religious man became obsessed with an excessive inferiority complex."[68] Religious education must not allow itself to be marginalized as a relic of antique reasoning. The vitality of religious education is to be found in the fact that its message is not old, but eternal. Therefore, if religious education finds itself peripheral to the changing fashions of secular reason, it has failed to articulate that its message is always relevant, always engaged in a process of renewal. Religious education awakens man to the ultimate source, possibility, and responsibility of freedom.

To read Heschel's *The Insecurity of Freedom* is to be reminded that freedom is not a concept which is easily understood or a simple reality which is easily granted. Nor is it a tool or ideological device meant to divide humanity. Freedom comes from choices and struggles of men and women engaged in everyday life who reveal in their actions that humanity can be more than it is in the eyes of other men but can in fact be a humanity in the eyes of God. Heschel's point is that each human life is not a trivial point of fleeting interest, but instead that each human life offers the possibility for realizing the "uniqueness and sacred preciousness of man,"[69] a uniqueness that comes to life in the work of freedom.

---

66. Heschel, *Insecurity*, 236.
67. Heschel, *Insecurity*, 236–37.
68. Heschel, *Insecurity*, 230.
69. Heschel, *Insecurity*, 16.

YEHEZKEL LANDAU, HARTFORD SEMINARY (HARTFORD, CONNECTICUT)

Review of *Israel: An Echo of Eternity*, Abraham Joshua Heschel. Farrar, Straus and Giroux, 1967.

Abraham Joshua Heschel's *The Sabbath* is a classic in religious literature, weaving together theology, philosophy, biblical commentary, rabbinic storytelling, and practical spirituality, all in luminous prose. It is a book about holiness in time that is itself timeless. Readers a hundred or five hundred years from now will be savoring Heschel's ideas and the elegance with which they are conveyed.

Can the same be said of Heschel's lengthy meditation on sacred geography, *Israel: An Echo of Eternity*? With deep sadness I would say, unfortunately not. My lament is prompted partly by my profound admiration for Heschel, whom I consider one of my most influential teachers and role-models. For me, as for so many others, he was a modern prophet—not only in his writings, which echoed the biblical prophets so powerfully, but also in the way he engaged the social issues of his time. In general, I find his writings to be intellectually and spiritually uplifting, worth reading again and again for their eloquence and wisdom.

Heschel's remarkable legacy, integrating thought and prophetic activism, is a source of inspiration for human rights and peace activists everywhere. Yet a rereading of his book on Israel deepens my dismay over how one-sided it is. He is passionate about Jews and Israel, but he lacks the *com*passion for Palestinians that he exhibited toward African Americans and Vietnamese. A more inclusive vision of freedom and justice could have made the volume a resource for the central Jewish and Zionist imperative of our time: healing the tragic conflict over God's Holy Land. Genuine peace between Israel and Palestine will require a truth-and-reconciliation process that allows these two traumatized peoples to finally end their debilitating and demoralizing war. Shared remorse, rather than mutual recrimination, is essential to this process. Not having Heschel as a teacher and ally in this struggle for real *shalom* deepens my sadness.

Both the beauty and the flaws in Heschel's book are largely due to its historical context. Had he lived another ten or twenty years (he died in 1972), he might well have rewritten portions of it. As it stands, the book is a personal manifesto of Jewish fidelity to the people, land, and state of Israel written shortly after the Six-Day War in 1967. The swift success of the Israel Defense Forces followed weeks of collective dread, as Israelis and Jews everywhere saw in Gamal Abdul Nasser's belligerent rhetoric the ominous prospect of mass slaughter. The haunting memory of the Six Million vied with a messianic hope for redemption in Heschel's soul. "Auschwitz is in our veins," he asserted. "It abides in the throbbing of our hearts. It burns in our imagination. It trembles in our conscience. We, the generation that witnessed the holocaust, should stand by calmly while rulers proclaim their intention to bring about a new holocaust?"[70] With this moral claim on his conscience, Heschel saw Nasser and Israel's other adversaries as genocidal agents, without factoring into his worldview the assault on Arab dignity caused by the displacement and dispossession of hundreds of thousands of Palestinians in 1948. The 1956 Suez Campaign, in which Israel joined with Britain and France against Egypt, left unhealed wounds which are also ignored by Heschel. As a result, his book tends to incriminate the Arabs while romanticizing the Israelis, as in the following passage:

> The State of Israel from the very beginning sought peace and desired peace. During many years its voice calling for peace and cooperation was a voice calling in the wilderness Again and again was the State of Israel thrust into war against her will, in self-defense confronted with the choice to be or to cease to be . . .
> But the Arab states have consistently refused to recognize Israel's existence, have subjected it to military harassment, infiltrating the land and killing civilians. They have received arms from Soviet Russia in the amount of almost $4 billion— and the avowed purpose proclaimed by the Arab rulers was to throw the population of Israel into the sea.[71]

The claims in this passage, as in many others like it, require historical contextualization and nuancing. Both the benevolence of self-interested Israeli intentions (however justified) and the literal interpretation of Arab rhetoric (however inflammatory) need to be questioned and qualified. But Heschel was not a historian like Benny Morris, and his book was not meant as an objective account. It comes across as a passionate appeal for sympathy and support, especially on the part of Christians, for Israel's basic right to exist in peace and security.

Heschel's outlook was shared by millions of fellow Jews in the immediate aftermath of the Six-Day War. The threat of a second Holocaust was amazingly averted, and Israel found itself, in less than a week, ruling over four times as much territory as it had controlled before the war. This lightning fast transition from existential dread to collective euphoria has skewed Jewish sensibilities at the expense of Palestinians until today. Over

---

70. Heschel, *Echo*, 206.
71. Heschel, *Echo*, 216.

the same period, it must be added, most Palestinians have not relinquished their aversion to Jewish sovereignty in even part of historic Palestine. My critique of Heschel's partisan viewpoint is tempered by an awareness that the Six-Day War was radically disorienting for all of us. Close to forty years later, we can better appreciate what a mixed blessing that "victory" was and how opportunities for negotiating a lasting peace were missed by leaders on all sides. The establishment of Jewish settlements in the occupied areas of Judea, Samaria, Gaza, the Golan, and Sinai further complicated efforts to reach negotiated compromises with Israel's neighbors.

Heschel's shortcomings as a political visionary reflect a struggle to reconcile his love of Zion, and his primary loyalty to Jews, with his commitment to alleviate human suffering everywhere. This is a cautionary lesson for Jews, Christians, or Muslims who are so immersed in this tragic conflict that they succumb to partisan polemics. At best, all attempts to tell inclusive truth or achieve inclusive justice will be colored by subjective perceptions and loyalties. To use one of Heschel's favorite terms, human *pathos*, unlike God's, tends to be self-referencing; and so, we Jews are tempted to ascribe to God a favoritism rooted in the covenantal love affair between God and Israel. Here is another illustrative statement from the book:

> The love of this land was due to an imperative, not to an instinct, not to a sentiment. There is a covenant, an engagement of the people to the land. We live by covenants. We could not betray our pledge or discard the promise.
>
> When Israel was driven into exile, the pledge became a prayer; the prayer a dream; the dream a passion, a duty, a dedication.
>
> Intimate attachment to the land, waiting for the renewal of Jewish life in the land of Israel, is part of our integrity, an existential fact. Unique, *sui generis*, it lives in our hopes, it abides in our hearts ...
>
> To abandon the land would make a mockery of all our longings, prayers, and commitments. To abandon the land would be to repudiate the Bible.[72]

This statement of love and loyalty is profoundly true—from a Jewish standpoint rooted in the Bible and in our own history. A Palestinian could write similar words, invoking the Arab and Islamic heritage, a parallel sense of covenantal particularity, and a national experience of exile and oppression.

---

72. Heschel, *Echo*, 44.

As a Jew, a religious Zionist, and a dual Israeli American citizen, I share Heschel's love of Zion and his yearnings for ultimate redemption. With him, I mourn two millennia of Jewish exile, vulnerability, and frequent victimization, culminating in the Holocaust. And with him, I exult in the re-establishment of Jewish sovereignty in Jerusalem and the ingathering of exiles from our global Diaspora. I, too, can affirm a transcendent consecration of God's Name in the Zionist homecoming, seeing in it a fulfillment of biblical prophecy and centuries of Jewish prayer. We are indeed like messianic dreamers, rejoicing in the spirit of Psalm 126.

But our Zionist dream will remain unfulfilled so long as we do not address wisely and compassionately the nightmare that Palestinians have been living since 1948. They certainly bear considerable responsibility for their own misery, but so do we. The first step toward recognizing our mutual obligations toward one another is a courageous stretching of our hearts and imaginations. For us Jews, it means entertaining the idea that the Palestinians' attachment to the land and their loyalty to God, grounded in their own sacred texts, are no less valid than our own. Ultimately, this leads to an awareness (in the spirit of Exodus 19:5–6) that the land belongs to God, and that we Jews, together with Palestinian Christians and Muslims, belong to the land. Biblically speaking, our residence in the land is contingent on our ethical behavior under the terms of the Sinai covenant. The Palestinians, also, are called to create a society characterized by justice and lovingkindness—in Hebrew, *mishpat* and *tzedakah*. These fundamental virtues were exemplified by our common forefather Abraham/Ibrahim and reiterated by all the Hebrew prophets (cf. Gen. 18:19 and Isa. 1:27).

The tragic reality is that our sense of justice, together with our loves and loyalties, are not sufficiently inclusive. They tend to privilege our own claims and our own aspirations, as expressed in our subjective narratives. For both Jews and Palestinians, those narratives focus too often on historic victimhood and ultimate vindication. To make sense of our own pain, and to find solace, we create elaborate mythologies. These symbolic dramas can engender massive suffering if they conflict with another group's mythology.

Jews played the role of villain in Christian passion plays for many centuries. This kind of negative, essentialist Othering bedevils the Israeli-Palestinian conflict and makes diplomacy so difficult. Sadly, it also colored Heschel's worldview. For him, the Arabs were either intransigent enemies or, paradoxically, they were absent from the stage entirely. For example, on page 138 he writes: "the reclamation of the land from the aridity and barrenness to which most of its soil had been condemned by the spoliation and neglect of man and nature, is an act of sanctification." It is true that Zionist pioneers drained swamps and made desert land bloom through dedicated labor and, over time, drip-irrigation technology. But for Palestinians, who tended the terraced hillsides for centuries, it adds insult to injury to say that the land was neglected by human beings, requiring a collective Jewish return and sanctification to be redeemed.

Here is another passage[73] that is reminiscent of the early Zionist perception, naively and tragically blind, of a "land without a people for a people without a land":

> Ancient cities erased, fields desolate, the soil forsaken, unloved by its inhabitants. Instead of "flowing with milk and honey," it was a land teeming with ruins, infested with malaria, a country without trees.
>
> Any man who traveled from Dan to Beersheba would cry: this is all arid, hopelessly sterile.
>
> Indeed, Zionism was a dream, a Utopia. Practical people could not but scoff at those who were ready to be intoxicated with a mere dream, who left the fleshpots of Europe to settle in the sands of Palestine, to drain the swamps—in the process of which so many people died of malaria.
>
> The Holy Land which some of the older people among us can still remember as a place of desolation and ruins has responded to the toil of the pioneers as if to carry out the prophet's prediction:

The wilderness and the dry land shall be glad, the desert shall rejoice and blossom;...(Isaiah 35:1)
The renewal of the land, the act of making the desert blossom, is bound to serve as an inspiration to underdeveloped lands all over the world.
Israel reborn is an answer to the Lord of history who demands hope as well as action, who expects tenacity as well as imagination.

This kind of self-glorifying rhetoric, with stirring biblical resonances, warms the Jewish heart and assures us of transcendent meaning in our lives. This can indeed produce an intoxicating effect. But, at the same time, it violates the prophetic imperatives that Heschel himself emphasized in his other writings: the injunctions to care for the stranger and the vulnerable and to work for justice. Selective memory and truth-telling, as in the passage just cited, angers Palestinians, for they are either invisible or typecast as mortal enemies in our own redemption drama.

73. Heschel, *Echo*, 117–18.

One of the requirements for diminishing the enmity that fuels the horrific violence is for Jews and Arabs to hear each other's testimonies, and to find in their respective love affairs with God and the land a common vocabulary of the heart that transcends partisan ideologies. For if we fail in meeting on that deeper human level, where we touch the Divine within us, we will remain stuck in self-justifying theologies of history and geography. We will continue to sacrifice our loved ones on an idolatrous altar: either the altar of nationalism or the altar of "territoriolatry," which is akin to the deification of trees and stones that led the Canaanites to forfeit their hold on the land in ancient times.

We need to share our deepest Jewish dreams with the Palestinians, and to listen respectfully to theirs, so that neither collective dream turns into a nightmare. Our dreams are reflections of our messianic *midrashim*, the sacred stories that fuel our deepest hopes and longings. The aim of true messianism is not victory or vindication. It is *shalom*, peace, wholeness, the integration of disparate elements or realities, even apparent opposites like Israel and Palestine. We are reminded of this Divine purpose within Creation every *Shabbat*. And here is where we come full circle in our understanding of Heschel. For whom is a better teacher on the messianic promise of *Shabbat* than he? It is Heschel who reminds us that the first act of consecration in Creation was the hallowing of the Sabbath by God. Holiness in time precedes, and transcends, all consecrations within space.

Toward the end of his book on Israel, Heschel cites the prophecy in Isaiah 19:23–25 that envisions Israel, Egypt, and Assyria coexisting in harmony. Heschel himself, trying to reconcile Jewish particularity with prophetic universalism, envisions a day when the peoples of the Middle East will live in peace. He asserts: "The wonder of the risen Israel and the gratitude to Him who has raised martyred Israel from the dead belong together. We are witnesses of the resurrection. And being a witness is a transformation."[74]

But how have we Jews been transformed? We are no longer passive victims, thank God, yet peace and security elude us. In fact, in the name of security or survival we (here I speak as an Israeli who served in the IDF) are too often trapped in situations where we victimize others. The sad reality is that Jews and Arabs alike are both victims and victimizers. Only as partners committed to ensuring a better future for our children, putting life before land and God before nationalism, can we hope to break this tragic cycle.

In closing his volume, Heschel writes: "The ultimate meaning of the State of Israel must be seen in terms of the vision of the prophets: the redemption of all [humanity]. The religious duty of the Jew is to participate

---

74. Heschel, *Echo*, 220.

in the process of continuing redemption, in seeing that justice prevails over power, that awareness of God penetrates human understanding."[75] On page 215, he excerpts a passage from the book *Siach Lohamim*—"Soldiers' Talk," published shortly after the Six-Day War and later translated into English as *The Seventh Day*—which demonstrates the "deep concern over the moral questions, uneasiness about being a 'conquering army' " By citing this self-reflective conversation among IDF soldiers, Heschel seemed to recognize that moral dilemmas and struggles lay ahead, that the Six-Day War was both a deliverance of biblical proportions and a profound moral challenge to Jews everywhere. He even asks the question: "Is Judaism as presently understood equipped to confront the challenge of the world?"[76] This remains an open question for all of us, but Heschel points the way toward an answer when he declares: "The six days of war must receive their ultimate meaning from the seventh day, which is peace and celebration."[77]

MORRIS M. FAIERSTEIN, (ROCKVILLE, MARYLAND)

Review of *Kotsk: In Gerangel far Emesdikeit*, Abraham Joshua Heschel. Tel Aviv: Ha-Menorah, 1973. 2 vols.

The last two books completed by Abraham Joshua Heschel and published posthumously were about R. Menahem Mendel of Kotsk (1787–1859), one of the most challenging and intriguing figures in the history of Hasidism. *A Passion for Truth* (New York: Farrar, Straus & Giroux, 1973) was written in English and intended for a general audience. It highlighted the similarities between R. Menahem Mendel and his contemporary, the Danish philosopher and theologian Soren Kierkegaard. *Kotsk*, the other book about R. Menahem Mendel, was written in Yiddish. It was twice the size of *A Passion for Truth* and written in a rich, rabbinically inflected style that could be appreciated by a small handful of readers. Unfortunately, Heschel did not offer an explanation for this seemingly unusual choice of language. He mentions in his Introduction the difficulties faced by R. Menahem Mendel's disciples when he asked them to preserve his writings in written form. They felt it unseemly to write in Yiddish, but at the same time they found it extremely difficult to translate his aphoristic teachings into Hebrew. The result was that there is no comprehensive corpus of R. Menahem Mendel's teachings. Instead, his teachings were preserved as oral traditions that were eventually

---

75. Heschel, *Echo*, 225.
76. Heschel, *Echo*, 223.
77. Heschel, *Echo*, 218.

collected and published many years later. This is the closest Heschel comes to an explanation of why he wrote the book in Yiddish.

The first part of the book, comprising the first eight chapters, explores the theology of Kotsk, both in comparison to the teachings of the Baal Shem Tov, the founder of Hasidism, and in its own context. It is easy to understand the attraction of the Besht's teachings, based on *hesed* (loving-kindness) and his openness to people on all spiritual levels. Kotsk, on the other hand, was in many ways the antithesis of Beshtian Hasidism. It was elitist and even anti-mystical in some respects. The Besht wanted to bring Heaven down to the people, while the Kotsker wanted to raise people to the Heavens. The Kotsker was uncompromising, both with himself and with others. When a destitute *Hasid* asked him for a blessing for financial success, R. Menahem Mendel asked if he had *tefillin* and a *talit*. If he did, then he could pray to God directly, without anyone's intercession. Heschel writes that his heart was with the Besht in Medzibozh, but his head, his intellect, was in Kotsk. This book is his attempt to explain his attraction to the spiritual path of Kotsk.

There is a Hasidic legend that R. Menahem Mendel would spend all year writing a book that would summarize and systematize his teachings. On the eve of Passover every year he would take his writings of the past year and burn them along with the *hametz*, because he felt that he had not adequately expressed his ideas. The written form was not amenable to the transmission of his ideas. It was a combination of his perfectionism and the inability of mere words to express the complexity and depth of his ideas.

Heschel follows what might be called a Kotsker method in his exposition of R. Menahem Mendel's teachings. Rather than a systematic exploration of concepts and ideas, he selects a brief statement or teaching, often no more than a sentence or two. He then analyzes it, explores its theological concerns, and reflects on its spiritual meaning. Each of these reflections is relatively brief, typically two to four pages in length. From ten to twenty of these brief expositions are brought together to form a chapter. Sometimes the transition from one discussion to the next is readily apparent and other times the connection is less clear.

Truth was the central concept of R. Menahem Mendel's teachings. His spiritual path was the search for truth. Whatever stood in the way of this search was to be discarded or ignored, whether it was family obligation or social convention. The study of Torah was central, but one had to be careful that one should not become full of oneself, arrogant or self-satisfied, from the knowledge acquired or the respect accorded scholars. For Menahem Mendel this would be a form of idol worship, the worst sin one could commit.

The second part of *Kotsk*, comprising ten chapters, is historical in orientation. It offers an overview of R. Menahem Mendel's teachers, the Holy

Yehudi of Przysucha and Simhah Bunem of Przysucha. Their teachings and practices are the foundation on which Kotsker Hasidism was built. R. Menahem Mendel became a follower of Hasidism despite his father's strong opposition. He visited the Seer of Lublin and like many other young men seeking spiritual and intellectual fulfillment was attracted to the Seer's disciple, the Holy Yehudi of Przysucha. He followed the Yehudi after he left Lublin after a disagreement with the Seer and remained a devoted disciple of the Yehudi's successor, R. Simhah Bunem. There was some debate about the succession after R. Simhah Bunem's death in 1827. A minority of the disciples, led by R. Isaac of Worka, accepted R. Abraham Moses, R. Simhah Bunem's son, as their leader. However, the majority chose R. Menahem Mendel as their *rebbe*.

R. Simhah Bunem had a warm, outgoing personality that attracted disciples. R. Menahem Mendel was dour, withdrawn, and uncompromising. Disciples were attracted to him by the force of his intellect and ideas, despite his difficult personality. R. Menahem Mendel was not interested in a mass following. He was an unabashed elitist who wanted a small group of disciples who would attain great intellectual and spiritual heights. R. Menahem Mendel once said that he only wanted fifty disciples who would stand on the rooftops and declare the greatness of God.

He led his disciples for thirteen years until the autumn of 1839, when he secluded himself in his study and had little contact with the outside world for the rest of his life, a period of twenty years. He did see members of his immediate family and a handful of his closest disciples. The event that was supposed to have precipitated this seclusion was the so-called "Friday night incident," the subject of much myth and speculation. Heschel argues convincingly that this incident was not on a Friday night, and had nothing to do with antinomianism. Rather, R. Menahem Mendel had a nervous breakdown on Simhat Torah of that year, and the precipitating event was the final rupture between himself and his close disciple, R. Mordecai Joseph of Izbica. They had grown apart over differences of personality and theology. R. Menahem Mendel had a history of depression, and this conflict with his old friend sent him into a deep depression from which he never emerged. My own independent study confirms the accuracy of Heschel's analysis and the falsity of the antinomian legends.

The study of R. Menahem Mendel's life and teachings are complicated by the problematic nature of the sources. He left behind no writings, and as Jacob Levinger has demonstrated, the references to Menahem Mendel's teachings in the writings of his close disciples are minimal and uninformative, for the most part. What are left are collections of brief teachings and aphorisms collected and published many years after his death. These collections are notorious for attributing the same teaching or aphorism to several different people, in different parts of the collection. Heschel argued in his Introduction that he could resolve many of these problems because he had been privileged to have heard in his youth authentic oral Kotsker traditions from old Kotsker *Hasidim*. This first-hand knowledge lends great importance to Heschel's study.

The significance of Heschel's study and the increasingly smaller number of Yiddish readers makes an English translation an urgent desideratum. At the same time, it is to be hoped that the few items needing revision or correction will be attended to during translation. There are some paragraphs that are repeated, sometimes verbatim, in several places in the text. The light hand of a good editor would be very helpful. The other area needing review is the footnotes. Many are fragmentary, with incomplete bibliographical information, and some need further review. The addition of comprehensive indices would also add significantly to the usefulness of the book. The book was written for a learned audience, familiar with Rabbinic and Hasidic thought. A glossary of terms and explanatory footnotes where needed would also add to the accessibility of the work.

Abraham Joshua Heschel's *Kotsk: In Gerangel far Emesdikeit* is the most important study of this major Hasidic teacher and is likely to remain so for the foreseeable future. It is to be hoped that it will be properly translated and reach the wide audience that this major work of scholarship and spirituality richly deserves.

STEPHEN D. BENIN, UNIVERSITY OF MEMPHIS

Review of *Maimonides: A Biography*, Abraham Joshua Heschel, translated by J. Neugroschel. New York: Farrar, Straus and Giroux, 1982.

Abraham Joshua Heschel wrote this biography of Maimonides in German when he was a young man of only twenty-eight, the first major work of Heschel's rich and varied career. It is now almost seventy-five years old, and yet it still speaks clearly, cogently, and coherently. It also demonstrates how the academic study of Judaism has changed—many would say declined—in the intervening years. From Heschel's biography, which is long and strong on reading and analysis of primary sources, lacking in theory—the be all and end all of modern scholarship—Maimonides emerges as incredibly human. A lonely man of faith and intellect, who encompassed all Jewish learning, classical philosophy, and mathematics, Maimonides was and remains the most important Jewish thinker in the post-biblical period. Indeed, as

Heschel himself once quipped, if Maimonides were not a man, he would have to be a university.

The geographical course of Maimonides' life from Andalusia to North Africa to Egypt—and a possible visit to Jerusalem, debated by scholars as to whether it occurred—was, in some ways, matched by his intellectual journey. For Maimonides the goal of his intellectual wandering was to come to know God as far as humans are able. Blessed with a remarkable mind, prodigious memory, and insatiable desire to absorb all he could, Rambam moved freely through all spheres of knowledge, sacred and profane. As scions of the family of Yehuda ha-Nasi, the Maimonides clan saw itself as having a special calling.

To escape the Almohade fanaticism of Fez, the family moved to Alexandria and then settled in Fustat, outside Cairo. Maimonides was devoted to his brother, David, who was the merchant of the family and whose business success enabled Rambam to engage in his studies. His brother's death plunged Maimonides into depression, from which he was slow to emerge. It was in Fustat that Maimonides undertook his greatest projects.

As a descendant of the redactor of the Mishnah, Maimonides undertook a similar redactive enterprise, the editing of a major legal compendium, the *Mishneh Torah*, about which Maimonides famously wrote that his codex coupled with a Bible would be all any Jew would need in order to come to an understanding of legal issues. Seeing his place in the lineage of R. Yehuda, Maimonides wrote, correctly and no doubt proudly, that he was emulating the style and language of the Mishnah. This compilation was an educational reform of sweeping magnitude, and for him, a major contribution to the Jewish religious tradition. Such bravado and boldness did not curry favor within all rabbinic circles. And it was the *Mishneh Torah*'s scholarly sin of omission, in his case sources, footnotes, and other scholarly trappings, that infuriated his adversaries. Would that Heschel had devoted more pages to this text, since Maimonides considered the *Mishneh Torah* the monumental achievement of his life.

It was in Fustat, thanks to his brother's work, that Maimonides had the time to devote to his numerous studies. Visits by various peripatetics could not erase what he saw as the vapid intellectual climate of Egypt, and yearning for Andalusia never seems to have waned completely. Nevertheless, Maimonides continued to write, including a commentary on the Mishnah written in Arabic, a well-known and controversial letter to the Jews of Yemen concerning messianic stirrings, and various other works.

For Maimonides a burning question was: how does a human reach the highest level of perfection possible? Maimonides wrote Joseph ibn Aknin, scholar, poet, and physician well-known for his commentary on the Song of

Songs, that he would write a text to guide him on this perplexing issue. For Maimonides, such a quest would of course entail a full-blown encounter with philosophy and its greatest teacher, Aristotle. The resulting *Guide for the Perplexed* ensured Maimonides fame in the non-Jewish world. Maimonides tackled issues of concern to all religious thinkers, and they, in turn, came to be in his debt. Heschel explicates this encounter in a remarkably clear, concise and illuminating manner.

As Heschel observes, the *Guide* is a not a goal, but a lodestar whose path leads to God. To settle down comfortably in religion, in tradition, is to be lazy. Maimonides' goal, as he stresses repeatedly, was not to create a philosophy or to erect a philosophical system, but rather to point out and pave the way to knowledge of God. He did not invent new and original elements of thought. He lived in the intoxicating wealth of universal science and was satiated with that. He was profoundly aware that reason has limits. Yet for him the realm of reason was not some narrow, hidden place, but a prominent neighborhood in the kingdom of God, perhaps not in the center, but certainly not on the periphery.

Maimonides, as Heschel understood him, well realized the intellectual contribution of Talmudic study, but seeking to subordinate ethics to theory was unique and unparalleled in Jewish thought. That is, making the contemplation of God the very goal of life, the purpose of all the commandments and actions was revolutionary.

According to Heschel, the *Mishneh Torah* and *Commentary on the Mishnah* presented philosophical teachings in the guise of religious commandments. The *Guide* attempted a marriage of Torah and Aristotle—a mixed marriage that was ultimately rejected, but not without exerting unrivaled influence in many quarters. The ideas of the *Guide*, written in Arabic, would reverberate for centuries in Latin and Hebrew translations.

Maimonides did not attempt to provide an all-encompassing answer. For him, thinking is a religious act which is no less important than the object of thought. But this entire project, as Heschel realized, was for a select few and did not go on to world-wide acclaim and acceptance. His ideas could be, and were, misunderstood, misinterpreted, and misconstrued by lesser and smaller intellects. Yet his influence was not restricted to particular periods or communities. As Heschel asserted, perhaps somewhat wistfully, it was not Maimonides' *Guide* but Rashi's commentary which won the hearts and minds of his people. Rashi became the most precious teacher, shaper, and commentator for the Jewish people. Maimonides' metaphysics would yield pride of place to mysticism and Hasidism, the *Guide* would yield to the *Zohar*. The mystical approach of Kabbalah and the fervent enthusiasm of

Hasidism would direct Jewish minds back to the commandments, as Maimonides had desired, but by a vastly different path than he would have taken.

For Maimonides the life of thought was supreme and thinking a religious duty; it was a fundamental motif of his life. Every act of thinking enabled greater revelation, and this profound insight made him realize the uniqueness of prophecy. Prophecy was beyond all philosophy, and it was the link between the divine and human. Thus, philosophy was but a prelude and prophecy was the culmination.

As he wished he was buried in the Holy Land near the city of Tiberias, a city frequented in his life by Yehudah ha-Nasi. An anonymous epitaph stated:

> Here lies a man and not yet a man:
> If thou wert a man, then heavenly creatures created thee.
> This inscription was later replaced by another:
> Here lies Moses Maimuni, the banished heretic.
> The people erected a monument for him that read:
> From Moses to Moses, there was no one like Moses.

JACOB YUROH TESHIMA, GILBOA INSTITUTE OF THE HUMANITIES (FUJISAWA, JAPAN)

Review of *The Circle of the Baal Shem Tov: Studies in Hasidism*, Abraham Joshua Heschel, edited by Samuel H. Dresner. Chicago: University of Chicago Press, 1985.

It is an exceptional honor to write a review of the book by my teacher, my master, Rabbi Abraham Joshua Heschel of blessed memory. I was his last doctoral student at the Jewish Theological Seminary of America, where he taught about the Kotzker Rebbe in the course on Hasidism in 1972.

The Circle of the Baal Shem Tov contains Heschel's four essays on Hasidism originally written in Hebrew in different periods: "Rabbi Pinhas of Korzec," 1948–52; "Rabbi Gershon Kutover: His Life and Immigration to the Land of Israel," 1950–51; "Rabbi Nahman of Kosow, Companion of the Baal Shem," in 1965; and "Rabbi Isaac of Drohobycz," in 1957. In their original Hebrew, these four essays were different from each other in syntax, tone, and style; each reflected Heschel's passion for his subject.

These essays serve as Heschel's fierce rebuttal to scholars such as Gershom Scholem, who criticized Hasidism for "departing from the rabbinical scale of values, namely their conception of the ideal type of man to which they ascribe the function of leadership. For rabbinical Jewry . . . the ideal type recognized as the spiritual leader of the community is the scholar, the student of the Torah, the learned Rabbi."[78] In all four essays Heschel demonstrates that the early leaders of Hasidism were scholars and kabbalists highly respected by their communities. If his first English book, *The Earth is the Lord's*, was his eulogy for East European Jewry, these essays were his prescription for the remedy of Jewish piety after the Holocaust (*The Earth is the Lord's* was first published in Yiddish in 1946). The first essay speaks of Rabbi Pinhas of Korzec, who was descended from Rabbi Nathan Shapiro (b. 1633), a renowned kabbalist and rabbi of Krakow. Rabbi Pinhas had mastered not only the Talmud and the Zohar and other Kabbalistic works, "but also several of the secular branches of knowledge. An expert in the disciplines of grammar, geometry, mathematics, and other subjects, he was among the few of his time who urged that 'one must acquire such learning in one's youth.'"[79] In this he resembles Rabbi Elijah, the Vilna Gaon, who was eager to acquire the knowledge of secular sciences such as geometry, geography, astronomy and medicine.[80]

R. Pinhas was nominated by the Besht to succeed him (alongside Rabbi Dov Ber, the Maggid of Miedzyrzez) but he declined the nomination.[81] He questioned the Maggid's interpretation of Hasidism and his way of conduct. The Maggid introduced the method of the Lurianic Kabbalah and taught that the essence of serving the Creator was *devekut* and *hitlahavut* through wisdom and meditation, while Rabbi Pinhas preferred to teach his students honesty and humility and purification of one's character as the way to serve God. Despite the disagreement between Rabbi Pinhas and the school of the Maggid, Hasidism continued to develop as a unified movement. Indeed, polemic and polarity became a part of Hasidism's character and tradition.

In the essay "Rabbi Gershon Kutover: His Life and Immigration to the Land of Israel,"[82] Heschel illuminates the figure of Rabbi Abraham Gershon by using information from several manuscripts that he discovered. R. Gershon spent many years in the town of Kuty (Kutov), where he was a member of the Society of Hasidism headed by the kabbalist Rabbi Moses. Later he moved to the city of Brody, where he became a member of the famed Kloiz of Brody. He was a presiding judge at one of the four rabbinical courts in Brody.

78. Scholem, *Major Trends*, 333.
79. Dresner, *Circle*, 4.
80. Klausner et al, "Elijah ben Solomon Zalman," 341.
81. Dresner, *Circle*, 9–10.
82. Dresner, *Circle*, 44–112.

As the title shows, one of the main purposes of this essay was to analyze Gershon's mission in the land of Israel. It is generally accepted that Gershon first journeyed to Israel in 1746–47, but Heschel assumes that his first visit in Israel was probably before 1741–42.[83] Heschel says, "The view that he went there to propagate the teaching of the Besht is incorrect."[84] He was merely one in a continuous migration of Diaspora pietists and kabbalists who settled in the Holy Land. Gershon lived in Jerusalem, Safed, and Hebron and joined Bet El of Jerusalem, the most prestigious center of kabbalah. In Jerusalem, the Ashkenazim asked him to take on a rabbinate and to assume control of their financial affairs even though he was Sephardic.

As proof of Gershon's rabbinical scholarship, Heschel points to his instructions to R. Tzvi, the scribe of the Besht, dealing with the problem of the inversion of the Hebrew letter "nun" in the Torah scroll.[85]

In the essay "Rabbi Nahman of Kosow,"[86] Heschel focuses on the original Hasidic teaching that Rabbi Nahman shared with the Besht. R. Nahman was the most prominent member of the Society of Hasidim (*hevrah shel Hasidim*) of Kuty, from which the first disciples of the Besht were drawn. The beginnings of the emerging Hasidic movement can be traced to this society. The Besht gave great respect to the head of the "society," Rabbi Moses. R. Nahman held no religious office. He was a prosperous grain dealer. He traveled with his merchandise in the cities of Galicia and Podolia.

It was Rabbi Nahman's custom when he came to a city to go to the synagogue and lead the congregation in prayer, sometimes even without the permission of the synagogue officials. He demonstrated for them prayer with passion, *hitlahavut* and sincerity in the Hasidic way.[87] Once Rabbi Nahman asked the Besht, "What am I thinking about at this moment?" The Besht answered: "If you focus your mind on one thing, then I will know." Nahman did so. The Besht said: "The name YHVH is in your mind." Nahman said: "You would know this is any case. For I must always think that thought, as it is written, and I have set the Lord (YHVH) before me always. If I put aside all other thoughts and concentrate my mind on only one, it must be the name YHVH." After that he became close to the Besht.[88] The constant awareness of God was a central concern of early Hasidism.

---

83. Dresner, *Circle*, 90–97.
84. Dresner, *Circle*, 62.
85. Dresner, *Circle*, 106–12.
86. Dresner, *Circle*, 131–51.
87. Dresner, *Circle*, 133, 87.
88. Dresner, *Circle*, 120.

Although the Besht and Rabbi Nahman were the fathers of the new movement, the way of Rabbi Nahman was different from that of the Besht. While the Besht faced the world with love, joy, and compassion, and sought to understand the way of each man, Rabbi Nahman approached the world with tension, bitterness, and revulsion. He was short-tempered and demanded that men live their lives uncompromisingly. Heschel spends a large portion of the essay analyzing the differing approaches of the Besht and Nahman, specifically, their ways of dealing with the problem of the *yetzer hara*, including self-interest and *keri* (involuntary nocturnal seminal emission).[89]

Heschel's essay "Rabbi Isaac of Drohobycz"[90] may leave a strange impression. As Dresner comments, Rabbi Isaac "remained somewhat distant until the end."[91] Nevertheless, Heschel counted Rabbi Isaac "among the movement's founders." The presence of Rabbi Isaac was important to the early Hasidim because he was the one person who possessed a spiritual power equivalent to that of the Besht. He once issued a ban on the Besht's amulets because he felt their magical use was a serious abuse of the sacred names written in them. But when the Besht met Rabbi Isaac, he revealed to Rabbi Isaac that there were no oaths nor any names in the Besht's amulets save his own name, "Israel, son of Sarah, Baal Shem Tov" (Usually, Baal Shem Tov is translated as "the Master of the Good Name." This is an incorrect translation; it should be translated as "the good Master of the Name.") Rabbi Isaac immediately rescinded his ban. From that time forth, the Besht again worked mighty deeds by means of his amulets.[92] R. Isaac's reversal of his own ban against the amulets attested to the legitimacy of the Besht's activity as an authentic expression of Hasidism.

This original work on Hasidism by Heschel is a major contribution to our understanding of the Hasidic movement. Also, the introduction and supplemental notes by Samuel H. Dresner are a useful resource for students of Heschel as well as of Hasidism.

---

89. Dresner, *Circle*, 136–48.
90. Dresner, *Circle*, 152–81.
91. Dresner, *Circle*, xl.
92. Dresner, *Circle*, 167–70.

AARON GROSS, UNIVERSITY OF CALIFORNIA (SANTA BARBARA, CALIFORNIA)

Review of *Moral Grandeur and Spiritual Audacity: Essays*, Abraham Joshua Heschel, edited by Susannah Heschel. New York: Farrar, Straus, Giroux, 1996.

Susannah Heschel's edited collection of forty short essays and two interviews spanning the full range of Abraham Joshua Heschel's career does much more than bring together previously difficult-to-find material with a fine biographically oriented and detail-rich introduction; *Moral Grandeur and Spiritual Audacity* has itself become a major work. No other volume conveys the breadth of Heschel's work so fully—both his writings and his activism—or provides so many powerful and pithy summaries of concepts elaborated elsewhere in his corpus. The volume's main demerit is technical: the lack of an index.

Here we find Heschel standing on one foot speaking to German Jews in 1936 as Hitler hosted the first televised Olympics and to the American people in a nationally televised interview more than 35 years later as the country reflected and reeled in response to the Vietnam War and the civil rights movement. Heschel speaks to seekers—Jewish, Christian, and secular—as well as scholars and to the leaders of Reform, Reconstructionist, Orthodox, and, especially, Conservative Judaism. One of the volumes great merits is its presentation of some of Heschel's most recurrent themes—God is in search of the human being and the need to be more than human to avoid being less than human—from multiple vantages as Heschel speaks in different contexts.

Susannah Heschel, Heschel's daughter and one of his foremost expositors, has admirably organized these essays under five headings: Existence and Celebration; No Time for Neutrality; Toward a Just Society; No Religion is an Island; and The Holy Dimension.

The bookend sections, one and five, contain especially wide-ranging material marked by Heschel's sustained effort to reformulate the basic questions and assumptions that propel inquiry about and into religion. Encapsulating the broad arc of Heschel's work, the first section emphasizes the Jewish context, while the fifth and final section emphasizes the religious situation more generally.

In the first section, the essays speak to such issues as what it means to be a Jew; the theological primacy of events over ideas; the Hasidic message of "hope and exultation"; "Israel as memory"; a critique of Reform, secular, and Orthodox Judaism; the meaning of *tshuvah*; and a poetic meditation on Nazi anti-Semitism. Ranging over wide terrain, Heschel argues that "[t]he very existence of a Jew is a spiritual act";[93] blasts Jewish demographers with his insistence that "[t]here are two words I should like to strike from our vocabulary: 'surveys' and 'survival'";[94] and offers a phenomenology of Talmud study, suggesting that *pilpul* "represented a desire to sublimate feelings into thoughts, to transpose dreams into syllogisms."[95] The final section is of special interest to the historian and philosopher of religion, for here themes such as piety, holiness, faith, prayer, and death are approached as basic human phenomena. In "An Analysis of Piety," Heschel summarizes a fundamental aspect of his analysis of religion: "man's affinity with God is his persistent aspiration to go beyond himself ... to live for an ideal."[96] Religion is imagined here as a vehicle to actualize this aspiration that may manifest in devotion to "the family, a friend, a group, the nation ... art, science, or social service..."[97]

The second essay in the final section, *The Holy Dimension*, contains the volume's most pointed critique of religious studies, which is also touched on elsewhere in the volume through Heschel's critique of symbolism "as the supreme category in understanding religious truth."[98] Heschel laments: "Modern man seldom faces things as they are.... We investigate the relation of religion to economics, history, art, libido. We ask for the origin and development, for its effect upon psychical, social, and political life.... We forget to inquire: What is religion itself?"[99]

His call to the scholar, like his call to the seeker, is to return to fundamental questions and the eschewing of answers that would reduce religion to another category. "Religion is more than a creed or a doctrine, more than faith or piety; it is an everlasting fact in the universe, something that exists outside knowledge and experience, an *order of being*, the *holy dimension* of existence [R]eligion cannot be totally described in psychological or sociological terms."[100]

Speaking to philosophers of religion in the essay *The Biblical View of Reality*, Heschel insists that "[p]hilosophy or religion is primarily not ... the philosophy of a doctrine ... but the philosophy of concrete events, acts,

---

93. Heschel, *Moral Grandeur*, 55.
94. Heschel, *Moral Grandeur*, 29.
95. Heschel, *Moral Grandeur*, 36.
96. Heschel, *Moral Grandeur*, 316.
97. Heschel, *Moral Grandeur*, 316.
98. Heschel, *Moral Grandeur*, 88, 128; see also 92.
99. Heschel, *Moral Grandeur*, 319.
100. Heschel, *Moral Grandeur*, 322.

insights, of that which is immediately given with the pious man."[101] In passages that can be read as an anticipation of aspects of Emmanuel Levinas's critique of Heideggerian thought, Heschel insists that all questioning, even the most profound, is secondary to confrontation with the mystery "in which the mind stands *face to face* with the world."[102] In *Death as Homecoming*, Heschel further argues that more primary than "man's being in the world is man's being known to god,"[103] and that it is a distortion "to characterize the life of man as moving toward death."[104]

Sandwiched between these broad ranging bookends are three more focused sections. The second section, "No Time for Neutrality," brings together essays which move from articulating a vision of fundamental human dilemmas to practical advice and commentary of immediate relevance to Jewish communal life and, as always, an emphasis on foundational theological issues. In the first essay, "No Time for Neutrality," Heschel opens with the observation that, "One of the lessons we have derived from the events of our time is that we cannot dwell at ease under the sun of our civilization, that man is the least harmless of all beings."[105] In the face of this situation, "Judaism is both an assurance and an urge.... It tells us that righteousness can be achieved..."[106]

In "Symbolism and Jewish Faith," Heschel offers his response to those who would reduce religion to symbolism; the essay functions as a guide for the Jew to navigate the language of religion as symbolism. "Symbols have their place," he insists, "in the outer court of religion."[107] While acknowledging a place for symbolism as "man's reference to God," Heschel calls for a focus on mitzvah, "God's reference to man" (93).

In "The Spirit of Jewish Prayer" Heschel issues a call for what he terms a "sympathetic prayer book exegesis," critiquing modern movements centered on liturgy reform for worrying more about "what to say" than "how to pray."[108] In an address to the Central Conference of American Rabbis, " Toward an Understanding of Halacha," Heschel critiques the Reform abandonment of normative halacha, emphasizing the limits of rationality and arguing for the "absolute relevance of human deeds" against "the view that

101. Heschel, *Moral Grandeur*, 354.
102. Heschel, *Moral Grandeur*, 364.
103. Heschel, *Moral Grandeur*, 372.
104. Heschel, *Moral Grandeur*, 375.
105. Heschel, *Moral Grandeur*, 75.
106. Heschel, *Moral Grandeur*, 77.
107. Heschel, *Moral Grandeur*, 91.
108. Heschel, *Moral Grandeur*, 119.

the essence of the good is in the good intention."[109] Other essays speak to the meaning of Yom Kippur; discuss Heschel's experience teaching religion to American Jews; provide a remarkable overview of Heschel's basic understanding of Jewish theology; survey "The Mystical Element in Judaism"; succinctly summarize Heschel's doctrine of the biblical God's search for the human; and offer an overview of the concepts "God, Torah, and Israel."

The third and fourth sections, "Towards a Just Society" and "No Religion Is an Island," are the most focused in the volume; they highlight respectively Heschel's political activism and his commitment to interreligious dialog. The opening essay, "The Meaning of This War" (World War II), blasts war as proceeding from and contributing to the demise of our humanity. "The outbreak of this war was no surprise. It came as a long-expected sequel to a spiritual disaster."[110] In the "Moral Dilemma of the Space Age," Heschel insists that humanity is "ill-prepared spiritually and morally for the vast accumulation of power which we are achieving through science."[111] In "Required: A Moral Ombudsman," Heschel inveighs against U.S. war crimes. In "The Reasons for My Involvement in the Peace Movement," Heschel emphasizes his conviction that "[e]ven the high worth of reflection in the cultivation of inner truth cannot justify remaining calm in the face of cruelties that make the hope of effectiveness of pure intellectual endeavors seem grotesque."[112] "In Search of Exaltation" interprets and critiques "the young people's escape to drugs."[113] In "A Prayer for Peace," Heschel calls the war in Vietnam "our most urgent, our most disturbing religious problem" and in a remarkable comment Heschel declares, "At this moment . . . we are spiritually Vietnamese. Their agony is our affliction, their hope is our commitment."[114]

The third section in the volume, "No Religion Is an Island," includes discussions of "the systematic liquidation of man's sensitivity to the challenge of God" as a shared interreligious challenge; an analysis of the inner dimensions of prayer; a plea for a Christian "confrontation with Judaism"; Heschel's interpretation of ecumenism; argument for areas of interreligious cooperation to manifest "in applied religion, particularly as they relate to social action";[115] and Heschel's pathos-filled eulogy to Reinhold Niebuhr.[116]

109. Heschel, *Moral Grandeur*, 140.
110. Heschel, *Moral Grandeur*, 210.
111. Heschel, *Moral Grandeur*, 218.
112. Heschel, *Moral Grandeur*, 224.
113. Heschel, *Moral Grandeur*, 228.
114. Heschel, *Moral Grandeur*, 232.
115. Heschel, *Moral Grandeur*, 297.
116. Heschel, *Moral Grandeur*, 301–2.

The gem of this section, though, and one of the great gems of this volume is the first essay in the section, "No Religion Is an Island" (previously published with helpful explanatory essays in an edited volume of the same name by Harold Kasimow and Byron Sherwin. At the opening of the essay, Heschel proclaims that "[t]he supreme issue is today not the *halacha* for the Jew or the Church for the Christian—but the premise underlying both religions..."[117] Here Heschel insists that the most characteristic aspect of his theology, his constant return to fundamental issues, is at root a shared inter-religious problem. In a starting formulation, Heschel proclaims, "Religion is a means, not an end.... To equate religion and God is idolatry."[118] Heschel concludes, in a striking phrase that characteristically melds traditionalism and radicalism, "In this eon diversity of religions is the will of God."[119]

REUVEN KIMELMAN, BRANDEIS UNIVERSITY

Review of *Torah min Hashamayim Ba-aspaklaria shel Hadorot (Theology of Ancient Judaism)* [Hebrew], Abraham Joshua Heschel. Vols. 1–2, London: Soncino Press, 1962–65; vol. 3, New York: Jewish Theological Seminary of America, 1995. English Translation: *Heavenly Torah as Refracted Through the Generations*, edited and translated by Gordon Tucker with Leonard Levin. New York: Continuum, 2005.

I am unaware of any other scholar of the twentieth century besides Abraham Joshua Heschel who contributed to the theological understanding of the four pivotal periods of pre-modern Jewish existence: Biblical, Rabbinic, Medieval-Philosophic, and Kabbalistic-Hasidic. The first two warranted major books. For the Biblical period, *The Prophets* articulates the Divine pathos of the Most Moved Mover's involvement in the affairs of man. For the Rabbinic period, *Torah Min HaShamayim BeAsplaqariah Shel HaDorot*, traces the internal dialectic of Jewish theology throughout its history. This is Heschel's magnum opus, for it presents the understanding of the woof and warp of Judaism which informs his writings on contemporary theology. Heschel not only had an overarching thesis about Rabbinic Judaism but adopted the strategy of exegeting it from within by writing it in Hebrew in native categories. Many of the subsections are titled with Rabbinic quotations. This

---

117. Heschel, *Moral Grandeur*, 236.
118. Heschel, *Moral Grandeur*, 243.
119. Heschel, *Moral Grandeur*, 244.

reflects his understanding of the intersect between language and thought, for as words and language inform thinking so do categories structure thought. The distinctiveness of Heschel's contribution can be gauged by comparing his chapter headings with three other major works on Rabbinic thought.

Solomon Schechter, *Aspects of Rabbinic Theology*:

1. Introductory
2. God and the World
3. God and Israel
4. The Election of Israel
5. The Kingdom of God (Invisible)
6. The Visible Kingdom (Universal)
7. The Kingdom of God (National)
8. The "Law"
9. The Law as Personified in the Literature
10. The Torah in its Aspect of Law (Mizwoth)
11. The Joy of the Law
12. The Zacuth of the Fathers. Imputed Righteousness and Imputed Sin
13. The Law of Holiness and Law of Goodness
14. Sin as Rebellion
15. The Evil Yezer: The Source of Rebellion
16. Man's Victory by the Grace of God, over the Evil Yezer Created by God
17. Forgiveness and Reconciliation with God
18. Repentance: Means of Reconciliation

George Foot Moore, *Judaism in the First Centuries of the Christian Era*:
Introduction

1. Historical
2. The Sources

Part I: Revealed Religion

1. Nationality and Universality
2. The Scriptures

3. The Unwritten Law
4. The Perpetuity of the Law
5. The Synagogue
6. The Schools
7. The Conversion of Gentiles

Part II: The Idea of God

1. God and the World
2. The Character of God
3. Ministers of God
4. The Word of God. The Spirit
5. Majesty and Accessibility of God

Part III: Man, Sin, Atonement

1. The Nature of Man
2. Sin and its Consequences
3. The Origin of Sin
4. Ritual Atonement
5. Repentance
6. The Efficacy of Repentance
7. Motives of Forgiveness
8. Expiatory Suffering

Part IV: Observances

Part V: Morals Part VI: Piety

Part VII: The Hereafter

Ephraim Urbach, *The Sages: Their Concepts and Beliefs* [Hebrew]; *The Sages: The World and Wisdom of the Rabbis of the Talmud* [English Translation]:

1. The Study of the History of the Beliefs and Concepts of the Sages.
2. The Belief in One God
3. The Shekhina—The Presence of God in the world
4. Nearness and Distance—Omnipresent and Heaven

5. The Epithet Gevura [Might] and the Power of God
6. Magic and Miracle
7. The Power of the Divine Name
8. The Celestial Retinue
9. He Who Spoke and the World Came into Being
10. Man
11. On Providence
12. The Written Law and the Oral Law
13. The Commandments
14. Acceptance of the Yoke of the Kingdom of Heaven, Love and Reverence
15. Man's Accounting and the World's Accounting
16. The People of Israel and its Sages
17. On Redemption

Abraham Joshua Heschel, *Torah Min HaShamayim BeAspaqlariah Shel HaDorot*. (The chapter numbering follows *Heavenly Torah as Refracted through the Generations*.):

1. Introduction
2. Two approaches to Torah Exegesis
3. Miracles
4. The Sacrifices
5. The Abode of the Shekhinah
6. Teachings concerning the Shekhinah
7. Afflictions
8. Torah and Life
9. In Awe and Trembling
10. Duties of the Heart
11. Issues of Supreme Importance
12. Scriptural Language Not Befitting God's Dignity
13. The Language of Torah
14. Transcendental and Terrestrial Perspectives
15. Go 'round the Orchard!

16. Beholding the Face of God
17. The Torah that Is in Heaven
18. Moses' Ascent to Heaven
19. The Descent of the Divine Glory
20. Torah from Heaven
21. The Ways of the Sectarians
22. Moses Did Things on His Own Authority
23. Two Methods of Understanding "Thus Says the Lord"
24. Is it Possible That It Was on His Own Say-so
25. The Book of Deuteronomy
26. The Maximalist and Minimalist |Approach
27. Is the Prophet a Partner or a Vessel
28. "See, How Great was Moses' Power!"
29. Moses' Prophecy
30. How the Torah Was Written
31. The Maximalist Approach to the Principle "Torah from Heaven"
32. The Minimalist |Approach to the Principle "Torah from Heaven"
33. Lost Books
34. It Is Not in the Heavens
35. Renewal of Torah
36. Both These and Those are the Words of the Living God
37. Against Multiplying Rules
38. Stringencies and Leniencies
39. Former and Latter Authorities
40. Theology in the Legal Literature
41. Interpersonal Relationships

The two volumes that were published during Heschel's lifetime reach chapter 33.

Schechter's work is based on four axes: God, Israel, Torah, and issues in human nature. The structure of parts one to three of Moore's book is also basically Israel, God, Law, and issues in human nature. Parts four to six deal with the religious life and part seven with the future. The general outline of

Urbach's work also reflects the order of God and the heavenly realm, Man, Torah, their interrelationship, and the future. In this sense, Urbach's work can be understood as the consummation of Schechter's project.

Even though Heschel's first two volumes were published five or so years prior to Urbach's, they made no impact on it. A glance at the chapter headings of Heschel's work shows how much his agenda differs. Two major differences are the chapters on the nature of revelation and the divine pathos, i.e., the Divine reality concerned with human destiny. The former takes up over half of the first two volumes. In this sense, Heschel's work on Rabbinic thought continues his work on Biblical thought. Both focus on the pathos in the divine-human relationship and how revelation results from the interaction of the Divine and human. Although the Biblical work is concerned with the prophetic understanding of the Divine and the Rabbinic work with the Rabbinic understanding of the Torah, the dynamics surprisingly overlap. *The Prophets* ends with "The Dialectic of the Divine-Human Encounter." The chapter that begins the third volume of *Torah Min Ha-Shamayim*, chapter thirty four of *Heavenly Torah,* is entitled "It Is Not in the Heavens," and its opening subsections are "Without Sages There Is No Torah," and "The Sages are the Finishing and the Completion of the Torah" (*The Heavenly Torah*: "The Sages Finish and Complete the Torah"). As prophecy results from the encounter between prophet and God, so Judaism results from the encounter between sage and Torah.

Heschel's work differs from the others also in its modality of presentation. It is more explorative than definitive. Chapters frequently present contrasting sides of an issue under the rubrics of R. Ishmael or R. Akiva, names used sometimes typologically or paradigmatically, sometimes historically. Chapters can stand in dialectical relationship. For example, Chapter 18, "Moses' Ascent to Heaven," contains the subsections: "Rabbi Akiva's View: Moses Was in Heaven" and "Moses Ascended to Heaven" along with "Moses Did Not Ascend to Heaven" and "How Could a Person Ascend to Heaven?" On a more mundane level, Chapter 37 contains a subsection "Against Those Who are Stringent," while chapter 38 has "Beloved Are Prohibitions." Heschel's perspective is infused with this sense of polarity. While he may advocate "a covenant between opposites" he is quite cognizant of the difficulty if not impossibility of holding both ends of a stretched rope. For those who cannot rise to such dialectical heights, realize, entreats Heschel, that a half a loaf is not a full loaf, and no perspective exhausts reality. In this manner Heschel seeks to expands our horizons, keep alternatives open, and prevent premature closure by training us to theologize dialectically. The problem is that someone strong in one pole of the dialectic is unlikely to do full justice to the other. Each pole needs the other to correct itself. Together they exemplify the complexity and fullness of the issue. One never knows when it might be the case when, as the third volume is subtitled and chapter 36 titled, "Both These and Those Are the Words of the Living God." Sometimes, a different perspective, even a competing one, can supplement one's understanding of the truth. Such an understanding can lead to a collaborative pluralism. For a pluralism to be collaborative, however, the commonality of goals must overshadow the divergence of means. With non-finality as his watchword, Heschel invites the reader to engage in the ongoing Rabbinic quest for the meaning of revelation and of God's involvement with humanity.

Back in 1968, after Heschel had seen my essay, "Non-violence and the Talmud," he asked me to undertake the translation of *Torah Min HaShamayim*. I protested my inability. I did not see how one could translate a work in which expression after expression rang with echoes of other expressions. To translate the work would be like translating evocative poetry into dry prose or transposing a symphony into a melody. Besides the problem of mapping a polysemous Hebrew into one-dimensional English "there is," as Tucker notes in his Preface, "the matter of capturing not only the meaning of the words but the cultural bells that they ring when put into combination." The answer is, as Tucker and Levin have so well executed, an annotated translation providing the reader with the cultural bells that ring in the ears of the intended Hebrew reader.

MONIKA ADAMCZYK-GARBOWSKA MARIA CURIE-SKŁODOWSKA, UNIVERSITY LUBLIN (POLAND)

Review of *The Ineffable Name of God: Man: Poems*, Abraham Joshua Heschel. Translated from the Yiddish by Morton M. Leifman. Introduction by Edward K. Kaplan. New York and London: Continuum: 2004.

In his autobiographical novel *Ven Yash iz geforn* (1938), Jacob Glatstein, a renowned Yiddish poet and critic, reminisces on his youth in Lublin just before the outbreak of World War I. He recalls how he and his friends wrote poetry and imagined themselves as romantic heroes from European literature. It is not unusual that young, sensitive people write poetry, and in Europe in the 1920s and 1930s it was perhaps even more common than anywhere else. It is no wonder that Abraham Heschel (1907–1972), at that time a young sensitive student of Hasidic background, exposed to vibrant secular life in Vilna where he studied in the Real Gymnasium before entering universities in Berlin, tried his hand at poetry. While there he was loosely associated with the Yung Vilna group. His poetry was more traditional, and so were his views compared with some very radical members of that group.

Heschel's oeuvre is well known to American readers. He had a great impact on shaping the image of pre-war East European Jewish life through his poetic prose. Even if readers of his prose do not know about his youthful poetic attempts, it should not come as a surprise that he had such aspirations. Now, thanks to this beautiful bilingual edition translated by Morton J. Leifman, with a preface by Edward K. Kaplan, the English-speaking reader has a chance to get to know Heschel's poetic work, and readers who know Yiddish can take pleasure in comparing the two versions. As Kaplan puts it: "Poetry can become a form of prayer, sharpening vision, transforming lives. Prayer can become poetry, emancipating words that illuminate the world's fullness." The latter was true of Heschel, for whom poetry was undoubtedly a way of rendering his thoughts.

The sixty-six poems are grouped in six sections. The titles of most of them testify to their religious, philosophical, and contemplative character: for example, "Man is Holy," "Bearing Witness," "Between Me and the World," "Repairing the World." But there is also the mysterious "Lady in a Dream," to which ten poems are dedicated (some with erotic content), as well as those devoted to nature grouped in the section entitled "Nature Pantomimes." Some poems are not very original in their philosophical content and express typical dilemmas of a young idealist looking at injustice and the crisis of values. For example, in the poem "Untitled" from the part "Repairing the World," Heschel talks about human selfishness and lack of faith and wonders if poetry is still possible in a world where "man sentences man to death" and "children suffer hardships" and where "no one knows what's good, what's right."[120]

But in others—for example, "People's Eyes Wait" from the section "Man Is Holy"—he foreshadows his future vocation in the following expression of mission:

> Shamed brothers beg my help,
> Deceived sisters dream of consolation.
>
> And I, with stubborn boldness have promised
> That I will increase tenderness in this world—
>
> And it seems to me that I will, in time
> Move on through this earth

---

120. Heschel, *ineffable*, 181.

With the brightness of all the stars
In my eyes!¹²¹

Paradoxically, some of Heschel's poems sound better in the English translation, in which they are devoid of the rhymes which are not always very fortunate in the original. This concerns mainly poems with philosophical and lyrical contents. For example, "In the Palace of Your Face" opens in its English rendition with the lines: "Your face is my palace,/Your eyes—blue, near—/A pillow for my soul."[122]

Perhaps not very original, perhaps a bit too lofty for modern sensibilities, but still acceptable as poetry from earlier times. Compare these lines with the Yiddish version: "Dayn gezikht iz mayn palats/Oygn nonte bloe dayne—/A kishn far neshome mayne."

Those grammatical rhymes (*mayne—dayne*), not very elaborate, make it sound like a very youthful poetry. No wonder that the well-known Yiddish poet Moshe Kulbak was supposed to have said after reading some of Heschel's verse that he would never become a great poet, but he would become a good philosopher. The same might be true of "Snow on the Fields": "The gentle snow/Falls like sawdust. /Still, like holy/Nomads,/Comrades of my words."[123]

In English, this fragment sounds and looks like a piece of Imagist poetry, reminiscent of haiku. In the Yiddish original we have a marching rhyme: "Shtil vi heylike/Nomadn, /Mayne verters/Kameradn."[124]

On the other hand, there are some poems which do not come across well in translation. This is especially true of those rooted in Jewish folklore, like the one about *shlimazl*, the proverbial "ne'er do well." Devoid of rhymes and rhythm, the poem does not make much sense. Let us compare the two versions, this time starting with the Yiddish original:

> Di mame flegt shreyen: —a kholere,
> Dos hot a pisk, freseruk!
> Hob ikh genekhtikt oyfn bruk
> Un gezingen "bayadere."
>
> [Zits ikh mir azoy un trakht:
> Es iz mir kalt, es iz yitzt nakht.
> Un emetz iz dokh fort gerekht.
> Nor got! Nor mame! Mir iz shlekht . . .[125]

---

121. Heschel, *Ineffable*, 39.
122. Heschel, *Ineffable*, 93.
123. Heschel, *Ineffable*, 157.
124. Heschel, *Ineffable*, 156.
125. Heschel, *Ineffable*, 178.

In this case the simple rhymes and rhythm created by means of short lines of equal length are most fitting. Furthermore, the two rhyming words in the first stanza quoted above (*kholere—bayadere*) require footnotes. The first is a common curse derived from Polish and the other is a very popular air from an operetta with music by Emmerich Kálmán and libretto by Julius Brammer and Alfred Grünwald. Overall, in the Yiddish original we get a grotesque image of a *shlimazl* singing an operetta song on the sidewalk. We could imagine this poem as a song sung in a pre-war cabaret. In English it seems rather awkward, and for this it is hard to blame the translator. Some works are simply untranslatable:

> My mother used to scream a curse at me—"Cholera!
> This one's got a mouth, that glutton!"
> I spent the night on a cobblestone pavement
> And sang a *Bayadere*.
>
> I sit like this and think:
> "I'm cold, it's night now.
> And someone is certainly right . . .
> But, God! But Momma! I'm so bad off . . .

Also, some concepts are simply untranslatable. How should one render *moyre-shkhoyre* (in "Promise")? In English we have "black fear" with a note that this is a Yiddish idiom referring to deep depression, but this is not the same as the sound and tenor of the original expression. Or with *di klamke*, which means a door handle, we can imagine it trembling when it is compared to a heartbeat.[126] But its American counterpart, the doorknob, which it is hard to imagine trembling, is very rare in East European households.

Heschel's poetry was first published in Warsaw in 1933. One should admire the care given to the editing and preparation of this new edition of the book. Everything was kept as in the first edition, even the original spelling as it was used before standardization in 1935–1936. But the cover of the modern bilingual edition is slightly misleading. It is illustrated with a photograph of Warsaw supposedly from the 1920s according to a note on the jacket. However. in the foreground of this half-empty sleepy street scene we see shop signs in Russian, which obviously means that this is a picture from before World War I, when Warsaw was still under Russian partition. The Warsaw in which Heschel wrote and published his poems was quite different, much more cosmopolitan and vibrant. The Warsaw of Heschel, with its Jewish intellectual life, was well-described by Heschel's contemporaries Melech Ravitch, Isaac Bashevis Singer, and Zusman Segalovitch in

---

126. Heschel, *Ineffable*, 40, 118.

their recollections of the Yiddish Writers and Journalists Association at 13 Tlomackie Street, where Heschel turned for advice as early as 1924 with his first poetic attempts.

It is rather obvious that this volume is a kind of tribute to Heschel as a philosopher. One is inclined to read these youthful poems more as a curiosity or as a footnote to Heschel's writing than for their poetic quality. The Polish poet and Nobel Prize laureate Wisława Szymborska in a humorous tribute to her sister praises her for not writing poetry. After having read this volume we do not need to regret that at a certain stage Heschel stopped writing poetry and found his voice in different genres.

Bibliography

Ballard, Bruce W. "Heidegger, Otto and the Phenomenology of Awe." *Philosophy Today* 32 (Spring 1988) 62–74.
Banks, Gary Michael. "Rabbi Heschel Through Christian Eyes" *Conservative Judaism* 50, 2–3 (Winter/Spring 1998) 100–11.
Barnard, David. "Abraham Heschel's Attitude toward Religion and Psychology." *Journal of Religion* 63, 1 (January 1983) 26–43.
Bar-Sela, Shraga. "Yahaduto Nanevuit-Meshiḥit shel Hillel Zeitlin." *Da'at.* 26 (1991) 109–24.
Ben-Horin, Meir "The Ineffable: Critical Notes on Neo-Mysticism." *Jewish Quarterly Review* 46, 4 (1956) 321–54.
———. "Of New Space and Time." *Judaism,* 8, 1 (Winter 1959) 28–32.
———. "Via Mystica." *Jewish Quarterly Review* 45, 3 (January 1955) 249–58.
Bennett, John C. "Agent of God's Compassion." *America* 128, 9 (March 1973) 205.
———. "Heschel's Significance for Protestants." In *No Religion is an Island: Abraham Joshua Heschel and Interreligious Dialogue,* edited by Harold Kasimow and Byron L. Sherwin, 124–34. Maryknoll, NY: Orbis, 1991.
Berger, Alan L. *Children of Job.* Albany: State University of New York Press, 1997.
Berkovits, Eliezer. "Dr. A. J. Heschel's Theology of Pathos." *Tradition,* 6, 2 (Spring-Summer 1964) 67–104.
Bialik, Hayim Nahman. *Collected Letters* [Hebrew]. Tel Aviv: Dvir, 1939.
Blumenthal, David R. "Abraham Joshua Heschel: The Inadequacy of the Ecumenical Perspective." *Journal of Ecumenical Studies,* 29, 2 (Spring 1992) 249–53.
Borodowski, Alfredo Fabio. "Hasidic Sources in Heschel's Conception of Prayer." *Conservative Judaism* 50, 2–3 (Winter/Spring 1998) 36–47.
Borowitz, Eugene. *Choices in Modern Jewish Thought: A Partisan Guide.* West Orange, NJ: Behrman, 1983/1995.
———. *Judaism After Modernity: Papers from a Decade of Fruition.* Lanham, MD: University Press of America, 1999.
———. *A New Jewish Theology in the Making.* Philadelphia: Westminster Press, 1968.
———. *Renewing the Covenant: A Theology for the Postmodern Jew.* Philadelphia: Jewish Publication Society, 1991.

———. *Studies in the Meaning of Judaism*. Philadelphia: Jewish Publication Society, 2002.

Bregman, Marc. "Mishnah and LXX as Mystery: An Example of Jewish-Christian Polemic in the Byzantine Period." In *Continuity and Renewal: Jews and Judaism in Byzantine-Christian Palestine*, edited by Lee I. Levine, 333–42. Jerusalem: Dinur Center for Jewish History, 2004.

Breslauer, S. Daniel. *The Impact of Abraham Joshua Heschel as Jewish Leader in the American Jewish Community from the 1960s to His Death: A Social, Psychological and Intellectual Study*. PhD diss., Brandeis University (1974).

———. "Kaplan, Abraham Joshua Heschel, and Martin Buber: Three Approaches to Jewish Revival." In *The American Judaism of Mordecai M. Kaplan*, edited by Emanuel Goldsmith, et al., 234–53. New York: New York University Press, 1990.

———. "Spinoza's Theologico-Political Treatise and A. J. Heschel's Theology of Biblical Language." *CCAR Journal* 24, 1 (1977) 19–26.

———. "Theology and Depth-Theology: A Heschel Distinction." *CCAR Journal* 21, 3 (1974) 81–86.

Bridges, Hal. *American Mysticism from William James to Zen*. New York: Harper and Row, 1970.

Brill, Alan. "Aggadic Man: The Poetry and Rabbinic Judaism of Abraham Joshua Heschel." *Meorot* 6, 1 (2007) 2–21.

Buber, Martin. *Torat Hanevi'im*. Tel Aviv: Dvir, 1961.

Carroll, James. *Constantine's Sword: The Church and the Jews: A History*. Boston: Houghton Mifflin, 2001.

Chester, Michael A. *Divine Pathos and Human Being: The Theology of Abraham Joshua Heschel*. London: Vallentine Mitchell, 2005.

———. "Heschel and the Christians." *Journal of Ecumenical Studies* 38, 2–3 (Spring-Summer 2001) 246–70.

Cohen, Adir. "Torah min Hashamayim." *Hahinukh* 2–3 (1981) 174–83.

Cohen, Arthur A. *The Natural and Supernatural Jew*. New York: Pantheon, 1962.

Cohen, Gerson D. "Abraham Joshua Heschel: The Interpreter of Classical Jewish Thought." *Proceedings of the Rabbinical Assembly* 45 (1983) 105–11.

Croner, Helga, ed. *Stepping Stones to Further Jewish-Christian Relations*. London and New York: Stimulus, 1977.

Davidovich, Adina. *Religion and a Province of Meaning: The Kantian Foundations of Modern Theology*. Minneapolis: Augsburg Fortress, 1993.

Davies, William David. "Conscience, Scholar, Witness." *America* 128, 9 (March 10, 1973) 213–15.

Dolna, Bernhard. *An die Gegenwart Gottes preisgegeben: Abraham Joshua Heschel Leben und Werk*. Mainz: Grünewald, 2001.

Dresner, Samuel H. "Abraham Joshua Heschel: The Man." In *Prayer and Politics: The Twin Poles of Abraham Joshua Heschel*, edited by Joshua Stampfer. Portland, OR: Institute for Judaic Studies, 1985.

———. *Heschel, Hasidism and Halakha*. New York: Fordham University Press, 1992.

Dresner, Samuel H., ed. Abraham J. Heschel *The Circle of the Baal Shem Tov: Studies in Hasidim*. Chicago: University of Chicago Press, 1985.

Eisen, Arnold. "Prophecy as Vocation: New Light on the Thought and Practice of Abraham Joshua Heschel." [Hebrew]. In *The Path of the Spirit: The Eliezer Schweid*

Jubilee Volume, volume 2, edited by Yehoda Amir, 835–50. Jerusalem: Magnes, 2005.

———. "Re-reading Heschel on the Commandments." *Modern Judaism* 9, 1 (February 1989) 1–33.

———. "Seeing the World from God's Perspective: A.J. Heschel's Prophetic Witness." *Tikkun* 13, 4 (1998) 70–72.

Eisen, Robert. "A. J. Heschel's Rabbinic Theology as a Response to the Holocaust." *Modern Judaism* 23, 3 (2003) 211–25.

Even-Chen, Alexander. "Mysticism and Prophecy According to Abraham Joshua Heschel." *Kabbalah* 5 (2000) 359–70.

Fackenheim, Emil L. Review of *God in Search of Man*, by Abraham Joshua Heschel. *Conservative Judaism* 15, 1 (Fall 1960) 50–53.

———. Review of *Man Is Not Alone*, by Abraham Joshua Heschel. *Judaism* 1, 1 (January 1952) 85–89.

———. *To Mend the World: Foundations of Future Jewish Thought*. New York: Schocken, 1982.

Faierstein, Morris M. "Abraham Joshua Heschel and the Holocaust." *Modern Judaism* 19 (1999) 255–75.

———. "'God's Needs for the Commandments' in Medieval Kabbalah." *Conservative Judaism* 36, 1 (Fall 1982) 45–59.

Fernando, Antony. "An Asian Perspective: The Novelty of Heschel's Views on Interreligious Dialogue." In *No Religion is an Island: Abraham Joshua Heschel and Interreligious Dialogue*, edited by Harold Kasimow and Byron L. Sherwin, 175–84. Maryknoll, NY: Orbis, 1991.

Fisher, Eugene J. "Heschel's Impact on Catholic-Jewish Relations." In *No Religion is an Island: Abraham Joshua Heschel and Interreligious Dialogue*, edited by Harold Kasimow and Byron L. Sherwin, 110–123. Maryknoll, NY: Orbis, 1991.

Fleischer, Eva. "Heschel's Significance for Jewish-Christian Relations." In *Abraham Joshua Heschel: Exploring His Life and Thought*, edited by John C. Merkle, 142–64. London: Collier Macmillan, 1985.

Fox, Marvin. "Heschel, Intuition and the Halakhah." *Tradition* 3, 1 (Fall 1960) 5–15.

———. Review of *God in Search of Man*, by Abraham Joshua Heschel. *Judaism* 6, 1 (Winter 1957) 77–81.

Freedman, Harry, and Maurice Simon, trans. *Midrash Rabbah*. London: Soncino Press, 1951.

Freidenreich, David M. "The Use of Islamic Sources in Saadiah Gaon's Tafsir of the Torah." *Jewish Quarterly Review* 93, 3–4 (2003) 353–95.

Friedman, Maurice. "Abraham Heschel among Contemporary Philosophers." *Philosophy Today* 18 (Winter 1974) 293–305.

———. "Divine Need and Human Wonder: The Philosophy of Abraham Joshua Heschel." *Judaism* 25, 1 (Winter 1976) 65–78.

———. Review of *The Prophets*, by Abraham Joshua Heschel. *Judaism* 13, 1 (Winter 1964) 117.

———. *You Are My Witnesses: Abraham Joshua Heschel and Elie Wiesel*. New York: Farrar, Straus, and Giroux, 1987.

Frymer-Kensky, Tikva, et al., eds. *Christianity in Jewish Terms*. Boulder: Westview Press, 2000.

Galli, Barbara E. "Transmissibility of the Ineffable: Convergence in Heschel, Rosenzweig, Benjamin." Unpublished paper given at the 30th AJS Conference (December 1998).

Gillman, Neil. "Epistemological Tensions in Heschel's Thought." *Conservative Judaism* 50, 2–3 (Winter/Spring 1998) 77–83.

Glatzer, Nahum N. Review of *The Sabbath*, by Abraham Joshua Heschel. *Judaism* 1, 3 (1952) 284–285.

Goldberg, Harvey E. "Becoming History: Perspectives on the Seminary Faculty at Mid-Century." In *Tradition Renewed: A History of the Jewish Theological Seminary*, edited by Jack Wertheimer, 1:355–437. New York: Jewish Theological Seminary of America, 1997.

Goldberg, Hillel. "Abraham Joshua Heschel and His Times." *Midstream* 28, 4 (April 1982) 36–42.

———. *From Berlin to Slobodka: Jewish Transition Figures from Eastern Europe*. Hoboken, NJ: Ktav, 1989.

Goldman, Norman S. "The Metapsychology of Abraham J. Heschel." *Journal of Religion and Health*, 14 (1975) 106–12.

Goldstein, Jeffrey. "Buber's Misunderstanding of Heidegger: Being and the Living God." *Philosophy Today* 22 (Summer 1978) 156–167.

Goldy, Robert G. *The Emergence of Jewish Theology in America*. Bloomington: Indiana University Press, 1990.

Gorny, Yosef. *Between Auschwitz and Jerusalem*. Tel Aviv: Am Oved, 1998.

Goshen-Gottstein, Alon. "Judaisms and Incarnational Theologies: Mapping Out the Parameters of Dialogue." *Journal of Ecumenical Studies* 39, 3–4 (2002) 219–47.

Graeber, Bruce S. "Heschel and the Philosophy of Time." *Conservative Judaism* 33, 3 (Spring 1980) 44–56.

Green, Arthur. "Abraham Joshua Heschel: Recasting Hasidism for Moderns." *Tikkun* 14, 1 (1999) 63–69.

———. "Early Hasidism: Some Old/New Questions." In *Hasidism Reappraised*, edited by Ada Rapoport-Albert, 441–46. London: Littman Library of Jewish Civilization, 1996.

———. "Reply to Alon Goshen Gottstein." *Kabbalah* 5 (2000) 201–6.

———. "Three Warsaw Mystics." *Jerusalem Studies in Jewish Thought* XIII (1996) 1–58.

———. "Three Warsaw Mystics." In *Kolot Rabim: Sefer Hazikaron Le-Rivka Shatz-Uffenheimer* [Hebrew], edited by Rachel Elior and Joseph Dan, 1–58. Jerusalem: Hebrew University, 1996.

Greenberg, Irving. *The Jewish Way: Living the Holidays*. New York: Summit Books, 1988.

———. *The Third Era of Jewish History: Power and Politics (Perspective), A Clal Thesis*. New York: National Jewish Resource Center, 1980.

Griffith, Sidney Harrison. "Sharing the Faith of Abraham: The 'Credo' of Louis Massignon." *Islam and Christian-Muslim Relations* 8, 2 (1997) 193–210.

Hacohen, Aviad. "Schlemiel, Schlemazel . . ." [Hebrew]. *Ha'aretz* (April 24, 2000) Literature and Culture Section, 1.

Hartman, David. "Abraham Joshua Heschel: A Heroic Witness to Religious Pluralism." In *A Heart of Many Rooms: Celebrating the Many Voices Within Judaism*, 169–92. Woodstock, VT: Jewish Lights, 1999.

———. *Conflicting Visions: Spiritual Possibilities of Modern Israel*. New York: Schocken Books, 1990.

———. *A Heart of Many Rooms: Celebrating the Many Voices Within Judaism*. Woodstock, VT: Jewish Lights, 1999.

———. "Heschel's Religious Passion." In *Conflicting Visions: Spiritual Possibilities of Modern Israel*, 173–83. New York: Schocken Books, 1990.

———. "Prayer and Religious Consciousness: An Analysis of Jewish Prayer in the Works of Joseph B. Soloveitchik, Yeshayahu Leibowitz, and Abraham Joshua Heschel." *Modern Judaism* 23, 2 (May 2003) 105–25.

Hartshorne, Charles. *Omnipotence and Other Theological Mistakes*. Albany: State University of New York Press, 1984.

Harvey, Warren Zev. "The Return of Maimonideanism." *Jewish Social Studies* 42, 3–4 (Summer–Fall 1980) 249–68.

———. "Why Maimonides Was Not a *Mutakallim*." In *Perspectives on Maimonides*, edited by, Joel L. Kraemer, 105–14. New York: Oxford University Press, 1991.

Herberg, Will. "Jewish Theology in the Post-Modern World." *Judaism* 12, 3 (1963) 364–370.

Heschel, Abraham Joshua. "After Majdanek: On Aaron Zeitlin's New Poems." [Yiddish]. *Yiddisher Kemfer* 29, 771 (October 1, 1948) 28–30.

———. "An Analysis of Piety." In *Moral Grandeur and Spiritual Audacity: Essays by Abraham Joshua Heschel* edited by Susannah Heschel, 305–17. New York: Farrar, Straus and Giroux, 1996.

———. *Between God and Man: An Interpretation of Judaism*. New York: Free, 1959.

———. "Choose Life!" In *Moral Grandeur and Spiritual Audacity: Essays by Abraham Joshua Heschel* edited by Susannah Heschel, 251–56. New York: Farrar, Straus and Giroux, 1996.

———. "Death as Homecoming." In *Moral Grandeur and Spiritual Audacity: Essays by Abraham Joshua Heschel* edited by Susannah Heschel, 366–78. New York: Farrar, Straus and Giroux, 1996.

———. *Die Prophetie*. Berlin: Arthur Collignon, 1936.

———. *Don Jizchak Abravanel*. Berlin: Erich Reiss Verlag, 1937

———. *The Earth Is the Lord's*. New York: Farrar, Straus and Giroux, 1978.

———. *The Earth is the Lord's*. New York: Henry Schuman, 1950.

———. "The Eastern European Era in Jewish History." *YIVO Annual of Jewish Social Science* 1 (1946) 86–106.

———. "Existence and Celebration." In *Moral Grandeur and Spiritual Audacity: Essays by Abraham Joshua Heschel* edited by Susannah Heschel, 18–32. New York: Farrar, Straus and Giroux, 1996.

———. "Faith." In *Moral Grandeur and Spiritual Audacity: Essays by Abraham Joshua Heschel* edited by Susannah Heschel, 328–39. New York: Farrar, Straus and Giroux, 1996.

———. "From Mission to Dialogue?" *Conservative Judaism* 21 (1967) 1–11.

———. *God in Search of Man*. New York: Farrar, Straus and Giroux, New York, 1978.

———. *Heavenly Torah: As Reflected through the Generations*. Edited and translated by Gordon Tucker. New York: Continuum, 2005.

———. "The Holy Dimension." In *Moral Grandeur and Spiritual Audacity: Essays by Abraham Joshua Heschel* edited by Susannah Heschel, 318–27. New York: Farrar, Straus and Giroux, 1996.

———. *The Ineffable Name of God: Man*. Translated by Morton M. Leifman. London: Continuum, 2004.

———. *The Insecurity of Freedom: Essays in Applied Religion*. Philadelphia: Jewish Publication Society, 1966.

———. *Israel: An Echo of Eternity*. New York: Farrar, Straus and Giroux, 1974.

———. *Israel: Present and Eternity*. Jerusalem, 1973.

———. "Jewish Theology." In *Moral Grandeur and Spiritual Audacity: Essays by Abraham Joshua Heschel* edited by Susannah Heschel, 154-63. New York: Farrar, Straus and Giroux, 1996.

———. *Kotzk: The Struggle for Integrity*. [Yiddish]. Tel Aviv: Menorah, 1973.

———. *Man Is Not Alone*. New York: Farrar, Straus, Giroux, 1984.

———. *Man Is Not Alone*. New York: The Jewish Publication Society of America, 1951.

———. "Man's Quest for God." *Judaism* 4, 2 (Spring 1955) 180–182.

———. *Man's Quest for God*. Santa Fe: Aurora Press, 1998.

———. *Man's Quest for God: Studies in Prayer and Symbolism*. New York: Scribner, 1954.

———. "The Meaning of Repentance." In *Moral Grandeur and Spiritual Audacity: Essays by Abraham Joshua Heschel* edited by Susannah Heschel, 68–70. New York: Farrar, Straus and Giroux, 1996.

———. "The Meaning of This War." In *Moral Grandeur and Spiritual Audacity: Essays by Abraham Joshua Heschel* edited by Susannah Heschel, 209–12. New York: Farrar, Straus and Giroux, 1996.

———. "The Mystical Element in Judaism." In *Moral Grandeur and Spiritual Audacity: Essays by Abraham Joshua Heschel* edited by Susannah Heschel, 164-84. New York: Farrar, Straus and Giroux, 1996.

———. "No Religion Is an Island." *Union Seminary Quarterly* (January 1966) 117–34.

———. "No Religion Is an Island." In *No Religion is an Island: Abraham Joshua Heschel and Interreligious Dialogue*, edited by Harold Kasimow and Byron L. Sherwin, 3–22. Maryknoll, NY: Orbis, 1991.

———. "No Religion Is an Island." In *Moral Grandeur and Spiritual Audacity: Essays by Abraham Joshua Heschel* edited by Susannah Heschel, 235–50. New York: Farrar, Straus and Giroux, 1996.

———. "On Jews in the Soviet Union." In *The Insecurity of Freedom: Essays in Applied Religion*, 262–73. Philadelphia: Jewish Publication Society, 1966.

———. "On the Holy Spirit in the Middle Ages (until the time of Maimonides)." In *Alexander Marx Jubilee Volume* [Hebrew Section] edited by Saul Lieberman, 117–208. New York: Jewish Theological Seminary, 1950.

———. *A Passion for Truth*. New York: Farrar, Straus and Giroux, 1974.

———. "*Pikuach Neshama*: To Save a Soul." In *Moral Grandeur and Spiritual Audacity: Essays by Abraham Joshua Heschel* edited by Susannah Heschel, 54–67. New York: Farrar, Straus and Giroux, 1996.

———. "The Plight of Russian Jews." In *Moral Grandeur and Spiritual Audacity: Essays by Abraham Joshua Heschel* edited by Susannah Heschel, 213–15. New York: Farrar, Straus and Giroux, 1996.

———. "Prophetic Inspiration." In *To Grow in Wisdom: An Anthology of Abraham Joshua Heschel* edited by Jacob Neusner and Noam M. M. Neusner, 53–69. Lanham, New York, London: Madison, 1990.

———. *The Prophets*. 2 vols. New York: Harper & Row, 1975.

———. "Reason and Revelation in Saadia's Philosophy." *Jewish Quarterly Review* New Series, 34, 4 (April 1944) 391–408

———. "The Reasons for My Involvement in the Peace Movement." In *Moral Grandeur and Spiritual Audacity: Essays by Abraham Joshua Heschel* edited by Susannah Heschel, 224–26. New York: Farrar, Straus and Giroux, 1996.

———. "Religion and Race." In *The Insecurity of Freedom: Essays in Applied Religion*, 85–100. Philadelphia: Jewish Publication Society, 1966.

———. "The Religious Message." In *Religion in America: Original Essays on Religion in a Free Society*, edited by John Cogley, John, 244–71. New York: Meridian Book, 1958.

———. *The Sabbath*. New York: Farrar, Straus, Giroux, 1975.

———. "Sacred Image of Man." In *The Insecurity of Freedom: Essays in Applied Religion*, 150–67. Philadelphia: Jewish Publication Society, 1966.

———. "Teaching Religion to American Jews." In *Moral Grandeur and Spiritual Audacity: Essays by Abraham Joshua Heschel* edited by Susannah Heschel, 148–53. New York: Farrar, Straus and Giroux, 1996.

———. "A Time for Renewal." In *Moral Grandeur and Spiritual Audacity: Essays by Abraham Joshua Heschel* edited by Susannah Heschel, 47–53. New York: Farrar, Straus and Giroux, 1996.

———. "To Be a Jew: What Is It?" In *Moral Grandeur and Spiritual Audacity: Essays by Abraham Joshua Heschel* edited by Susannah Heschel, 3–11. New York: Farrar, Straus and Giroux, 1996.

———. "Toward an Understanding of Halakhah." In *Moral Grandeur and Spiritual Audacity: Essays by Abraham Joshua Heschel* edited by Susannah Heschel, 127–45. New York: Farrar, Straus and Giroux, 1996.

———. "The Two Great Traditions: The Sephardim and the Ashkenazim." *Commentary* 5:5 (May 1948) 416–22.

———. "The White Man on Trial." In *The Insecurity of Freedom: Essays in Applied Religion*, 101–11. Philadelphia: Jewish Publication Society, 1966.

———. *Who is Man?* Stanford: Stanford University Press, 2004.

———. "Yisrael: Am, Eretz, Medinah: Ideological Evaluation of Israel and the Diaspora." *Rabbinical Assembly of America Proceedings* 22 (1958) 118–36.

Heschel, Susannah. "My Father." In *No Religion is an Island: Abraham Joshua Heschel and Interreligious Dialogue*, edited by Harold Kasimow and Byron L. Sherwin, 23–41. Maryknoll, NY: Orbis, 1991.

———. "Social Justice—The Theme of Heschel." In *Prayer and Politics: The Twin Poles of Abraham Joshua Heschel*, edited by Joshua Stampfer. Portland, OR: Institute for Judaic Studies, 1985.

———. "Theological Affinities in the Writings of Abraham Joshua Heschel and Martin Luther King, Jr." *Conservative Judaism* 50, 2–3 (1998) 126–43.

Heschel, Susannah, ed. *Moral Grandeur and Spiritual Audacity: Essays by Abraham Joshua Heschel*. New York: Farrar, Straus and Giroux, 1996.

Holtz, Avraham. "Hillel Zeitlin: Critic, Mystic, Social Architect." *Conservative Judaism* 20, 3 (1965) 50–65.

———. "Religion and the Arts in the Theology of Abraham Joshua Heschel." *Conservative Judaism* 28, 1 (1973) 27–39.

Horowitz, Rivka. "Abraham Joshua Heschel on Prayer and His Hasidic Sources." *Modern Judaism* 19 (1999) 293–310.

———. "David Hartman, Paul Van Buren and Franz Rosenzweig on Jewish-Christian Dialogue." In *Judaism and Modernity: The Religious Philosophy of David Hartman*, edited by Jonathan W. Malino, 241–69. Aldershot: Ashgate, 2004.

Hunsinger, George. *How to Read Karl Barth: The Shape of His Theology*. Oxford: Oxford University Press, 1991.

Husserl, Edmund. *Ideas Pertaining to a Pure Phenomenology and to a Phenomenological Philosophy*. Dordrecht: Kulwer, 1982.

Hyman, James. *Alienation and the Trope of Meaning*. PhD diss., Stanford University, 1996.

———. "Meaningfulness, the Ineffable and the Commandments." *Conservative Judaism* 50, 2–3 (1998) 84–99.

Idel, Moshe. *Kabbalah: New Perspectives*. New Haven & London: Yale University Press, 1988.

Ignatowski, Grzegorz. *Kościoły wobec przejawów antysemityzmu*. [Polish]. Lodz: 1999.

International Council of Christians and Jews. "The Ten Points of Seelisburg." In *An Address to the Churches*. Seelisberg, Switzerland, 1947. http://www.jcrelations.net/An_Address_to_the_Churches__Seelisberg__Switzerland__1947.2370.0.html?id=960

Jaeger, John. "Abraham Heschel and the Theology of Jurgen Moltmann." *Perspectives in Religious Studies* 24 (Summer 1997) 167–79.

Jeanrond, Werner G. *Theological Hermeneutics: Development and Significance*. London: Macmillan, 1991.

Kahana, Menahem I. "Midreshi Halakhah." In *Encyclopedia Judaica*. Keter, Israel: Judaica Multimedia.

Kaplan, Edward K. "The American Mission of Abraham Joshua Heschel." In *The Americanization of the Jews*, edited by Robert M. Seltzer and Norman J. Cohen, 335–74. New York: New York University Press, 1995.

———. "Confronting the Holocaust." In *Holiness in Words: Abraham Joshua Heschel's Poetics of Piety*, 115–31. Albany: State University of New York Press, 1996.

———. "Heschel as Philosopher: Phenomenology and the Rhetoric of Revelation." *Modern Judaism* 21 (2001) 1–14.

———. *Holiness in Words: Abraham Joshua Heschel's Poetics of Piety*. Albany: State University of New York Press, 1996.

———. "Mysticism and Despair in Abraham J. Heschel's Religious Thought." *Journal of Religion*, 57 (1977) 33–47.

———. "Readiness Before God: Abraham Heschel in Europe." *Conservative Judaism* 50, 2–3 (Winter/Spring 1998) 22–35.

———. "Sacred Versus Symbolic Religion: Abraham Joshua Heschel and Martin Buber." *Modern Judaism* 14 (1994) 213–31.

———. "The Spiritual Radicalism of Abraham Joshua Heschel." *Conservative Judaism* 28 (1973) 40–49.

Kaplan, Edward K., and Samuel H. Dresner. *Abraham Joshua Heschel: Prophetic Witness*. New Haven: Yale University Press, 1998.

Kaplan, Mordecai M. *Judaism as a Civilization*. New York, London: Thomas Yoseloff, 1934.

Kasimow, Harold. "Abraham Joshua Heschel and Interreligious Dialogue." *Journal of Ecumenical Studies* 18, 3 (1981) 423–34.

———. "Heschel's Prophetic Vision of Religious Pluralism." In *No Religion is an Island: Abraham Joshua Heschel and Interreligious Dialogue,* edited by Harold Kasimow and Byron L. Sherwin, 79–96. Maryknoll, NY: Orbis, 1991.

Kasimow, Harold, and Byron L. Sherwin, eds. *No Religion is an Island: Abraham Joshua Heschel and Interreligious Dialogue.* Maryknoll, NY: Orbis, 1991.

———. *No Religion is an Island* [Polish edition] *Żadna religia nie jest samotną wyspą. Abraham Joshua Heschel i dialog międzyreligijny.* Krakow: WAM, 2005.

Katz, Steven T. "Abraham Joshua Heschel and Hasidism." *Journal of Jewish Studies* 31 (1980) 82–104.

———. "Eliezer Berkovits and Modern Jewish Philosophy." In *Post-Holocaust Dialogues: Critical Studies in Modern Jewish Thought,* 94–140. New York: New York University Press, 1983.

Kaufman, William E. "A. J. Heschel, Hasidic Prayer, and Process Philosophy." *Proceedings of the Rabbinical Assembly of America* 45 (1983) 163–68.

———. "Judaism and Process Theology: Parallel Concerns and Challenging Tensions." In *Jewish Theology and Process Thought,* edited by Sandra Lubarsky and David Griffin, 59–74. Albany: State University of New York Press, 1996.

Kimelman, Reuven. "Rabbis Joseph B. Soloveitchik and Abraham Joshua Heschel on Jewish-Christian Relations." *Modern Judaism* 24 (2004) 251–71. An electronic version in *The Edah Journal* 4, 2 (2004). http://www.edah.org/backend/coldfusion/displayissue.cfm?volume=4&issue=2

King, Martin Luther, Jr. "Conversation with Martin Luther King." *Conservative Judaism* 22 (Spring 1968) 1–19.

Klapper, Naomi (Wilon). *On Being Human: A Comparative Study of A. J. Heschel and Viktor Frankl.* PhD diss., Jewish Theological Seminary of America, 1974.

Klausner, Israel, et al. "Elijah ben Solomon Zalman." In *Encyclopaedia Judaica 2nd edition* 6:341–46. http://www.jevzajcg.me/enciklopedia/Encyclopaedia%20Judaica,%20v.%202006%20(Dr-Feu).pdf

Klein, Roger C. "Abraham Joshua Heschel: Universal Hasidism." In *Modern Jewish Thinkers: An Introduction,* edited by Alan T. Levinson, 255–65. Northvale NJ: Jason Aronson, 2000.

Kolberg, Tamar. "From Research to Theology in *Torah min Hashamayim* by A. J. Heschel" [Hebrew], *Daat* 31 (1993) 65–82.

Krajewski, Stanislaw. "Christian-Jewish Dialogue: Heschel, *Dabru Emet* and We." In *Słowo pojednania, a Festschrift for Michal Czajkowski.* Warsaw, 2004.

———. "Polish Rabbi, American Activist and Thinker, World-wide Prophet of Dialogue." [Polish]. In *No Religion is an Island* [Polish edition] *Żadna religia nie jest samotną wyspą. Abraham Joshua Heschel i dialog międzyreligijny,* edited by Harold Kasimow and Byron L. Sherwin. Krakow: WAM, 2005.

Lauterbach, Jacob. *Mekilta de-Rabbi Ishmael.* Philadelphia: Jewish Publication Society, 1933.

Levenson, Jon D. "The Contradictions of A. J. Heschel." *Commentary* 106, 1 (July 1998) 34–38.

———. "How Not to Conduct Jewish-Christian Dialogue." *Commentary* 112, 5 (2001) 31–37.

———. "Religious Affirmation and Historical Criticism in Heschel's Biblical Interpretation." *AJS Review* 25, 1 (2000/2001) 25–44.

Levin, Leonard. "Heschel's Homage to the Rabbis: *Torah min hashamayim* as Historical Theology." *Conservative Judaism* 50, 2–3 (Winter/Spring 1998) 56–66.

Liebman, Charles S. "The Training of American Rabbis." *American Jewish Year Book*, 69 (1968) 3–112.

Lookstein, Joseph H. "The Neo-Hasidism of Abraham J. Heschel." *Judaism* 5, 3 (Summer 1956) 248–55.

Lorberbaum, Yair. *Tzelem Elohim* [Hebrew]. Jerusalem: Schocken, 2004.

Mackler, Aaron L. "Symbols, Reality and God: Heschel's Rejection of a Tillichian Understanding of Religious Symbols." *Judaism* 40, 3 (Summer 1991) 290–300.

Magid, Shaul. "Abraham Joshua Heschel and Thomas Merton: Heretics of Modernity." *Conservative Judaism* 50, 2–3 (Winter/Spring 1998) 112–25.

Marmur, Michael. "Heschel's Rhetoric of Citation: The Use of Sources in *God in Search of Man*." PhD diss., Hebrew University of Jerusalem, 2005.

McBride, Alfred. *Heschel: Religious Educator*. Denville NJ: Dimension Books, 1973.

———. *The Transcendental Themes of Abraham Heschel and Their Value for Religious Education*. PhD diss., Catholic University of America, 1972.

Meir, Ephraim. "Ahava ve-Emet be-toda'a hayehudit." *Hagut be-hinukh Hayehudi* 3–4 (2002) 141–49.

———. "David Hartman on the Attitudes of Soloveitchik and Heschel Towards Christianity." In *Judaism and Modernity: The Religious Philosophy of David Hartman*, edited by Jonathan W. Malino, 262–73. Aldershot: Ashgate, 2004.

Merkle, John C. *The Genesis of Faith: The Depth Theology of Abraham Joshua Heschel*. New York: Macmillan, 1985.

———. "Heschel's Attitude toward Religious Pluralism." In *No Religion is an Island: Abraham Joshua Heschel and Interreligious Dialogue*, edited by Harold Kasimow and Byron L. Sherwin, 97–109. Maryknoll, NY: Orbis, 1991.

———. "Heschel's Monotheistic Perspective vis-à-vis Pantheism." Unpublished paper from the 30th AJS Conference (December 1998).

———. "The Sublime, the Human, and the Divine in the Depth-Theology of Abraham Joshua Heschel." *The Journal of Religion* 58, 4 (1978) 365–79.

Merkle, John C., ed. *Abraham Joshua Heschel: Exploring His Life and Thought*. London: Collier Macmillan, 1985.

Moore, Deborah Dash. *East European Jews in Two Worlds*. Evanston, IL: Northwestern University Press, 1990.

Moore, Donald J. *The Human and the Holy: The Spirituality of Abraham Joshua Heschel*. New York: Fordham University Press, 1989.

Morgan, Michael L. *Beyond Auschwitz:Post-Holocaust Jewish Thought in America*. Oxford: Oxford University Press, 2001.

Nanstad, Donald F. *Heschel and Whitehead on God and Good*. PhD diss., Boston University, 1994.

National Conference of Catholic Bishops USA. *Statement on Catholic-Jewish Relations*. 1975. http://www.jcrelations.net/NCCB__USA__Statement_on_Catholic-Jewish_Relations.2414.0.html

Neusner, Jacob. "Abraham Joshua Heschel: The Man." In *To Grow in Wisdom: An Anthology of Abraham Joshua Heschel*, edited by Jacob Neusner and Noam M. M. Neusner, 3–12. Lanham, New York, London: Madison, 1990.

———. "Faith in the Crucible of the Mind." *America* 128, 9 (10 March 1973) 207–9.

———. "The Intellectual Achievement of Abraham Joshua Heschel." In *To Grow in Wisdom: An Anthology of Abraham Joshua Heschel*, edited by Jacob Neusner and Noam M. M. Neusner, 13–22. Lanham, New York, London: Madison, 1990.

———. Review of *Theology of Ancient Judaism*, by Abraham Joshua Heschel. *Conservative Judaism* 20, 3 (1965) 66–73.

———. *Stranger at Home: "The Holocaust," Zionism and American Judaism*. Chicago: University of Chicago Press, 1981.

Neusner, Jacob, and Noam M. M. Neusner, eds. *To Grow in Wisdom: An Anthology of Abraham Joshua Heschel*. Lanham, New York, London: Madison, 1990.

Neusner, Jacob, et al., eds. *From Ancient Israel to Modern Judaism: Intellect in Quest of Understanding*. Atlanta: Scholars Press, 1989.

Niebuhr, Reinhold. "Masterly Analysis of Faith." *New York Herald Tribune Book Review* (April 1, 1951) 12.

Olan, Levi. Review of *Man's Quest for God*, by Abraham Joshua Heschel. *Judaism* 4, 2 (Spring 1955) 180–82.

Patai, Raphael, and Emanuel S. Goldsmith, eds. *Thinkers and Teachers of Modern Judaism*. New York: Paragon House, 1994.

Peli, Pinhas. "Heschel and the Hạsidic Tradition." In *Prayer and Politics: The Twin Poles of Abraham Joshua Heschel*, edited by Joshua Stampfer, 63–84. Portland, OR: Institute for Judaic Studies, 1985.

Peri, Paul F. *Education for Piety: An Investigation of the Works of Abraham J. Heschel*, EdD diss., Columbia University Teachers College, 1980.

Perlman, Lawrence. *Abraham Heschel's Idea of Revelation*. Atlanta: Scholars, 1989.

———. "As a Report about Revelation, the Bible Itself is a Midrash." *Conservative Judaism* 55, 1 (Fall 2002) 30–37.

———. "Heschel's Critique of Kant." *From Ancient Israel to Modern Judaism: Intellect in Quest of Understanding* 3 edited by Jacob Neusner et al., 213–26. Atlanta: Scholars Press, 1989.

Petuchowski, Jakob. "Judaism as "Mystery"—The Hidden Agenda?" *HUCA* 52 (1981) 141–52.

Piekarz, Mendel. *The Beginning of Hasidism: Ideological Trends in Derush and Musar Literature* [Hebrew]. Jerusalem: Bialik Institute, 1978.

Rapoport-Albert, Ada. "Hasidism after 1772: Structural Continuity and Change." In *Hasidism Reappraised*, edited by Ada Rapoport-Albert, 76–140. London: Littman Library of Jewish Civilization, 1996.

Ratzabi, Shalom. "Heschel's Depth Theology" [Hebrew]. *Iton 77* (November–December 1993) 22–25.

Rodin, Samuel. "Two Types of Faith: Martin Buber on Judaism and Christianity." In *Judaism and Christianity: Toward Dialogue*, edited by Douglas Pratt and Dov Bing, 131–69. Hamilton, NZ: University of Waikato, 1987.

Ronen, Shoshana. *In Pursuit of the Void: Journeys to Poland in Contemporary Israeli Literature*. Cracow: 2001.

———. *Nietzsche and Wittgenstein: In Search of Secular Salvation*. Warsaw: Dialog, 2002.

Rosen, David. "Orthodox Judaism and Jewish-Christian Dialogue." https://www.bc.edu/content/dam/files/research_sites/cjl/texts/center/conferences/soloveitchik/sol_rosen.htm

Rosenak, Michael. *Roads to the Palace: Jewish Texts and Teaching*. Oxford: Berghahn, 1995.

Rosenberg, James B. "Time, Space and Abraham Joshua Heschel." *CCAR Journal* 15, 2 (Spring 1973) 103-4.

Rotenstreich, Nathan. "On Prophetic Consciousness." *Journal of Religion* 54 (July 1974) 186-95.

Rothschild. Fritz A. "Architect and Herald of a New Theology." *Conservative Judaism* 28, 1 (1973) 55-60.

———. "The Religious Thought of Abraham Heschel." *Conservative Judaism* 23 (Fall 1968) 12-24.

———. "Varieties of Heschelian Thought." In *Abraham Joshua Heschel: Exploring His Life and Thought*, edited by John C. Merkle, 87-102. London: Collier Macmillan, 1985.

Rothschild. Fritz A., ed. *Between God and Man: An Interpretation of Judaism*. New York: Free, 1959.

———. *Jewish Perspectives on Christianity*. New York: Continuum, 1996.

Rubenstein, Richard. *After Auschwitz: Radical Theology and Contemporary Judaism*. New York: Bobbs-Merrill, 1966.

———. *Power Struggle*. New York: Scribner's, 1974.

Sacks, Jonathan. *Tradition in an Untraditional Age: Essays on Modern Jewish Thought*. London: Vallentine Mitchell, 1990.

Sanders, James A. "Apostle to the Gentiles." *Conservative Judaism* 28, 1 (Fall 1973) 61-63.

Schachter, Zalman S. "Hasidism, and Neo-Hasidism." *Judaism* 9, 3 (Summer 1960) 216-221.

Schatz-Uffenheimer, Rivka. *Ḥasidism as Mysticism: Quietistic Elements in Eighteenth Century Hasidic Thought*. Princeton: Princeton University Press and Jerusalem: Magnes, 1993.

Scholem, Gershom G. *Major Trends in Jewish Mysticism*. London: Thames and Hudson, 1953.

Schremer, Oded. "Perek ba-Retorika ha-hinukhit shel Heschel" [Hebrew]. *Zehut* 3 (1983) 95-105.

Schulweis, Harold M. "Charles Hartshorne and the Defenders of Heschel." *Judaism* 24, 1 (Winter 1975) 58-62.

Schweid, Eliezer. "'Prophetic Mysticism' in Twentieth-Century Jewish Thought." *Modern Judaism* 4, 2 (May 1994) 139-174.

———. *Prophets for their People and Humanity: Prophecy and Prophets in 20th Century Jewish Thought*. Jerusalem: Magnes, 1999.

Shandler, Jeffrey. "Heschel and Yiddish: A Struggle with Signification." *Journal of Jewish Thought and Philosophy* 2, 2 (1993) 245-99.

Shapira, Avraham. *Between Spirit and Reality: Dual Structures in the Thought of M. M. Buber* [Hebrew]. Jerusalem: Bialik Institute, 1994.

Shapiro, Marc B. "Scholars and Friends: Rabbi Jehiel Jacob Weinberg and Professor Samuel Atlas." *Torah u-Madda Journal* 7 (1997) 105-121.

Sharma, Arvind. "Hindu-Jewish Dialogue and the Thought of Abraham Heschel: At Grassroots and Mountaintop." In *No Religion is an Island: Abraham Joshua Heschel and Interreligious Dialogue*, edited by Harold Kasimow and Byron L. Sherwin, 163-74. Maryknoll, NY: Orbis, 1991.

Sherman, Franklin. *The Promise of Heschel*. Philadelphia: J. B. Lippincott, 1970.
Sherwin, Byron L. *Abraham Joshua Heschel*. Atlanta: John Knox, 1979.
———. *Makers of Contemporary Theology: Abraham Joshua Heschel*. Atlanta GA: John Knox, 1979.
———. "My Master." In *No Religion is an Island: Abraham Joshua Heschel and Interreligious Dialogue*, edited by Harold Kasimow and Byron L. Sherwin, 42–62. Maryknoll, NY: Orbis, 1991.
Shorsch, Rebecca. "The Hermeneutics of Heschel in Torah min Hashamayim." *Judaism* 40, 3 (Summer 1991) 301–308.
Siegel, Seymour. "Abraham Joshua Heschel's Contributions to Jewish Scholarship." *Proceedings of the Rabbinical Assembly of America* 29 (1968), 72–85.
———. "Divine Pathos, Prophetic Sympathy." *Conservative Judaism* 28, 1 (Fall 1973) 70–74.
Soloveitchik, Joseph. "Confrontation." *Tradition: A Journal of Orthodox Thought*, 6 (1964) 5–29. https://www.bc.edu/content/dam/files/research_sites/cjl/texts/center/conferences/soloveitchik/
Stampfer, Joshua, ed. *Prayer and Politics: The Twin Poles of Abraham Joshua Heschel*. Portland, OR: Institute for Judaic Studies, 1985.
Staude, John Raphael. *Max Scheler 1874–1928: An Intellectual Portrait*. New York: Free, 1967.
Stegemann, Ekkehard. "Introduction (to Martin Buber)." In *Jewish Perspectives on Christianity*, edited by Fritz A. Rothschild, 111–21. New York: Continuum, 1996.
Stern, Harold. "A. J. Heschel, Irenic Polemicist." *Proceedings of the Rabbinical Assembly of America* 45 (1984) 169–177.
Ströker, Elisabeth. "Phenomenology as First Philosophy: Reflections on Husserl." In *Edmund Husserl and the Phenomenological Tradition*, edited by Robert Sokolowski, 249–63. Washington, DC: Catholic University of America Press, 1988.
Tanenzapf, Sol. "Abraham Joshua Heschel and His Critics." *Judaism* 23, 3 (Summer 1974) 276–86.
———. "A Process Theory of Torah and Mitzvot." In *Jewish Theology and Process Thought*, edited by Sandra Lubarsky and David Griffin, 35–58. Albany: State University of New York Press, 1996.
Tillich, Paul. *Dynamics of Faith*. New York: Harper & Row, 1957.
Tucker, Gordon. "Heschel's *Torah min ha-shamayim*: Ancient Theology and Contemporary Autobiography." *Conservative Judaism* 50, 2–3 (Winter/Spring 1998) 48–55.
Uffenheimer, Benjamin. *Ancient Prophecy in Israel* [Hebrew]. Jerusalem: Magnes, 1973.
———. "Buber and Modern Biblical Scholarship." In *Martin Buber: A Centenary Volume*. Edited by Haim Gordon and Jochanan Bloch, 163–211. New York: Ktav and Be'er Sheva: Ben Gurion University of the Negev, 1984.
Urbach, Ephraim E. *The Sages* [Hebrew]. Jerusalem: Magnes, 1971.
Wertheimer, Jack, ed. *Tradition Renewed: A History of the Jewish Theological Seminary*, Vol. 1. New York: Jewish Theological Seminary of America, 1997.
Wolf, Arnold Jacob. "What We Learned in the 70s II." *Sh'ma* 10:185 (January 11, 1980).
Wolok, Davin Levi. *Meeting and Mystery: Toward a Synthesis of Buber and Heschel*. PhD diss., State University of New York at Stony Brook, 1988.

World Council of Churches. *The Christian Approach to the Jews*. Amsterdam: World Council of Churches, 1948. http://www.jcrelations.net/The_Christian_Approach_to_the_Jews.2584.0.html?id=720

Zuesse, Evan M. "The Gate to God's Presence in Heschel, Buber and Soloveitchik." In *Thinkers and Teachers of Modern Judaism*, edited by Raphael Patai and Emanuel S. Goldsmith, 121–49. New York: Paragon House, 1994.

www.ingramcontent.com/pod-product-compliance
Lightning Source LLC
Chambersburg PA
CBHW070320230426
43663CB00011B/2183